"In *Holy Living: Jonathan E*[...] has once again accented [...] his pastoral sensitivities. This book has many [...] features, and it is smartly organized. The introduction gives the reader a helpful overview of the life of Jonathan Edwards and his 'Resolutions' within their historical context. The resolutions are wonderfully organized into thematic groupings. Moreover, Everhard's commentary on the Resolutions is patient, interesting, and clearly from the pen of an Edwards scholar. The symbiotic relationship between Edwards's Resolutions and Diary is presented well, and Everhard's treatment of Edwards's discontinuation of his self-scrutiny with the Resolutions is instructive. Reading this book is time well spent."

—Jonathan S. Marko, Associate Professor
Philosophical and Systematic Theology, Cornerstone University

"Matthew Everhard embodies the commitment of a pastor and the intellectual rigor of a theologian. Notably, his scholarship on Jonathan Edwards has pioneered several areas that help Christians think about how they should view the world. His work is therefore twofold, serving both the church and the academy."

—John T. Lowe, Adjunct Professor, University of Louisville
Coeditor of *Jonathan Edwards within the Enlightenment*

"A great emphasis on sanctification is needed in the modern church. *Holy Living* makes a superb contribution to this end. For Matthew Everhard takes Edwards's famous Seventy Resolutions, helpfully categorizes them, and then brings them to lively understanding and application using Edwards's own life events and writings. From now on, one will not want to have Edwards's Resolutions in hand without Matthew's work in the other!"

—Barry York, President
Reformed Presbyterian Theological Seminary

"Matthew's writing strikes an enviable balance between being studiously informed and yet accessible. Readers of *Holy Living* will not only learn much about Jonathan Edwards but, under Matthew's skillful and keen guidance through Edwards's Resolutions, will also learn much from Edwards."

—Joshua Schendel, Executive Editor
***Modern Reformation* magazine**

HOLY LIVING

Jonathan Edwards's Seventy Resolutions *for* Living *the* Christian Life

MATTHEW EVERHARD

an imprint of Hendrickson Publishing Group

Holy Living: Jonathan Edwards's Seventy Resolutions for Living the Christian Life

© 2021 Matthew Everhard

Published by Hendrickson Publishers
an imprint of Hendrickson Publishing Group
Hendrickson Publishers, LLC
P. O. Box 3473
Peabody, Massachusetts 01961-3473
www.hendricksonpublishinggroup.com

ISBN 978-1-68307-33-6

Unless otherwise noted, all Scripture citations are taken from the King James Version of the Bible.

Printed in the United States of America

First Printing — October 2021

Library of Congress Control Number: 2021945497

CONTENTS

Acknowledgments

I would like to thank a number of people for helping me on this project. First, I would like to thank Hendrickson Publishers this opportunity to share my gleanings of Edwards's Seventy Resolutions with a broader audience. Thanks especially to Dr. Jonathan Kline, Hendrickson's academic editor, for working with me through the acquisition process.

Second, I would like to express my most sincere thanks to Patricia Anders, editorial director at Hendrickson, who took a rough draft and made it far more readable with her careful and diligent help. Thanks also to assistant editor Marco Antunes for his helpful work on the book. Of course, any remaining faults here are my own.

Third, I would like to thank the elders of Gospel Fellowship PCA, the church I serve as pastor. I hope that all of my writing projects are an extension of our local church's witness of Christ's love to the world.

Fourth, I would like to thank my three children—Soriah, Elijah, and Simone—for bringing such joy into my life. I love you all.

Finally, I want to express my love for my wife Kelly. We have had more than twenty years together now and only an eternity together will be enough.

ABBREVIATIONS

The Works of Jonathan Edwards Series

WJE 1   *Freedom of the Will.* Edited by Paul Ramsey. New Haven: Yale University Press, 1957

WJE 2   *Religious Affections.* Edited by John E. Smith. New Haven: Yale University Press, 1959

WJE 3   *Original Sin.* Edited by Clyde A. Holbrook. New Haven: Yale University Press, 1970

WJE 4   *The Great Awakening.* Edited by C. C. Goen. New Haven: Yale University Press, 1972

WJE 5   *Apocalyptic Writings.* Edited by Stephen J. Stein. New Haven: Yale University Press, 1977

WJE 6   *Scientific and Philosophical Writings.* Edited by Wallace E. Anderson. New Haven: Yale University Press, 1980

WJE 7   *The Life of David Brainerd.* Edited by Norman Pettit. New Haven: Yale University Press, 1984

WJE 8   *Ethical Writings.* Edited by Paul Ramsey. New Haven: Yale University Press, 1989

WJE 9   *A History of the Work of Redemption.* Edited by John F. Wilson. New Haven: Yale University Press, 1989

WJE 10   *Sermons and Discourses, 1720–1723.* Edited by Wilson H Kimnach. New Haven: Yale University Press, 1992

WJE 11   *Typological Writings.* Edited by Wallace E. Anderson, Mason I. Lowance Jr., and David Watters. New Haven: Yale University Press, 1993

WJE 12   *Ecclesiastical Writings.* Edited by David D. Hall. New Haven: Yale University Press, 1994

WJE 13   *"The Miscellanies," a–500.* Edited by Thomas A. Schafer. New Haven: Yale University Press, 1994

WJE 14   *Sermons and Discourses, 1723–1729.* Edited by Kenneth P. Minkema. New Haven: Yale University Press, 1997

WJE 15   *Notes on Scripture.* Edited by Stephen J. Stein. New Haven: Yale University Press, 1998

WJE 16   *Letters and Personal Writings.* Edited by George S. Claghorn. New Haven: Yale University Press, 1998

WJE 17   *Sermons and Discourses, 1730–1733.* Edited by Mark Valeri. New Haven: Yale University Press, 1999

WJE 18   *"The Miscellanies," 501–832.* Edited by Ava Chamberlain. New Haven: Yale University Press, 2000

WJE 19   *Sermons and Discourses, 1734–1738.* Edited by M. X. Lesser. New Haven: Yale University Press, 2001

WJE 20   *"The Miscellanies," 833–1152.* Edited by Amy Plantinga Pauw. New Haven: Yale University Press, 2002

WJE 21   *Writings on the Trinity, Grace, and Faith.* Edited by Sang Hyun Lee. New Haven: Yale University Press, 2002

WJE 22   *Sermons and Discourses, 1739–1742.* Edited by Harry S. Stout and Nathan O. Hatch, with Kyle P. Farley. New Haven: Yale University Press, 2003

WJE 23   *"The Miscellanies," 1153–1360.* Edited by Douglas A. Sweeney. New Haven: Yale University Press, 2004

WJE 24   *The "Blank Bible" (Parts 1 and 2).* Edited by Stephen J. Stein. New Haven: Yale University Press, 2006

WJE 25   *Sermons and Discourses, 1743–1758.* Edited by Wilson H. Kimnach. New Haven: Yale University Press, 2006

WJE 26   *Catalogues of Books.* Edited by Peter J. Thuesen. New Haven: Yale University Press, 2008

Works cited as "WJE" are sourced from the printed editions of the Yale works above; those cited as "WJEO" in the footnotes are sourced from the digital archives, *The Works of Jonathan Edwards Online*, at Edwards.Yale.edu.

The Works of Jonathan Edwards

Works I   *The Works of Jonathan Edwards: Volume 1.* Edited by Edward Hickman. 2 vols. 1834. Reprint ed. Edinburgh: Banner of Truth, 1974

Works II   *The Works of Jonathan Edwards: Volume 2.* Edited by Edward Hickman. 2 vols. 1834. Edinburgh: Banner of Truth, 1974

Other Abbreviations

ESV	Holy Bible, English Standard Version
HC	The Heidelberg Catechism
JEE	*The Jonathan Edwards Encyclopedia.* Edited by Harry S. Stout, Kenneth P. Minkema, and Adriaan C. Neele. Grand Rapids: Eerdmans, 2017
KJV	The King James Version (Also: AV)
WCF	Westminster Confession of Faith
WLC	Westminster Larger Catechism
WSC	Westminster Shorter Catechism

"Resolved"

An Introduction to the Life of Jonathan Edwards

An Overview of Edwards's Life

The history of the world is the story of billions of regular people with just a smattering of geniuses and uniquely gifted people mixed in. A true genius comes around only every hundred years or so. A genius is a person with an extraordinary mind who leaves his or her indelible mark in at least one significant area of human thought; perhaps in philosophy, literature, science, art, mathematics, theology, film, or choreography. Rarer still are those sprinklings of people who come around every millennium or so and contribute markedly to multiple fields. Da Vinci was one such genius: he was an extraordinary painter, sculptor, inventor, and architect. About this creator of such masterpieces as the *Mona Lisa* and *The Last Supper*, it was said that he could write in Greek with one hand and in Latin with the other. Or if he preferred, Da Vinci could sketch a new inventive design with his right hand and take notes on the same project with the other. Indeed, there are really very few genuinely remarkable people!

Jonathan Edwards (1703–58) was in that small handful of one-in-a-million people.

If the hallmark of such extraordinary lives is that these people impacted not just one field of human knowledge but *many*, then Jonathan Edwards certainly qualifies. Some consider him America's first incomparable intellect. Edwards left a legacy in the following areas: philosophy, natural science, theology, pastoral ministry, and missiology. He was, in a word, a polymath—a brilliant scholar in multiple disciplines. It is not a stretch to say that Jonathan Edwards may have been the American Colonies' most gifted individual, though with personalities like Benjamin Franklin, George Whitefield, and George Washington alive in the same window of history, it is easy to see how Edwards could be outshined.

The famed preacher Martyn Lloyd-Jones once said of Edwards, "I am tempted, perhaps foolishly, to compare the Puritans to the Alps, Luther and

Calvin to the Himalayas, and Jonathan Edwards to Mount Everest. He has always seemed to me to be the man most like the Apostle Paul."[1] Allow me to brag about him just a bit to back up such vivid claims. When Jonathan Edwards was just a teenager, he wrote a detailed scientific analysis of the creaturely habits of arachnids. It *almost* made it into the premier scientific journal of his day. Consumed by the writings of scientists like Isaac Newton, Edwards wrote some penetrating early essays on the properties of light, refraction, and color waves. As a mature philosopher, he wrote the definitive treatise on the relationship between the sovereignty of God and human responsibility. *The Freedom of the Will*[2] has still never been bettered. Once, he wrote a state-of-the-art essay on the nature of human moral virtue, capturing the very essence of right living.[3]

Though many remember him only as the fire and brimstone preacher of "Sinners in the Hands of an Angry God,"[4] indisputably America's most famous sermon, many forget that Edwards was also a loving and careful missionary to the indigenous peoples of the frontier, and that his ideas on human dignity were developed by his followers to further the cause of the abolition of slavery.[5] Truly, Jonathan Edwards possessed an incredibly gifted mind, as well as an enormous heart for God and a love of his fellow human beings.

In this book, we will be working through one of his earliest writings, and perhaps also one of his shortest: Seventy Resolutions.[6] These are his personal life goals, written when he was only nineteen years old. In the next section, I will say much more about these Resolutions and their composition, but for the moment, we simply need to know that they are comprised of seventy short, pithy goals by which the young minister-in-training determined to live his life. A framework for who he wanted to become in the presence of others, and especially before the all-seeing eyes of a holy God, the Resolutions are

---

1. Steven J. Lawson, *The Unwavering Resolve of Jonathan Edwards* (Lake Mary, FL: Reformation Trust, 2008), 1.
2. *The Freedom of the Will* is contained in WJEO 1.
3. *The Nature of True Virtue* is contained in WJEO 8:539ff.
4. "Sinners in the Hands of an Angry God" can be found in WJEO 22:404–18.
5. For more on Edwards and race, see my article "Jonathan Edwards's Complex Views on Race," *Modern Reformation*, Web Exclusive Articles, July 1, 2020, https://modernreformation.org/resource-library/web-exclusive-articles/the-mod -jonathan-edwards-complex-views-on-race/.
6. The "Resolutions" are contained in the *Two Volume Works of Jonathan Edwards* (Banner of Truth) in I:xx–xxiii and the Yale Editions of the *Works of Jonathan Edwards* in 16:753–59. Hereafter, the two volumes will be cited as *Works I* or *Works II* followed by page numbers. The printed Yale Editions (vols. 1–26) will be cited as WJE with a volume and page number following, and the digital-only volumes will be cited as WJEO with the same convention of volume and page number. All volumes, both print and digital only, can be found online at Edwards.yale.edu.

a helpful insight into the heart and mind of this verifiable genius just as he was emerging into full bloom.

Before we get to the Resolutions, however, it would be helpful for us to take a bit of a closer look at their author. Jonathan Edwards is often called America's greatest scholar. This is a fitting moniker, I think, given that Edwards was born into the colonies—Connecticut, to be precise—and lived his entire life in New England. In that sense, he was truly American. Although he died eighteen years before the founding of the United States of America in 1776, he would have considered himself a faithful subject of the British Crown. Despite his loyalties, his influence helped shape the American Colonies in their pre-Revolutionary years in ways beyond measure.

Edwards's Youth and Conversion to Christ

Edwards was the maternal grandson of one of the most renowned preachers in New England, the famed and feared Solomon Stoddard, himself revered as the "Puritan Pope of the Connecticut River Valley."[7] Edwards's own father, Timothy Edwards, was likewise a Harvard-trained Puritan minister, who zealously raised young Jonathan to be an inscrutably precise thinker.[8] Incidentally, Jonathan was the only male child alongside ten sisters, all of whom were over six feet tall! Raised among the "sixty feet" of his sisters,[9] Jonathan was able to combine his father's strident intellect with his mother and sisters' deep affections. This term, "affections," would become a key idea in Edwards's thought as he analyzed the human heart. He later defined the affections as the deep inclinations and desires of the soul. So, as a precocious young child, he was raised to both *think* clearly and *feel* deeply. Head and heart. Brain and soul. Thinking and loving.

At about the age of seventeen, he had a profound conversion experience. First Timothy 1:17 impacted him like never before, and he had a "new apprehension" of the glory of Christ, the power of God, and the grace of the gospel. Striking him with its beauty and power, he felt Christ renovate his entire life as he mused on it:

> Now unto the King eternal, immortal, invisible, the only wise God, be honour and glory for ever and ever. Amen.

He knew he must live for such a great and mighty God.

---

7. George Marsden, *Jonathan Edwards: A Life* (New Haven: Yale University Press, 2003), 11. For more information on Solomon Stoddard, see JEE 553.
8. For more information on Timothy Edwards, see JEE 185–86.
9. Marsden, *A Life*, 18.

It's rather surprising that Edwards didn't convert earlier, especially having a pastor for both his father and his grandfather! But in those days, Puritan theology conceived of conversion as a far deeper transformation of one's life and heart; it was much more than simply signing a pledge card or raising one's hand at the end of an evangelistic meeting. The "altar call" had yet to be invented as a mode of evangelism, and true conversion was thought to take place in a series of somewhat predictable "steps," ranging from the dread of hell, to the guilt of conscience, to recognizing one's need for a Savior, to understanding the gospel, to finally resting and receiving Jesus Christ as Savior and Lord. For some, these steps (the Puritan morphology of conversion) were thought to take months or even years to work through; and when Edwards told his father about his new experience of grace, his minister father had his doubts about their veracity, since his ingenious son seemed to have skipped over some of the steps too quickly.[10] The tension between young Jonathan and his father on this matter later prompted him to deeply and thoughtfully study the Bible's account of the nature and process of real conversion (or salvation) in Christ.[11]

Edwards graduated from Yale twice, once at age seventeen with his bachelor's degree (1720), and then at nineteen with his master's degree (1722). He wrote his master's thesis in Latin (as expected at that time) on the doctrine of justification by faith alone, a standard and cherished Protestant and Calvinistic theme. Edwards fell in love with the much younger Sarah Pierpont, to whom he devoted a rather fanciful love poem,[12] later marrying her and treasuring her as the love of his life (1727). Together, they raised eleven children of their own, bringing up their own "sixty feet" of godly progeny. After a couple of short pastoral internships (see more below) and a few years of serving the Reverend Stoddard as his associate pastor, Edwards finally became the senior pastor of the Church of Northampton (1729), one of the most prestigious churches west of the important city of Boston.

The Great Awakening

The single most significant event that transpired in Edwards's life and ministry was the 1740 "First Great Awakening," in which a massive spiritual revival poured out on the colonies. In one sense, we can say that his whole life up until that time anticipated this event and that he spent the rest of his

---

10. See the appendix for an explanation of the Puritan "morphology" of conversion.

11. Edwards fixated on this doctrine, writing several powerful works on the process of conversion, especially *The Religious Affections,* which comprises WJEO 2.

12. "Apostrophe to Sarah Pierpont" or "On Sarah Pierpont" is contained in WJE 16:789–90. For more information on Sarah, see JEE 184–85.

life reflecting on it. Even his own conversion seemed to be an anticipation in microcosm of the dynamic outpouring of God on the emerging nation in 1740. This revival was what Solomon Stoddard had been yearning for his entire life, having seen but a few smaller "harvests" (as he called them) in his many decades of pastoral ministry. It was what Timothy Edwards had hoped for his entire life as well—and now, the third-generation pastor was unexpectedly in the very center of it all.

Of course, the Great Awakening was far bigger than Jonathan Edwards. George Whitefield was the central preacher and the most galvanizing personality, perhaps the most famous man alive on the planet at that time. Depending on one's perspective, either Whitefield followed the revival or it followed him! John and Charles Wesley were likewise contemporary, leading their blooming branches of Methodism, toggling back and forth between the Colonies and their beloved England. Gilbert Tennant, a fiery Presbyterian, was a notable revival preacher then too. There were many others as well. But the work of analyzing the revival from a biblical and theological perspective was the primary responsibility of the sharp-minded Jonathan Edwards.

Edwards's revival-oriented writings drove him to international renown just before, but especially *during*, the peak of the revival years. In 1734–35, Northampton itself had experienced a smaller-scale revival, which was a harbinger of what was to come five years later. His description of those preceding events became sought-after literature, much acclaimed in its own time.[13] This book, *A Faithful Narrative of the Surprising Works of God*, put Edwards on the map internationally as Christians everywhere were eager to read of such shocking good news. A local revival like that in Northampton was an exciting beacon of hope!

In 1740, when the large-scale revival shook the Colonies with full force, Edwards rose to prominence as the cautious, well-balanced, but clearly optimistic advocate of this burgeoning movement. He had already been recognized as somewhat of an "expert" on revival, having led his own church through a renewal of fervor those short years earlier. Now, the outpourings of individual conversions, renewed communities, and revitalized local churches were taking place on an unprecedented scale. We would have to go back more than two hundred years to the time of the Reformation itself for comparable events!

This new revival, however, came with great controversy and even some bitter argumentation as Edwards fought off criticism from all quarters. Some thought the revivals were uncontrolled fanaticism. Others thought they didn't go far enough. But Edwards ably defended the events as a legitimate outpouring of God's gracious hand on an undeserving people. He managed to balance biblical fidelity with passionate devotion. Again, both head and heart were aglow with love for God and man.

13. See *A Faithful Narrative*, WJE 4:95–211.

The Great Awakening drew out Edwards's true intellectual genius and foisted his learning on an eager world hungry to discuss the current events that were both impossible to quench and difficult to ignore. Hardly a town, a church, or even a family were left without a member who was deeply renewed in religious zeal and the blessings of joy. Through it all, Edwards wrote significant letters, sermons, tracts, theological essays, and long philosophical works, mastering nearly every literary genre to which he lent his hand. He thought clearly, loved deeply, and wrote abundantly, pouring out what is contained today in the twenty-six official printed volumes of his written works. If we include the digital volumes that have not yet been printed, then Edwards's extant works would span wider than a basketball player's reach, from fingertip to fingertip, numbering around seventy volumes of written works.

Edwards's Removal and Death

Ironically, in 1750, the uniquely gifted Pastor Edwards was fired by his own congregation over a dispute over the Lord's Supper. Wanting to strengthen his grandfather Solomon Stoddard's requirements to participate in the sacrament of the Table, Edwards sought to limit participation to only those baptized church members who had also publicly professed their faith in Christ.[14] Stoddard allowed baptized persons to participate at the Table as long as their lives were scandal free. This move to strengthen communion requirements was perceived as too hostile, and in a congregational church vote, Edwards lost by a landslide.

Although Edwards and Sarah considered a possible calling in Scotland, ultimately they chose to move their large family toward the fringe of society to serve as a missionary to the indigenous peoples. In Stockbridge, Massachusetts, he pastored a small congregation of English settlers and ministered kindly to the native peoples. In God's good grace, Edwards used these years to re-preach some of his simpler sermons and focus instead on writing some of the major treatises over which he had long been ruminating, sealing his reputation as a next-level thinker and the truly great mind of his century.

In 1758, at the age of fifty-five, just after he had been named the new president of Princeton, Edwards died after being inoculated for smallpox. Although the science of inoculation was good in principle, it hadn't yet been fully refined in practice, and the pastor-philosopher's optimism in the emerging technology led to his own untimely death after he contracted the disease

---

14. For an excellent chapter on Edwards's firing, see Mark Dever, "How Jonathan Edwards Got Fired, and Why It's Important for Us Today" in *A God Entranced Vision of All Things: The Legacy of Jonathan Edwards*, eds. John Piper and Justin Taylor (Wheaton, IL: Crossway, 2004), 129–44.

and his throat closed up. Sadly, Sarah died just six months later, and the Edwards family was thrown into grief-filled upheaval.

Following his death, Edwards's legacy continued to rise sharply. His disciples carried on some of his ideas, applying them more courageously than he had in areas of social concern, especially his concept of "benevolence to being in general,"[15] which meant a love for God and humanity. His son Jonathan Edwards Jr. and his disciple Samuel Hopkins applied their concept of "disinterested benevolence" to race relations and slavery, working toward the abolition of that horrific institution.[16] Like their mentor, they were way ahead of their time.

Since the publication of his full *Works* in the twentieth century, Edwards's reputation has skyrocketed. Like many thinkers of his caliber, it took many generations for scholarship to catch up with his ideas in order to recognize his true worth in several vast fields of human knowledge.

The Early Pastoral Years

As we study the Seventy Resolutions, which Edwards began as a teenager in late 1722 and completed on August 17, 1723, we should be somewhat familiar with this general timeframe of his life. Much of what I say about the Resolutions will be framed by the context and events of this formative period.

By 1722, Edwards had formally completed both programs of study, although he didn't submit his master's thesis until September 1723. For our purposes in this book, I am calling the five years between 1722 and 1726 his "early pastoral years." They are "early," because Edwards had not yet ascended to his famed pastoral charge of the congregation at Northampton alongside his esteemed grandfather Rev. Solomon Stoddard. Serving this church for over twenty-three years would eventually become his primary life's work. But these years are nevertheless still "pastoral" since Edwards was already actively serving in the ministry with three unique training or preparatory roles (what we might call "internships"): first, as interim pastor at a small Scottish congregation in New York City (1722–23); second, in another temporary pastorate at a congregation in Bolton (1723–24) and other preaching opportunities locally; and third, as the student tutor at Yale College (1724–26).

---

15. This concept is unfolded in detail in *The Nature of True Virtue*, WJEO 8:539–627. In general terms, Edwards suggests that the moral person is the one who loves all things that God has made, but especially the Creator himself.

16. Some of the best research on Edwards and slavery is being done by John T. Lowe. See, for example, his chapter "Destruction and Benevolence: The New Divinity and Origins of Abolitionism in Edwardsean Tradition," in *Jonathan Edwards within the Enlightenment: Controversy, Experience and Thought*, ed. John T. Lowe and Daniel N. Gulotta (Göttingen: Vanderhoeck & Ruprecht, 2020), 87–110.

During these years, Edwards served and practiced for the ministry in ways that emulated the life and duties of a full-time pastor, which he hoped to someday become. He dealt with real people, their faults and frailties included. He counseled church members and students through the trials of life. He preached well-prepared sermons, some of which were considered excellent. He gave lectures on theology which disciplined unruly undergraduates. Most importantly, Edwards saw himself emerging into full, mature, Christian adulthood during this period. This self-awareness is probably what led him to put pen to paper and begin his Resolutions as the cold New England winds blew in November or December of that year. If there was a trajectory he needed to take in order to become a respectable pastor like his father and grandfather, then these life goals would serve as the proper route to get there.

His time serving in New York City (1722–23) in particular was among the spiritual high points of his life as the dynamic, growing port city refreshed him. The church, which met at the corner of Broadway and Wall Street, was challenging and invigorating. His job was to help a church splinter group work through reconciliation issues with another faction. He discharged this task so well that he essentially worked himself out of a job when the church came together again peaceably.

In New York, he found deep and true friendships with a certain Madam Smith and her son John, with whom he resided during those months, marking them among the most treasured Christian relationships he had yet found. Edwards often waxed eloquent thinking back to this short time in his life. In his "Personal Narrative" (1740), he described these joyful months in glowing terms. Writing about his own Christian growth and sanctification during this specific period, he fondly recalled the following:

> My sense of divine things seemed gradually to increase, till I went to preach at New York; which was about a year and a half after they began. While I was there, I felt them, very sensibly, in a much higher degree, than I had done before. My longings after God and holiness, were much increased. Pure and humble, holy and heavenly Christianity, appeared exceeding amiable to me. I felt in me a burning desire to be in everything a complete Christian; and conformed to the blessed image of Christ: and that I might live in all things, according to the pure, sweet and blessed rules of the gospel. I had an eager thirsting after progress in these things. My longings after it, put me upon pursuing and pressing after them. It was my continual strife day and night, and constant inquiry, how I should be more holy, and live more holily, and more becoming a child of God, and disciple of Christ. I sought an increase of grace and holiness, and that I might live an holy life, with vastly more earnestness, than ever I sought grace, before I had it. I used to be continually examining myself, and studying and contriving for likely ways and means, how I should live holily, with far greater diligence and earnestness, than ever I pursued anything in my life: but with too great a dependence on my own strength; which afterwards proved a great damage to me. My experience had not then taught me, as it has done since, my extreme feebleness and impotence,

every manner of way; and the innumerable and bottomless depths of secret corruption and deceit, that there was in my heart. However, I went on with my eager pursuit after more holiness; and sweet conformity to Christ.[17]

Clearly, this was a period in which he was excited about ministry, enthused with a newfound profundity in his relationship with Christ, relished preaching grand and joyful sermons, and was greatly strengthened by the spiritual friendships he had found with Madam Smith and her son John.[18]

The Writing of His Personal Resolutions

When the nineteen-year-old pastor-in-training wrote his first few Resolutions in November or December 1722, he was not necessarily doing something creative or original. Instead, he was participating in a typical Puritan-era practice that was well established at the time. It was then commonplace to write a set of short, punctiliar vows or goals to help govern one's life. George Claghorn defines the Resolutions as "firm determinations" and says that for Edwards, "they were neither pious hopes, romantic dreams, nor legalistic rules. They were instructions for life, maxims to be followed in all respects. Edwards depended on the sustaining strength of his omnipotent Deity to enable him to live up to them" (WJE 16:741).

Writing his own set of statements and guidelines put Edwards in the same class of other thought-leaders, who cared deeply about the meaning of life and the proper way to conduct themselves. George Washington, for instance, wrote one hundred and ten personal resolutions to guide his life. Most of Washington's resolutions contained rules for maintaining one's manly integrity in front of subordinates, such as not spitting in the fire, avoiding chewing one's nails, and refraining from falling asleep when others speak. Some are even a bit humorous to us today.[19]

Edwards's Seventy Resolutions have often been compared and contrasted with those of Benjamin Franklin. Franklin also wrote his own set of personal guidelines, although he wrote far fewer in number (thirteen). By way of comparison, both of these great intellects warned themselves against speaking afoul, sloth, and wasting time, while exhorting themselves toward maintaining good social comportment. We might summarize by saying that Franklin's personal written constitution reveals the modern influence of the progressive Enlightenment: forward thinking and more focused on being a good, productive citizen than a saint. By way of contrast, in his Resolutions, Edwards is

---

17. "Personal Narrative," WJE 16:795.

18. See WJE 16:797.

19. Washington's resolutions can be found at http://davidbrucesmith.com/george-washingtons-resolutions/.

far more concerned with his soul, his relationship with Christ, Scripture, and the things of God—especially holiness and eternity. Edwards's Resolutions reveal the influence of the Reformation, which was far more concerned with being a faithful pilgrim than a prosperous citizen.

Among all of the voluminous writings of Jonathan Edwards, the Resolutions provide the clearest view into the inner chambers of the young man's heart, especially when combined with his diary that he also penned in the early pastoral years. His "Personal Narrative," which he wrote many years later as a more mature preacher and pastor, is likewise intensely introspective. In his sermons, however—and unlike most sermons from pastors today—he almost never mentioned himself, his thoughts, or his personal experiences. No self-respecting Puritan pastor ever told a personal anecdote as a sermon illustration! Thus his "Resolutions," "Diary," and "Personal Narrative" combine in a unique way to "provide a direct window into Edwards's interior life,"[20] giving us the best view into his soul.

The influence of Edwards's Seventy Resolutions has left a long and glorious legacy. They were initially printed in his first biography by Samuel Hopkins (1721–1803) and in an early memoir edited by Sereno E. Dwight, who seems to have been particularly affected by reading them.[21] Both Hopkins and Dwight printed the Resolutions, although their versions differ slightly from each other. In the official version of Edwards's *Works* printed by Yale University (WJE 16), slight differences between Dwight and Hopkins are noted in brackets. Since Edwards's own original draft has now been lost, we have to trust that Hopkins and Dwight combined to reproduce them accurately from the papers left written in Edwards's own hand. After those printings, the Resolutions began to circulate somewhat freely in the nineteenth century (1805, 1807, 1808, 1823, 1841, and 1877), usually included alongside period-related collections of inspirational materials such as church covenants, confessions of faith, and other pious devotional content.[22] Today, many Christian believers still find them to be of great spiritual and personal value, and I trust that you too will find them helpful in your own walk with Christ.

---

20. Marsden, *A Life*, 50.

21. Sereno Edwards Dwight (1786–1850), the great-grandson of Jonathan Edwards, was a lawyer, Congregational minister, chaplain of the U.S. Senate (1816–17), and president of Hamilton College in New York. He inherited Edwards's papers and published several of his works, along with an insightful memoir. This memoir is contained in the two-volume *Works* (Banner of Truth), I:xi–ccxxxiv. In 1822, Dwight published an edited volume of *The Life of David Brainerd*, and in 1829, the new, enlarged version of Edwards's works. For more on Dwight, see David Komline, "Dwight, Sereno Edwards (1786–1850)" in JEE, edited by Harry S. Stout, 161.

22. This and other background material on the Resolutions can be found in WJE 16:750.

Notes on the Surviving Manuscripts

Although we have many of Edwards's own handwritten notes and manuscripts preserved at the Beinecke Rare Manuscript Library at Yale University, sadly we do not have the original handwritten set of the Resolutions. We have scores of his sermons in his own handwriting, many notebooks, and drafts of some of his best masterpieces, but his "Resolutions," "Diary," "Personal Narrative," and early love poem "On Sarah Pierpont" have all been tragically lost to antiquity.

Thankfully, these texts were preserved in other copies and reprints and passed down to us today. Edwards's early admirers, Hopkins and Dwight, are to be either thanked or blamed, since they both seem to have had access to the original manuscript at some point. We do still have the original cover of the Resolutions, which is labeled as manuscript number GEN MSS 151 at the Yale Manuscript Library. Interested scholars will have to content themselves to see this sole surviving scrap of the original draft, which Edwards himself made for his small notebook.

Other Early Works

The Diary

During his early pastoral years (1722–26), Edwards also began a number of other writing projects that would serve to steer the general direction of his life. Of course, we will be focusing on the Resolutions in this book, but it is difficult to separate this project from these other works that he began writing at about the same time.

Most notably, the Resolutions have a symbiotic relationship with his personal diary (WJE 10:263). This notebook served as the sounding board by which he checked himself against the Resolutions he had already written and, when necessary, chide himself for failing to live up to them. He began writing in his notebook on December 18, which is the same date as the earliest dated resolution (the 35th Resolution). If there was any section prior to this first entry, it is now lost. Early biographer and Sereno E. Dwight believed there might have been a lost section since Edwards's notebook begins abruptly, without introduction or front matter (Works I:xxiii). It seems slightly unusual for a diary in that day not to contain any sort of prefatory material.

In his diary, Edwards often graded his performance in keeping his Resolutions. These two documents intertwine with one another as a vine of clematis or morning glories climb a string toward the sun. If the Resolutions were the stringline providing guidance and direction, then the diary climbed all over it, blooming forth thoughts and reflections on his spiritual progress.

Edwards's frequent reflections in his Diary on previously written Resolutions often prompted him to write new Resolutions, especially as he saw himself failing in certain areas. The Resolutions and Diary therefore seem to be in constant conversation with each other.

Edwards began his Resolutions sometime before December 18, 1722, and finished the last of his seventy personal guidelines on August 17, 1723, just eight months later. He also began the diary around December 18, 1722 (noting that he just completed writing the 35th Resolution in his first diary entry), carrying on that project until 1735. The Diary outlived the Resolutions by ten years, although his entries grew fewer and fewer after the close of his early pastoral years. In the years 1726, 1728, 1734, and 1735, there are just a few solitary entries, which indicates that the diary's place in his life seems to have functionally lessened as the early pastoral years were closing in 1725.

The "Miscellanies" and "Notes"

Another writing project that will be of some interest to us as we go through the Resolutions is his outstanding collection of the "Miscellanies," which is in many ways truly an extraordinary project! For decades of his life, Edwards kept multiple volumes on his "miscellaneous" thoughts about Scripture, philosophy, natural science, history, and especially theology. Notably, the first miscellaneous thought was "On Holiness," which very much coincides with Edwards's striving for spiritual maturity and sanctification in his Diary and Resolutions.

Edwards also began two other projects during this time: his "Notes on the Apocalypse" (1723) and "Notes on Scripture" (1724).[23] Both of these are also cross-referenced notes systems on various biblical constructs.

Overall, his early pastoral years signify the commencement of a vast and voluminous lifetime of writing, evidencing an unusually bright and illuminated mind. By the end of this period and before he took up the call to the Northampton Church in 1726, this young pastor had already written significant works in multiple fields of human knowledge, including dozens of sermons that were both quintessentially Puritan and exemplary expositions.

When he was twenty-three, the Northampton Church called him to serve as the associate pastor to his grandfather Solomon Stoddard. By that time, Edwards had written the following literary gems: "The Spider Letter," "The Mind,"[24] his Latin master's *Quaestio*,[25] and "Apostrophe to Sarah Pierrepont [sic]," along with essays on light, rainbows, natural philosophy, atoms, and being/existence.

---

23. "Notes on the Apocalypse" can be found in WJEO 5, and "Notes on Scripture" comprises the whole of WJEO 15.
24. "The Spider Letter" and "The Mind" as well as other scientific papers can be located in WJEO 6.
25. The *Quaestio* is contained in WJEO 14:47–66.

The Beginning of the "Resolutions" Project

As stated above, Edwards wrote the first twenty-one Resolutions some-time before December 18, 1722, possibly all in the same sitting (Works I:xx). We know this because they are not individually dated, and they are all in the same pen and handwriting.[26] Although the original handwritten copy of his Resolutions has now been lost, Sereno Dwight, who inherited his great-grandfather's personal papers, recognized this fact as he examined the original document in his own hands. Those who handle the original handwritten manuscripts of any of Edwards's works often remark about how he varied his handwriting to suit particular purposes, changing over time, and even between particular writing sessions. At some points in the published version of the diary, Dwight mentions how Edwards wrote in an indiscernible script to purposefully make certain sections unreadable, a personal shorthand of sorts.[27] Dwight suggests that this was to conceal material considered too private for any other eyes than the Lord's (Works I:xxxiv; WJE 16:783).

Edwards wrote another dozen or so Resolutions (the 22nd Resolution and following) quite early, again sometime before December 18, completing his first undated batch of personal rules (Works I:xx). Beginning with the 35th Resolution, Edwards began dating the "Resolutions" individually, or in some cases, writing them in small flurries of twos or threes. He also periodically amended those he had previously written, tightening them up, and postdating them as he reflected on their meaning and importance to him.[28] Tight correspondence between the "Resolutions" and the diary allows us today to peer somewhat into what Edwards was thinking as he added to them. With these writings, we get a glimpse of Edwards's private life and thoughts as he wrote new Resolutions and reflected on his ability to keep them.

The "Preamble": Striking a Delicate Balance

Preceding the Resolutions in Edwards's notebook are two sentences that set the tone for the document as a whole and shed light on his purpose for writing them, along with a short encouragement to himself to then remember them. Similar to the opening words of two other famous eighteenth-century

26. By the same "pen," we mean the size of handwriting, manner of script, character similarity, and even the kind of ink he used with various shades and widths.
27. For example, see "Diary," Friday, January 10, 1724. See also Dwight's comment in Works I:xxxiv and the editor's comment in WJE 16:783.
28. This explains why the 33rd Resolution is dated December 26, 1722, but the 35th Resolution is dated earlier at December 18, 1722. The later dating of the lower numbered resolution is explained by the fact that Edwards would often slightly edit or amend the resolutions, dating them as he went.

documents, the Declaration of Independence and the U.S. Constitution, we will call Edwards's opening a "preamble." Where Edwards's Resolutions differ from these official political statements is the first sentence of his "preamble" is a short, humble prayer.

Taking several loose sheets of paper, nineteen-year-old Jonathan Edwards dipped his quill into a pot of ink and wrote the first sentence:

> Being sensible that I am unable to do anything without God's help, I do humbly entreat him by his grace to enable me to keep these Resolutions, so far as they are agreeable to his will, for Christ's sake. (WJE 16:253)

Critical to the whole text, this line is often skipped over too quickly by those who study the Resolutions. Yet it is this prayer that governs all Seventy Resolutions, as Edwards admits from the very beginning that he humbly relies on God's grace. He knows he can't do this alone. He will need divine help! Concerning this first sentence, his great-grandson Sereno Dwight commented in a rather laudatory manner:

> He was too well acquainted with human weakness and frailty, even where the intentions are most sincere, to enter on any resolution rashly, or from a reliance on his own strength. He therefore in the outset looked to God for aid, who alone can afford success in the use of the best means, and in the intended accomplishment of the best purposes. This he places at the head of all his other important rules, that his whole dependence was on the grace of God, while he still proposes to recur to a frequent and serious perusal of them, in order that they might become the habitual directory of his life. (Works I:xx)[29]

The second sentence in the preamble is likewise important to the whole. Ironically, it foreshadows the darker paradox that perhaps Edwards did not yet see in his earliest enthusiasm. It creates a tension between humble reliance on God, and dogged self-determination.[30] He wrote the second sentence giving himself an important assignment: "Remember to read over these Resolutions once a week" (WJE 16:754).

As we will see many times in the chapters that follow, the young pastor often toggled back and forth between making this a spiritual self-improvement project and graciously resting in and receiving the divine work of sanctification. This is especially evident as we read the symbiotic interaction between the Resolutions and the Diary. As we see later on, his diary makes it clear that he himself often lost sight of this delicate balance he intended in his opening

---

29. In this quotation, we can see Dwight's tendency to see Edwards's spiritual struggles from a "glass half-full" perspective. He tends to view the resolutions and the diary positively, emphasizing Edwards's desire for sanctification, but perhaps failing to note Edwards's own admitted failures.

30. See below on the 3rd Resolution.

preamble prayer. It reveals that this simple "review once a week" assignment would become a frustrating tug-of-war between Edwards's need to review and act on those Resolutions already in force, and the constant desire to make even stronger Resolutions that might fortify him against failure. Sometimes the Resolutions were like a school assignment, and Edwards had to grade himself on his own report card in his diary.

In the months that followed, Edwards often struggled with how exactly he should "review" his Resolutions: Should he simply go over what he had already written, or write newer, stronger Resolutions when he messed up and failed? Should he track his shortcomings in some mathematical way by writing down examples of his failures, or should he simply rejoice in his victories wherever and whenever he had them? Edwards went back and forth in his own mind as to whether these occasional reviews were even helpful in the first place, and what he could possibly do when he found himself falling short of his own goals.

Nevertheless, he had a general direction and by the time the new year rolled around in January 1723, the project was moving ahead full scale. Thus, for the most part, Edwards began his Resolutions with an optimistic trajectory, hopeful for his personal growth in grace. At the same time, he drafted a rather rigorous project of self-analysis. He then began a highwire balancing act between his dependence on divine grace (the first line of the preamble) and a dogged determination to further himself by his own efforts in his walk with Christ (the second line of the preamble).

Studying the Resolutions: Three Basic Categories

To this point, I have provided a basic biographical sketch of Jonathan Edwards's life, and we have considered the literary genre of his personal Resolutions, the colonial practice of writing and reviewing individual directives or "life goals."[31] We have also gone over the particular time period of Edwards's personal development in which he wrote the Seventy Resolutions, during his brief pastorate in New York City from 1722–23, when he was nineteen years old.[32]

Now we move to looking at each of the Seventy Resolutions both separately and in groups to see how they might apply to our own lives today and

---

31. See Donald S. Whitney, *Finding God in Solitude: The Personal Piety of Jonathan Edwards (1703–1758) and Its Influence on His Pastoral Ministry* (New York: Peter Lang, 2014), 87–93.

32. For more information about this period, see WJE 10:261–94 and WJE 16:6–8. In the introductions to the Yale Editions, see Edwards's *Sermons and Discourses, 1720–23,* ed. Wilson H. Kimnach; and *Personal Writings,* ed. George S. Claghorn. The respective editors provide excellent sketches that shed much light on this relevant period of Edwards's life.

help us grow in the faith. As we go through them, we will have to be careful that we don't forget about the grace of God. Whenever Edwards tried too hard and depended on his own willpower, he became stuck and frustrated. We need to be careful not to make the same mistake.

In the coming chapters, we will examine the "Resolutions" in three major categories, which I have organized not necessarily in the order they were written and numbered, but rather by larger themes. I am going to call these three categories "Existential Resolutions," "Ethical Resolutions," and "Eschatological Resolutions." The first main group, Existential Resolutions, takes up the challenge of considering what Edwards believed to be the main purpose of his life. We will think about why we exist, why we live, and what our purpose is in life. This set of Resolutions attempts to answer the question, as the Westminster Divines posed it in 1647, "What is the chief end (or purpose) of man?"[33] In this first category, we will look at the Resolutions related to our purpose in living, our questions of personal faith and assurance, and how to love God with our hearts and minds.

The second main category, Ethical Resolutions, considers what Edwards believed to be his ethical duty. Ethics is the part of philosophy or religion concerned with how we ought to live, especially in relationship to one another. In the most general terms possible, ethics helps us think about how to be a good (or better) person. In this major grouping of Resolutions, we will look at Edwards's life goals related to self-control, interpersonal relationships, controlling his speech, duty, and taking action—while asking ourselves how we likewise should then live.

Finally, in the third main category, Eschatological Resolutions, we look at those ideas related to the end of human life on earth. The word *eschatology* has as its root the Greek word *eschatos*, which means "end" or "last." Eschatology considers in detail what the Bible teaches in relationship to death, the afterlife, the return of Christ, heaven, and hell. Edwards wrote quite a bit about the end of life, thinking about death more than most do today. Of course, this is mostly due to the time period with low average lifespans. Edwards himself was only fifty-five when he died. This third cluster of Resolutions considers matters touching on the repentance of sin, the brevity of life, and the eternal world to come.

With that as our introduction, let's begin our study of his Seventy Resolutions!

---

33. Westminster Shorter Catechism, Q&A #1 in The Westminster Confession of Faith and Catechisms (Lawrenceville, GA: The Orthodox Presbyterian Church, 2007), 355. For an online edition, see https://reformedstandards.com/westminster/wsc.html. This helpful website contains several of the primary confessions of Reformed, confessional Protestantism.

1

EXISTENTIAL RESOLUTIONS: THE MEANING AND PURPOSE OF LIFE

❖ Why Do We Exist in the First Place?
Resolutions 1, 2, 3, 4, 22, 27, 43, 44, 63

As we launch into the first section of our study, we will be considering the first major category, the Existential Resolutions of Jonathan Edwards. The word *existential* has in its root the word *exist* or the idea of "existence." Tracing the Latin back to its origin, it means to stand (*sistere*) out (*ex*). To stand out of what? Nothingness, I suppose! Have you ever thought about the very idea that you exist? For eons there was no such thing as "you," and yet at the very moment you were conceived you began to exist. And now you are. Once, there was no you, and now you exist—whether you like it or not. This is incredible, really. Of course, we can consider the theoretical possibility that there may be a universe in which neither you or I never existed. I can easily imagine a scenario in which most of world history unfolded about the same without me. This, however, is the only universe we know—a universe where you and I exist.

But the very fact that we do exist, that we are, that we have presence, consciousness, take up physical space, and are composed of physical atoms and molecules—that we possess life and even a soul—all seem to conspire together to beg the question of why. "Who am I, and why do I exist?" are among the fundamental questions all philosophers must tackle. After all, if we cannot get a hold on why we exist in the first place, then it will be even more difficult to answer questions such as "How should I live my life?" (Ethical Resolutions in chapter 2) or "What will become of me when I die?" (Eschatological Resolutions in chapter 3).

To ask why we exist in the first place is one of the most foundational and critical questions we must seek to answer, for we do not want to roll through life haphazardly like a pinball, with no particular purpose or direction. Nor do we want to passively flow through life like a leaf fallen floating on a gentle river stream. One thing that we can be sure of is that we did not create ourselves. We did not call ourselves into existence on our own, nor did we do anything to make our existence possible or necessary. That was solely the work of God.

Existentialism is a philosophical theory that essentially says that we each define our own purposes for being. That we get to individually make up our own purpose for living, and assign ourselves our own reality. But this flies in the face of the fact that we did not make ourselves. Our Creator made us, and therefore he alone determines our purpose. Our goal as human beings, and especially as Christians, is to discover our original purpose and meaning in life as early as possible and fully live out that purpose forever. The young Jonathan Edwards, just now taking his first pastoral responsibilities in the fractured Scottish Presbyterian Church in New York in 1722, determined to discover and define his purpose for life, even as he found that purpose assigned to him by being created by Almighty God. Resolutions numbered 1, 2, 3, 4, 22, 27, 43, 44, and 63 are Edwards's early attempt to wrestle with this question.

After we look at these first nine Resolutions related to our reason for existing, we will then move on to two other small subgroupings in this category: Resolutions on "Faith and Assurance" (26, 30, 32, 42, 33, and 64) and on "Heart and Mind" (11, 14, 15, 24, 25, 28, 45, 60, and 65).

1. Resolved, that I will do whatsoever I think to be most to God's glory, and my own good, profit and pleasure, in the whole of my duration, without any consideration of the time, whether now, or never so many myriads of ages hence. Resolved to do whatever I think to be my duty, and most for the good and advantage of mankind in general. Resolved to do this, whatever difficulties I meet with, how many and how great soever.

The first resolution is glorious, beautiful, and complex. It is the Polaris of the whole document—a North Star of sorts—pointing toward a true and sure direction that the rest of the Resolutions will follow. In fact, this 1st Resolution can be thought of as summarizing the entire seventy. We might consider the other sixty-nine as an extended commentary on the first one, which makes it ever more specific and particular. Although Edwards touches on many facets of human existence, he continually returns to this touchstone: the glory of God.

Some general observations here are important as we take our first steps in this journey. First, we can see why categorizing the Resolutions under the three main headings of *existential, ethical,* and *eschatological* is a helpful format as they are all present already in the very first rule.[1] Edwards's *existential*

---

1. I borrow the idea of "tri-perspectivalism" from my professor, theologian John Frame, whose usual categories in his systematic theology and other works are the

purpose is set forth when he writes, "Whatsoever . . . is most to the glory of God, and my own good." His *ethical duty* is represented in the phrase, "My duty . . . for the good and advantage of mankind in general," and his *eschatological framework* is evident when he says, "In the whole of my duration . . . whether now, or never so many myriads of ages hence."

It is not surprising that Edwards immediately mentions the glory of God as the *summum bonum*, or "greatest good," of his whole life. Like most Puritan youth reared in Calvinist theology, Edwards was trained in the Westminster Shorter Catechism,[2] and probably knew from an early age that "man's chief end is to glorify God and enjoy Him forever." Although the Adopting Act of 1729,[3] which gave the Church of Scotland's famous doctrinal statement authority in the American Colonies, was still several years away, the shadow of the Shorter Catechism's influence was already growing long in Puritan homes and churches in early America. For this reason, the fact that Edwards mentions God's glory in the very first clause of his Resolutions is not surprising.

One serendipity in the 1st Resolution, however, is how accurately this paragraph anticipates several of his major works and treatises as a more mature pastor and theologian. The glory of God is the dominating motif of his masterpiece, *The End for Which God Created the World* (1755).[4] Not only that, but the "general good of mankind," what he later calls "benevolence to being in general," would likewise take shape in his philosophical treatise, *The Nature of True Virtue* (1755).[5] By focusing on both God and mankind, Edwards intentionally assumes a cruciform pattern for his life: the vertical axis is the prime motive to glorify God, and the horizontal axis is his desire to bless and

---

normative, the situational, and the existential. See Frame, *Systematic Theology* (Phillipsburg, NJ: P&R, 2013).

2. See Reagan Marsh, "Catechism," in JEE, 82–3. Here, Marsh notes several important places in the WJEO in which Edwards's use of and commentary on the process of catechism is extolled. Note especially WJE 16:205, 280, 409. For more on the use of the Westminster Catechism in Edwards's era, see Andreas J. Beck and Willem Van Vlastuin, "Sanctification between Westminster and Northampton," *Jonathan Edwards Studies* 2, no. 2 (2012): 3–27.

3. See "Adopting Act (1729)" in *Dictionary of the Presbyterian and Reformed Tradition in America*, ed. D. G. Hart (Phillipsburg, NJ: P&R, 1999), 13–14.

4. *The End for Which God Created the World* is contained in WJEO 8:403–536. This work is a theological masterpiece and gives a Trinitarian and theocentric explanation for the universe, citing the glory of God and the joy of his people in praise as the primary and secondary reasons that God created the universe.

5. *The Nature of True Virtue* is contained in WJEO 8:537–38. This is one of Edwards's unique works in that it is philosophical in nature and he does not utilize the Scriptures as nearly as much as he does in his other important works. This is because he wrote this in part to help combat the growing anthropocentrism of the Enlightenment. Here, Edwards argues that true virtue or morality must necessarily be grounded on a love for God, even before and above love for fellow man.

serve his fellow human beings. Or to say it another way, his ultimate end is to glorify his Creator, and his subordinate end is to work for the good of others. One cannot help but see some influence here too from the Lord's first and second greatest commandments:

> Jesus said unto him, Thou shalt love the Lord thy God with all thy heart, and with all thy soul, and with all thy mind. This is the first and great commandment. And the second is like unto it, Thou shalt love thy neighbour as thyself. On these two commandments hang all the law and the prophets. (Matt. 22:37–40)

The phrase "in the whole of my duration" is interesting. One application is apparent enough: life has a "duration," a time limit—like sands in an hourglass. This implies that the nineteen-year-old is already thinking about life's brevity. Our mortal existence has a shelf-life, with an expiration date known only to God (see Ps. 139:16). For those living during this time, death was a very present reality. They knew all too well that life does not go on forever and that sometimes it ends before it can even begin.

The contemplation of death will be a steadfastly recurring theme in the Resolutions, which we will consider in some depth in the latter part of this book. Why was death such a preoccupation for the young Edwards, when most teenagers are thinking about everything *but* their own demise? This can partly be explained by the fact that the sooner he discovered his purpose for living, the less time he wasted in general and more time fulfilling his purpose. Knowing that life is short, like a mist (James 4:13–17), Edwards determined to make the most of it.

2. Resolved, to be continually endeavoring to find out some new invention and contrivance to promote the forementioned things.

If Edwards failed to perfectly keep many of his directives, he did not fail to keep his second resolution at least. This is one he certainly made good on. But what does Edwards mean by "new invention and contrivance"? I take this phrase to correspond to the innovative ways the young Puritan began to record his thoughts, especially as he thought inventively with pen in hand. Throughout his life, he had a hard time setting aside his pen as he mulled gigantic concepts like God, heaven, hell, redemption, and the meaning of his life:

> My method of study, from my first beginning the work of the ministry, has been very much by writing; applying myself, in this way, to improve every important hint; pursuing the clue to my utmost, when any thing in reading, meditation, or conversation has been suggested to my mind, that seemed to promise light, in any weighty point; thus penning what appeared to me my best thoughts on innumerable subjects for my own benefit. (WJE 10:71)

Edwards was curious. He was a keen observer and a lifelong learner. The vast worlds of knowledge that could be observed and considered in creation, nature, books, the inner self, and Scripture would have to be dutifully studied and recorded. We know that during this New York period of his life, Edwards had an explosion of productive writing, most of which was driven by his own intellectual curiosity. He began several idea notebooks to record almost everything: his thoughts and feelings, sermon ideas, observations on Scripture, and more.[6] He wrote not so much for publication as for self-expansion and improvement. In some ways, Edwards's whole life was as a living human mind being carried around on "spindly" legs.

In 1722, he began an unedited masterpiece of personal observations on theology, Scripture, philosophy, titled the "Miscellanies."[7] Though Edwards is known primarily as a preacher and theologian, he probably deserves more credit as an organizational genius as well. His mind was a menagerie of beautiful concepts, and he needed "new inventions and contrivances" to organize his complex thoughts. These notebooks show Edwards at his organizational best. They are his "everything" folders—individually numbered, cross-referenced, indexed and dutifully annotated.

There are about 1,400 miscellaneous entries, some of which are as short as a line or a paragraph, and others as long as treatises or short books. The Miscellanies are thoughtful, deep, sublime, and imaginative. By 1723, Edwards had completed more than one hundred entries in this series of journals. By 1725, he had more than two hundred entries. One can only imagine what he would have done if he had had a computer!

Unlike the Resolutions (which he stopped composing in 1723) and the Diary (in which he ceased making entries by 1735, functionally as early as 1725), Edwards kept adding to his Miscellanies for the rest of his life.[8] Although I will have much more to say later on, suffice it to say for now that the Miscellanies provide a longitudinal look into his genius over the period of a few decades, in which he exhibited greater insight, depth, and perseverance in maintaining entries than we see in his diary. By the end of 1723, the prime year of both the Resolutions and Diary projects, Edwards had already begun the Miscellanies with entries A–Z and Aa–Zz. After he realized he needed a more advanced numbering system, he completed entries 1–94 by the end of that year. But there were more "inventions and contrivances" still to come.

---

6. Kenneth P. Minkema gives an outstanding overview of most of these personal writings in his chapter in *The Cambridge Companion to Jonathan Edwards*, ed. Stephen J. Stein (Cambridge: Cambridge University Press, 2007), 39–60.

7. In total, there are over 1,400 "Miscellanies." These comprise WJEO 13, 18, 20, and 23, which can be found in print and online (http://edwards.yale.edu/research/browse).

8. For an excellent volume on the "Miscellanies," providing several insightful articles into the main themes of this important note series, see *The "Miscellanies" Companion*, ed. Robert L. Boss (Fort Worth, TX: JESociety Press, 2018).

Edwards also began a *Catalogue of Books*, in which he detailed his reading plans for spiritual and intellectual edification.[9] He launched a journal titled *Notes on the Apocalypse*[10] for taking notes on all things eschatological. Edwards always had a hankering for end-time-related content and took copious notes on the book of Revelation, comparing these texts to current events in Europe and around the world that he thought fit in. In 1724, still within the purview of his prime Diary writing era, he began yet another journal project, *Notes on Scripture*,[11] which he replaced in 1730 by still another new note-taking project in the form of the "Blank Bible."[12] Both of these projects contain methods for his ever-expanding series of notes on biblical passages.

The 2nd Resolution, then, can be thought of as the launching pad of an entire written intellectual and theological project to which Edwards would continually contribute for the rest of his life.

3. Resolved, if ever I shall fall and grow dull, so as to neglect to keep any part of these Resolutions, to repent of all I can remember, when I come to myself again.

The vexing possibility that his initial passion might "grow dull" in his Resolutions was already considered by the time Edwards wrote the 3rd Resolution. No one should expect that their spiritual life is always up and never down. The young pastor knew that, but perhaps he simply didn't know how far down it could go! Edwards staved off these downturns as much as possible by examining himself against his own written rules, repenting and confessing every infraction he observed, hoping the Spirit would bring him back to "[him]self again." But Edwards's diary shows that this struggle would end up being more violent than the young, emerging minister may have originally anticipated. This battle raged back and forth: one day, Edwards rejoiced in his apparent sanctification, and the next, he lamented his soul's weak condition.

For instance, in Monday, December 24, just about a week after he began the project and had penned thirty-eight Resolutions, he added a new convention to the project:

> Monday, Dec. 24. Higher thoughts than usual of the excellency of Jesus Christ and his kingdom. Concluded to observe, at the end of every month, the number of breaches of resolutions, to see whether they increase or diminish, to begin from this day, and to compute from that the weekly account, my monthly in-

---

9. This record of Edwards's books is contained in WJEO 26. For more information on this, see Iain Murray, *Jonathan Edwards: A New Biography* (Carlisle, PA: Banner of Truth Trust, 200), 67–68.
10. *Notes on the Apocalypse* can be found in WJEO 5.
11. *Notes on Scripture* can be found in WJE 5.
12. The "Blank Bible" can be found in WJEO 24.

crease, and, out of the whole, my yearly increase, beginning from new year days. (WJE 16:760)

It seems he actually considered tracking the number of infractions of his Resolutions somehow to determine if there were any major trends. He keenly observed himself and his patterns, as he had done before when he analyzed the woodland spider and considered all of its habits and behaviors.[13] This seems to indicate that Edwards believed his infractions were limited enough to calculate by some tally-mark method. But soon, he began to lament the condition of his soul and cried out somewhat dolefully:

> Wednesday, Jan. 2, 1722–23. Dull. I find by experience, that let me make resolutions, and do what I will, with never so many inventions, it is all nothing, and to no purpose at all, without the motions of the Spirit of God: for if the Spirit of God should be as much withdrawn from me always, as for the week past, notwithstanding all I do, I should not grow; but should languish, and miserably fade away. I perceive, if God should withdraw his Spirit a little more, I should not hesitate to break my resolutions, and should soon arrive at my old state. There is no dependence upon myself. Our resolutions may be at the highest one day, and yet, the next day, we may be in a miserable dead condition, not at all like the same person who resolved. (WJE 16:760)

At the conclusion of this book, we will return to this topic as we consider why Edwards did eventually abandon the Resolutions/Diary project as a means of personal sanctification. For the moment, it is enough to note that at age nineteen, as his first pastoral duties in a Christian congregation were beginning to press in on him in the small New York Presbyterian Church, Edwards determined to drive forward in his new project, hoping that waves of grace combined with the steely determination of his will would help him override any "dullness." If nothing else, we can rightly commend Edwards for setting God's glory as his first and ultimate aim.

When we read Edwards's diary in conjunction with his Resolutions, it becomes apparent how very much like the psalmist the young pastor could be. Have you ever noticed how often the Psalms swing wildly from joy to lament, sometimes even within the same psalm? Open your Bible to one of the psalms of David in particular, and you will likely find the king of Israel extolling God in the happiest terms, as well as lamenting the sorrowful state of his own soul—in the same psalm!

Summarizing the potency of the 3rd resolution, Steve Lawson comments, "Of course, Edwards was concerned to deal with all sin in his life, not just violations of the 'Resolutions.' His writings indicate that whenever he became aware of any sin, he sought to turn away from it."[14] Sadly, since

---

13. See Edwards's early writings on spiders in WJEO 6:163–69.
14. Lawson, *Unwavering Resolve*, 80.

we are not often aware of all of our own shortcomings, Psalm 19:12 advises us to repent even of hidden faults. We should continually ask God to reveal to us those remote places in our hearts where we retain "autonomous zones" that do not want to submit to God's lordship. So far, Edwards has set a fairly determined course for his life. In the Existential Resolutions that follow, we will see him continue to refine his purpose and add ballast to his life's course, returning again to confessional language from the Reformed tradition.

4. *Resolved, never to do any manner of thing, whether in soul or body, less or more, but what tends to the glory of God; nor be, nor suffer it, if I can avoid it.*

In the 4th Resolution, part of the original twenty-one undated guidelines for personal growth, Edwards doubled down on what he had already written in the 1st Resolution. If this 1st Resolution was a positive statement (I *will* do this), then the 4th Resolution is its opposite (I will *not* do that). The force of this short, negative statement does not really add too much to what has been previously said, other than that it makes clear that Edwards steered his life far from anything that detracted from his God-glorifying direction. Part of godliness after all is not only doing what is right, but also avoiding what is wrong.

Since sin is often categorized by theologians in terms of both commission (whatever actively transgresses the law of God) and omission (whatever fails to undertake God's command), Edwards resolved to endeavor to walk the straight path between both pits. Although the phrase "nor be, nor suffer it" is slightly awkward to the modern reader, it implies that Edwards would not tolerate or permit within himself whatever failed to give God glory. Sereno Dwight, almost unfailingly approving, comments, "There is a remarkable tenderness of conscience discovered in every particular which has been stated. The man who could thus write, was not one who could easily trifle with sin, or who could enter any of its paths without the immediate reproofs of an offended conscience" (Works I:xxii).

One interesting note about the 4th Resolution is that it does once again hint toward confessional, catechetical language. When the Westminster Shorter Catechism considers the law of God, it often goes back and forth between positive statements (the law requires this) and negative statements (the law forbids that). For instance, in questions on third commandment, the Shorter Catechism tells us that it requires using God's name in ways that are reverent and holy and forbids using his name in ways that are profane and abusive. Edwards realized this, likely through reading the Shorter Catechism as a young man, and he saw fit to add a negative statement in the 4th Resolution to balance his positive statement in the 1st Resolution. Whether Edwards did this intentionally is uncertain. Perhaps it was just in his bloodstream, growing up with the catechism in the home and memorizing it in college at Yale.[15]

---

15. Murray, *A New Biography*, 31.

But there also may be an allusion to other confessional language with the wording of glorifying God with "body and soul." Here, Edwards glosses the first entry in the Heidelberg Catechism, which like the Westminster Shorter Catechism is memorable for its beauty and sublime quality:

> That I with *body and soul*, both in life and death, am not my own, but belong unto my faithful Saviour Jesus Christ; who, with his precious blood, has fully satisfied for all my sins, and delivered me from all the power of the devil; and so preserves me that without the will of my heavenly Father, not a hair can fall from my head; yea, that all things must be subservient to my salvation, and therefore, by his Holy Spirit, He also assures me of eternal life, and makes me sincerely willing and ready, henceforth, to live unto him.[16]

On the balance, it would seem that in the 4th Resolution, Edwards promises more than a mere mortal is realistically able to perform. By resolving not to "do any manner of thing" but "what tends to the glory of God," the ambitious young pastor would appear to be outpacing all human ability to comply. There is a danger in performance-based righteousness, isn't there? Looking back on his youthful ambition, a more mature Edwards would later write, "I made seeking salvation the business of my life. But yet it seems to me, *I sought after a miserable manner*" (WJE 16:791; italics mine).

And yet, if we fault him in this, the problem hardly lies in his aiming too high for his own sanctification. After all, Scripture *does* clearly call believers to aim highly toward lives of holiness (Lev. 11:44; 1 Pet. 1:16). Instead, the fault most likely lies in his placing too much confidence in his own mortal ability to actually carry out both his positive and negative Resolutions. Overall, though, it is hard to condemn Edwards for so loftily stating the primacy of the glory of God as the ultimate meaning and purpose for human existence.

22. Resolved, to endeavor to obtain for myself (as much happiness in the other world), as I possibly can, with all of the power, might, vigor, and vehemence, yea violence, I am capable of, or can bring myself to exert, in any way that can be thought of.

All human beings long to be happy. This is ubiquitous, without exception. Obtaining happiness is the universal quest that captivates all people, whether we attempt to fulfill this desire through adventure, travel, romance, or lesser and more dangerous pursuits such as drugs, alcohol, or fornication. It seems that the desire for joy is an inescapable and overwhelming part of being human. Ask any person on the street what they want to get out of life, and they will likely give you their story of a treasure hunt for whatever they believe gladdens the heart.

---

16. See the Heidelberg Catechism, https://reformedstandards.com/three-forms-of-unity/heidelberg-catechism.html (my italics).

As philosopher Blaise Pascal indicated, finding joy is the undergirding obsession that causes some men to rush into battle and others to flee; it is even the motivation of those who hang themselves.[17] Saint Augustine, in his own testimony of conversion, describes seeking after joy but finding it in all the wrong places: "For there is a joy not granted to the wicked but only to those who worship Thee thankfully—and this joy Thou Thyself art. The happy life is this—to rejoice to Thee, in Thee, and for Thee. It is this and there is no other."[18] Augustine found joy, but not after searching fruitlessly for it in petty theft, the violence of the gladiatorial games, or especially fornication and sexual pleasure. The young Edwards made sure not to make the same mistake. His happiness would be "in the other world." This is a mature recognition of truth, and one that few people so young discover.

Throughout his career, Jonathan Edwards wrote as much about joy (or as he more commonly styled it, "happiness") as practically any other topic.[19] Rather than finding the truth about joy the hard way as Augustine did, through trial and error, Edwards rooted his understanding about happiness in God's own joyful nature. He believed that mankind has a tremendous capacity for real, lasting joy, since we are beings created in the image of God (Gen. 1:27). For Edwards, this is crucial because God is an essentially joyful Divine Being. Edwards's writings on the Trinity[20] indicate that he viewed God as infinitely and personally joyful; happy in and among the three persons of Father, Son, and Holy Spirit. Rather than an angry, capricious God, or even a God who is aloof or above emotions and feelings, Edwards viewed the Lord as a perfectly joyful and harmonious being, because each of the divine persons essentially exist rejoicing in one another. For Edwards, the Holy Spirit, the most mysterious *persona* in the Godhead, is actually the joyful, interpersonal love between the Father and the Son.

One time, Edwards preached the following to his congregation:

> Man is of such a nature, that he is capable of an exceedingly great degree of happiness; he is made of a vastly higher nature than the brutes, and therefore he must have vastly higher happiness to satisfy. . . . It must be an incomprehensible object that must satisfy the soul; it will never be contented with that, and only

---

17. Quoted in John Piper, *Desiring God: Meditations of a Christian Hedonist* (Sisters, OR: Multnomah Books, 2003), 19.

18. St. Augustine's "Confessions," quoted in my *A Theology of Joy: Jonathan Edwards and Eternal Happiness in the Holy Trinity* (Fort Worth, TX: JESociety Press, 2018), 57.

19. I have done a vast amount of research to track Edwards's uses of joy, gladness, and happiness in his theology. See my *Theology of Joy*. See also my entry on "Happiness" in JEE, 273–74.

20. See, for instance, Edwards's "Treatise on Grace" and "Essay on the Trinity," both contained in the *Treatise on Grace and Other Posthumous Writings Including Observations on the Trinity*, ed. Paul Helm (Cambridge: James Clark & Co., 1971).

that, to which it can see an end, it will never be satisfied with that happiness to which it can find a bottom.[21]

Of course, he followed that statement with exhortations to find that joy in Christ alone. For Edwards, any joy that could be exhausted or terminated was no joy at all. Wine? Sex? A temperate autumn day? They all come to an end. As such, these are all merely finite sources of pleasure. Real joy—the substantial, unmitigated, and unadulterated happiness that the soul seeks—can never be fully obtained by hands and tongue. The pleasures of this life are at best types and shadows of the real experience found in Christ alone. At worst, they are damnable counterfeits sent by the evil one to distract and confuse our hearts. For this reason, as Edwards rightly recognized even as a young man, true happiness could only be obtained in the "other world"—the world that doesn't end. We fight and strive *now* to recognize and obtain what will really satisfy *then*.

Indeed, this life has its share of delights: weddings, childbirth, anniversaries, and holidays. But the best of these celebrations are those that point us to the One who alone can satisfy the soul. To truly pursue Christ, the believer must reject all counterfeits that manifest themselves as various temptations. They quench our thirst no better than a mirage of water in the desert. The true fountain, however, is Christ. "Man's highest happiness consists in holiness," Edwards wrote. "It is by this the reasonable creature is united to God, the fountain of all good. . . . But no other enjoyments or privileges whatever will make a man happy without this" (WJEO 8:161).

23. Resolved, frequently to take some deliberate action, which seems most unlikely to be done, for the glory of God, and trace it back to the original intention, designs and ends of it; and if I find it not to be for God's glory, to repute it as a breach of the 4th Resolution.

The force of this 23rd Resolution comes from the phrase "take some deliberate action." To paraphrase a famous shoe company that doesn't need any more advertising, "Just do *something*!" Many of us are guilty of being altogether too passive. If we are not careful, much of our life simply slips through our fingers like water. Too often, we resign ourselves to lethargy and inertia. We wait for life—for something good—to finally happen to us. We wait for opportunities to come our way. When they do come, we may even pass them by because they don't seem quite perfect. In so doing, we waste days, weeks, and even years. I once read of a particular genius who had written several books in his own mind, but he was too lazy to write them out. He had ideas, but he lacked initiative to see them through. Edwards determined

---

21. Jonathan Edwards, "Safety, Fullness, and Refreshment in Christ," *Sermons of Jonathan Edwards* (Peabody, MA: Hendrickson, 2005), 29–30.

not to make such foolish mistakes, and with the 23rd Resolution, he resolved
to be a man of "deliberate action."

But not just any action, he especially wanted to do those things that are
"most unlikely to be done." What he meant here is not exactly clear. Perhaps
he meant those things unlikely to be done by others. In this case, the thrust
of this resolution is to be the rare kind of person willing to do what others
refrain from doing out of fear or because of the sheer difficulty of the task.
Or perhaps Edwards meant he would do things that are unlikely to be done
by *himself* due to his lack of motivation or dread of the task. We all have
challenges in our lives we simply cannot muster up the strength to tackle: for
example, those stacks of papers or bills sitting right now on our desks. Either
way, Edwards roused himself above and beyond the lethargy of hesitation.
The one thing he does make clear in this resolution is that everything must
be done for the express glory of God.

In adding the lines "trace it back to the original intention, designs and
ends of it; and if I find it not to be for God's glory, to repute it as a breach of the
4th Resolution," Edwards is challenging himself to be honest about his own
internal motivations. Sometimes we do things uncritically. We never stop to
ask *why* we do them. We do not do the rigorous work of self-evaluation. We
must be brave enough to ask, "What exactly *was* my motivation for doing
this? Am I choosing this activity because it will make me look good before
others? Am I doing this to uphold my own reputation? Am I choosing this
activity over another because it allows me to put off a greater task that I
dread?" The godly person must first of all be an honest person.

Sometimes—and probably more often than we care to admit—when we
really "trace it back to the original intention," or the very source or spark of
our actions, we find the dreadful reality that we operate in a mode of self-
promotion or at least self-preservation. In these moments of duplicity, Jesus'
words take on a special power of conviction,

> Take heed that ye do not your alms before men, to be seen of them: otherwise
> ye have no reward of your Father which is in heaven. Therefore when thou doest
> thine alms, do not sound a trumpet before thee, as the hypocrites do in the syna-
> gogues and in the streets, that they may have glory of men. Verily I say unto you,
> They have their reward. (Matt. 6:1–2)

Just about the time Edwards wrote the following words for himself, he
preached the virtue of such critical introspection in his 1722/1723 sermon
"The Duty of Self-Examination":

> Thus, all our actions ought to be strictly examined and tried, and not only barely
> to consider the outward action as it is in itself: but also from what principle our
> actions do arise from; what internal principle we act and live [by], for actions
> are either good or bad according to the principle whence they arise. We must

consider whether what we do, we do from a love to God and his commands, or whether from a love to ourselves—that is, to our flesh—love to this world, and love to sin. (WJE 10:488)

It takes a great amount of introspection to admit this, and many aren't willing to analyze their intentions in such ways. We aren't brave enough to look at our own X-rays. We are afraid we might see a cancerous lump of self-love. We utter pious words or act in obviously praiseworthy ways for others to see, but the motivation rises no higher than "for me."

27. Resolved, never willfully to omit anything, except the omission be for the glory of God; and frequently to examine my omissions.

Growing up in a liturgical church, one of the first prayers I memorized as a child was this traditional form of corporate repentance: "We confess that we are in bondage to sin and cannot free ourselves. We have sinned against You in thought, word, and deed; by what we have done, *and by what we have left undone*" (my italics). In the 4th Resolution, although he already touched on the distinction between sins of commission and omission, Edwards returns to the same theme in this 27th Resolution.

Indeed, it is a biblical emphasis. If Eve committed the first sin of commission in taking the forbidden fruit and eating it (Gen. 3:6), then Adam had already failed by way of omission before her. Adam failed to defend the garden from the serpent, although he had been assigned as its gardener (Gen. 2:15). He failed to defend the purity of his wife from Satanic assault (Gen. 3:1), and he acted passively by failing to honor God's name from the lies and smears of Satan (Gen. 3:4). It is for this reason that as the covenant head of his family and humanity as a whole, Adam is considered guilty of the first breach of faith and is often described in Scripture as committing the archetypal sin (Rom. 5:14–21; 1 Cor. 15:22, 45).

Though we often think of sin in terms of overt actions, things we *do* (killing, lying, stealing, just to name a few), it is also true that failing to act in a godly way can be just as deadly to one's spiritual life, family, or church. Think of parents failing to discipline their children through their formative teens. Or consider an elder board that repeatedly declines to take action against a gossiping and divisive person. As Christians, we must also consider that we can do just as much harm through passivity and inertia as we can by action. Prayerlessness, timidity to boldly proclaim Christ's grace through evangelism, failing to show up dutifully for work at our jobs, and even a reticence to speak out when called on to be truth-tellers can have a deleterious effect on our relationship with God and others. Our homes and communities are all the weaker when we act as feeble, unmotivated spectators when decisive action is required.

Notice though that Edwards reserves the possibility that some omissions
are *not* sinful and instead can be for the glory of God. For instance, when
we overlook an insult instead of responding, we "omit" to the glory of God.
Scripture says, "Good sense makes one slow to anger, and it is his glory to
overlook an offense" (Prov. 19:11 ESV). Edwards's Authorized Version read,
"The discretion of a man deferreth his anger; and it is his glory to pass over a
transgression." Of course, we might think of Christ's commendation of "turning the other cheek" as a classic example in which an omission of justified
self-defense is positively commendable (Matt. 5:39).

But in line with Edwards's desire to closely monitor himself, he also
noted his commitment to "frequently examine his omissions." This accords
with his overall desire to critically evaluate his whole life. Why this continual,
morbid introspection? One possible explanation for this drive is that the Puritans in general, having failed to fully reform the Church of England in the
1600s, combined with their inability to thoroughly Christianize the societies
in which they lived, were forced to turn inwards to the heart to carry out their
spiritual reformation projects. In fact, the very name "Puritans" comes from
the drive toward "purification of the self and of society as well."[22] Donald
Whitney writes in proper balance,

> This examination was not for the purposes of discerning if one had reached an
> arbitrary level of separation from the world or sufficient conquest of sin in the
> pursuit of being acceptable to God, rather it was in order to detect whether the
> inner motions of the soul and its outworkings in the life were congruent with
> those who had experienced regeneration and the indwelling of the Holy Spirit.[23]

In other words, Edwards and the Puritans weren't checking in on themselves
merely to become proud of their accomplishments (though that is always a
temptation), as much as to ensure that the gracious operations of the Holy
Spirit were alive and well within themselves.

Overall, self-examination is probably good general advice for us. We
might do well to ask ourselves some hard questions from time to time about
our own sins of omission such as, "Why did I fail to speak my convictions
when others started gossiping?" Or "Why am I so afraid to invite my neighbor to church?" Or "Why am I not praying as often as I used to?" If Edwards
and the Puritans in general were a little bit too aggressive in self-monitoring,
then there are probably at least a few of us who could stand to become more
intentionally self-aware. It is necessary to ask ourselves why we do what we
do, as well as why we don't do what we don't do.

David, the sweet psalmist of Israel, encourages us wisely by his own
example when he prayed, "Search me, O God, and know my heart: try me,

---

22. Mark A. Noll, quoted in Whitney, *"Finding God in Solitude, "*11.
23. Noll, 15.

and know my thoughts: And see if there be any wicked way in me, and lead me in the way everlasting" (Ps. 139:23–24).

43. *Resolved, never henceforward, till I die, to act as if I were anyway my own, but entirely and altogether God's, agreeable to what is to be found in Saturday, Jan. 12.*

Fundamental to most modern Western philosophy and social theory is the idea that the individual is sovereign in and of himself. He is, as they say, "his own man." Painting with a broad brush, this may be the single defining and differentiating concept between the East and the West. The East tends to think of humans collectively, but the West tends to think of humanity individually. This is the big "aha!" that led nations such as Great Britain and especially the United States of America to encode civil liberties and human rights into the fabric of their constitutions and laws. Though Edwards lived in the time of the Enlightenment, the dawning of the enshrinement of individual autonomy, he did not fully or uncritically imbibe of all its principles. In this 43rd Resolution, Edwards asserts not his individual rights and autonomy, but rather his possession by God.

The Bible teaches that we do not belong to ourselves, but to God: "Know ye not that your body is the temple of the Holy Ghost which is in you, which ye have of God, *and ye are not your own? For ye are bought with a price:* therefore glorify God in your body, and in your spirit, which are God's" (1 Cor. 6:19–20; italics mine). In the context of this passage, Paul reminds us that we belong to the Lord in order to fortify us against temptations toward sexual immorality. How then could we yield up our own bodies back into the slavery of disordered sexual desires and behaviors? If Christ has saved us through his own blood and cross, then we now owe him a life-debt of service.

The primary confession of the Christian faith is that Jesus Christ is Lord (see Acts 10:36; Rom. 10:9; Phil. 2:11). This means that we confess him as master, owner, sovereign, our king. Therefore, we do not truly belong to ourselves. Even our bodies. We are owned by someone else. We are the rightful property and possession of another. Actually, this is doubly true of us who believe: first we belong to God, our Heavenly Father, as his creatures by virtue of creation, and now much more also through our redemption in Jesus Christ. In the face of Western individualism, Edwards reminded himself that more radical expressions of self-autonomy were only a deception. He knew we belong to God and none other.

That we are owned and controlled by our Lord and God is at first a terrifying thought, and only with much reflection and prayer does this become a consolation to us. If he is truly our rightful owner, then this means he can demand anything he wants from us. Anything. There is nothing Christ cannot command me to do that I would not be obliged to perform. But at the same time, this is also a greatly freeing thought because this means we cannot be owned or controlled by anyone else: not my boss, my rival, or any other human has the right to treat me like their possession, emotionally or otherwise.

One window into Edwards's emotional state as he wrote this profession of Christian lordship in the 43rd Resolution becomes clear in a corresponding diary entry he wrote on the same day, January 12, 1723:

> Now, henceforth I am not to act in any respect as my own. I shall act as my own, if I ever make use of any of my powers to anything that is not to the glory of God, and don't make the glorifying him my whole and entire business; if I murmur in the least at afflictions; if I grieve at the prosperity of others; if I am anyway uncharitable; if I am angry because of injuries; if I revenge; if I do anything, purely to please myself, or if I avoid anything for the sake of my ease; if I omit anything because it is great self-denial; if I trust to myself: if I take any of the praise of any good that I do, or rather God does by me; or if I am any way proud. (WJE 16:762–63)

Perhaps these "afflictions" and "injuries" had been more than theoretical of late for him, and he was wrestling mightily with his own pride due to a slight or offense received from someone important to him. It is possible he had been hurt by some words that cut him to the quick. He would have to remind himself of the importance of belonging wholly to another—to God. He did not live for the purpose of making others happy or to impress any other audience but one. The sooner we realize we cannot be controlled and manipulated by the whimsical opinions of others the sooner we take one step closer to true freedom.

44. Resolved, that no other end but religion, shall have any influence at all on any of my actions; and that no action shall be, in the least circumstance, any otherwise than the religious end will carry it. Jan. 12, 1723.

Poll any number of people today, and they will tell you that they are "spiritual but not religious." We bristle at the term "religion" or "religious." Most people simply are no longer comfortable with those words, and fewer and fewer use them to describe themselves. When I became a Christian in eighth grade, one of the first things I was told was that Christianity was not a religion but a relationship with God through Jesus Christ. This idea was profound at the time, and in some ways is still very helpful. If by "religion" we mean some sort of formal institution—a mere set of behavioral modifications and standards of external conformity—then Christianity is certainly so much more. One of the most revolutionary "aha!'" moments that can dawn on us is when we realize that God knows us personally and intimately through a saving relationship with Jesus. The last thing we would ever want is for our vibrant relationship with Christ to be anchored down by some dry, dusty system, so lifeless and stolid.

Our faith is deeply personal, and in the New Testament, we see the believers' relationship with God described in terms of a father to his children,
brother to brother, husband to wife, and even friend to friend.[24] Today, the
word *religion* has lost any sense of intimacy and communicates almost the
opposite of what it used to mean. But Edwards had no quarrel with that term.
In fact, he embraced it. In the 1700s, the term "religion" was synonymous for
Christianity as a whole, including its spiritual practices, beliefs, heart-filled
worship, humble service, and evangelistic mission. Consider for instance that
one of the most important books ever written for Protestant Christians was
John Calvin's 1559 work *The Institutes of the Christian Religion*. I am not sure
any publishers would select that particular title today!

The apostle James gives us as good a definition of the term "religion":

> But whoso looketh into the perfect law of liberty, and continueth therein, he
> being not a forgetful hearer, but a doer of the work, this man shall be blessed in
> his deed. If any man among you seem to be *religious*, and bridleth not his tongue,
> but deceiveth his own heart, this man's *religion* is vain. Pure *religion* and undefiled
> before God and the Father is this, to visit the fatherless and widows in their afflic-
> tion, and to keep himself unspotted from the world. (James 1:25–27; italics mine)

According to the brother of our Lord, the definition of "pure religion" consists
primarily in (1) living consistently before God our Heavenly Father, especially
as that life of faith is (2) carried out in consistent acts of grace and mercy, with
(3) a requisite attendance on the importance of personal holiness. For the
Puritans, then, this term would have not carried any of the baggage of connotations of stodginess, institutionalization, lukewarmness, or heartlessness
that it carries today. So, when Edwards spoke so highly of "religion," it may
be unsettling at first if we think that he was falling back into some dreary,
institutionalized concept of the Christian faith. He was not.

For the Puritans, the distinction between religion and relationship was a
false dichotomy; Christianity was self-evidently a soul-deep relationship with
the Living God through the work of Christ, empowered by the presence of
the Holy Spirit. The word *religion* was used with more joyful, more personal,
and far warmer overtones than we do today. Notice how Edwards says that
no other "end" (purpose, motive, goal) should affect his actions as highly as
religion. "Religion" should be the greatest motive, stirring and "carrying" him
to action as far as it would go.

It is not surprising, then, that Edwards uses this term in the loftiest of
categories. Notice how in this early miscellany, he uses the term "religion"
as synonymous for the whole of the Christian faith. In fact, Edwards sees
religion as the very *reason* God created intelligent beings in the first place:
so that we may love and serve him in the beautiful universe he has made.

---

24. See, for example, Matt. 12:46–50; John 15:15; Eph. 5:25–32.

Wherefore religion must be the end [purpose] of the creation, the great end, the very end. If it were not for this, all those vast bodies we see ordered with so excellent skill,[25] so according to the nicest rules of proportion, according to such laws of gravity and motion, would be all vanity, or good for nothing and to no purpose at all. For religion is the very business, the noble business of intelligent beings, and for this end God has placed us on this earth. If it were not for men, this world would be altogether in vain, with all the curious workmanship of it and accoutrements about it.[26]

May we all strive to be more religious!

63. On the supposition, that there never was to be but one individual in the world, at any one time, who was properly a complete Christian, in all respects of a right stamp, having Christianity always shining in its true luster, and appearing excellent and lovely, from whatever part and under whatever character viewed: resolved, to act just as I would do, if I strove with all my might to be that one, who should live in my time. Jan. 14 and July 13, 1723.

This is really an extraordinary statement, and it is a fitting place to conclude our review of this first group of Edwards's Existential Resolutions. He says here exactly what you fear he might be saying, in all of its audacity, in all of its holy desire. A thought you and I might dare to admit having from time to time, though we push it back into the recesses of our minds. It is at once both alarming and alluring: *Edwards is saying that if there was only one true Christian believer on the planet in each successive generation, then he would strive to be that one.*

Let's be clear. He is not saying that he *is* the only one or that he is the most deserving to be the one. What comes off at first as possibly quite arrogant is actually more tempered when fully considered. If there were only one true Christian (a fully hypothetical situation all parties admit), then Edwards would henceforth act as though he were striving to be that single individual. I am happy to report that this hypothetical is not real. The prophet Elijah was once truly terrified that he was the only faithful man left, until God reminded him that there were still seven thousand strong in a time of great moral collapse (see 1 Kings 19:18). Throughout the Old and New Testaments runs a doctrine of the "remnant," that God always preserves for himself a people in every generation (Gen. 45:7; Isa. 10:21; Jer. 23:3). Thankfully, we are never the only faithful one.

Referring back to his statement on being the "one" complete Christian, Edwards later tells us a little bit more about what he was feeling when he wrote this 63rd Resolution:

---

25. Here Edwards is referring to the created universe: sun, moon, stars, galaxies, etc.

26. "Miscellany gg," WJE 13:185.

While I was [in New York in 1723], I felt them, very sensibly, in a much higher degree, than I had done before. My longings after God and holiness, were much increased. Pure and humble, holy and heavenly Christianity, appeared exceeding amiable to me. I felt in me a *burning desire to be in everything a complete Christian*; and conformed to the blessed image of Christ: and that I might live in all things, according to the pure, sweet and blessed rules of the gospel. I had an eager thirsting after progress in these things. My longings after it, put me upon pursuing and pressing after them. It was my continual strife day and night, and constant inquiry, how I should be more holy, and live more holily, and more becoming a child of God, and disciple of Christ. (WJE 16:795; italics mine)

Edwards, though, was always very careful and precise with his language. Notice how he resolved to act "*as if [he] strove* with all [his] might to be that one" (italics mine). This is not a competition for Edwards, as though he were trying to outdo others; instead, it was a pursuit of God himself. On this concept of striving, Kyle Strobel helpfully comments, "For the believer, this striving is not for salvation but from within salvation. Furthermore, the nature of holiness leads one to desire more of it—communion with God satisfies even as it deepens the longing needing to be satisfied."[27]

The 63rd Resolution is dated as having been written on January 14, 1723. It must have made an impression on him again later that July 13, as he noted that date as well. But on that original date, Edwards's diary reveals that he had been dwelling on Romans 8 and how the mortification of the sinful nature led to greater growth in Christ. His thoughts then swelled and he boldly asserted, "Such little things as Christians commonly do will not show increase of much grace. *We must do great things for God*" (WJE 16:764; italics mine). He wanted to be more than average. Greater than normal. He wanted to fly like Icarus with wings of faith.

But if it still seems a bit arrogant for Edwards to think of himself in this manner, the more mature Edwards too saw some immaturity in these words. He then added,

I used to be continually examining myself, and studying and contriving for likely ways and means, how I should live holily, with far greater diligence and earnestness, than ever I pursued anything in my life: but with too great a dependence on my own strength; which afterwards proved a great damage to me. My experience had not then taught me, as it has done since, my extreme feebleness and impotence, every manner of way; and the innumerable and bottomless depths of secret corruption and deceit, that there was in my heart. (WJE 16:764)

Fly freely like Icarus, but be careful not to fly too close to the sun!

---

27. Kyle Strobel, *Jonathan Edwards: Spiritual Writings*, Classics of Western Spirituality (New York: Paulist Press, 2019), 36.

❖ Faith and Assurance
Resolutions 26, 30, 32, 42, 53, 64

The Bible provides us with two definitions of faith through the writer of the book of Hebrews in chapter 11, both of which work together: "Now faith is the substance of things hoped for, the evidence of things not seen" (v. 1), and "Without faith it is impossible to please him: for he that cometh to God must believe that he is, and that he is a rewarder of them that diligently seek him" (v. 6). According to this definition of faith, it is something substantial, not just a feeling or a vague impression. Faith relies on the content of the Bible being true—namely, that God exists, God saves, and God loves! As Christians, our faith is in Christ—his life, death, and resurrection. In this great event—the very work of Calvary—we put our hope.

At the same time, faith has also been described as a "leap." That is because much of what we believe is "not seen." Personally, I've never seen an angel, a prophet, an apostle, or a person walking on water. But just because I haven't seen them doesn't mean they aren't real. These things are historically verifiable, because Scripture speaks to their factuality. Yet what if we sometimes doubt whether our faith is really, well, *faithful?* Every believer I have ever met, or read about in Scripture, has experienced periods of doubt, worry, or concern. This, however, is where assurance comes in.

Assurance is an aspect of faith in which it grows and is strengthened to a point of clarity, if not complete certainty. Edwards believed (and I am convinced Scripture teaches) that we can come to a place of assurance in our walk with Christ where we know that we know. We are secure in his grace. In this next set of Edwards's Resolutions, we will consider those that touch on faith, believing, doubts, and ultimately our assurance that we belong fully and finally to God.

26. Resolved, to cast away such things, as I find do abate my assurance.

Of the many things over which the Puritan conscience could agonize, there was no topic more vexing than their assurance of personal salvation. While modern evangelicals are all too quick to put away any such worry—having walked down the aisle at an altar call or raised their hand while "every head down; every eye closed"—the Puritans gave much more careful consideration to the question, "How can I be assured that I am truly saved?" Many Puritans spent months or years worrying that the fate of their souls hung in the balance between heaven and hell. Edwards was no exception to this, and he spent several of his early years ardently searching his own heart to find credible evidence of genuine conversion.

Earlier Puritans such as William Perkins devised an exacting multistep process to discern if one was really saved and expected a person to predictably walk through successive periods of conviction, fear, humility, and faith before finally landing on the solid ground of assurance. His own father, Rev. Timothy Edwards, had taught such a scheme to Jonathan as a boy, and both father and son naturally expected this paradigm of identifiable steps to be lived out experientially.[28] But this only served to perplex the young Edwards further, because his own experience of saving grace seemed to defy the normative categories of the anticipated Puritan paradigm.

According to his diary entry on July 4, 1723, it was precisely the fact that his conversion did not accord with these prescribed steps that he was so vexed in his spirit:

The last night, in bed, when thinking of death, I thought, if I was then to die, that, which would make me die, in the least degree fearfully, would be, the want of a trusting and relying on Jesus Christ, *so distinctly and plainly, as has been described by divines*; my not having experienced so particular a venturing, and entirely trusting my soul on Christ, after the fears of hell, and terrors of the Lord, encouraged by the mercy, faithfulness and promises, of God, and the gracious invitations of Christ. . . . Whenever things begin to seem in the least out of order, when things begin to feel uneasy within, or irregular without, then to examine myself, by the strictest examination. (WJE 16:773; italics mine)

According to George Marsden, Edwards grappled long and hard with why his experience of saving grace did not fit with the expected pattern that Perkins and others had devised.[29] It seems that Edwards had omitted the conversion step called "legal terrors,"[30] or an overwhelming fear that the law of God could crush the sinner. In *Pilgrim's Progress*, Puritan writer John Bunyan dramatically portrays this fear when his protagonist, Christian, is nearly crushed by Mount Sinai and beaten to death by Moses.[31]

Did Edwards skip this step because he wasn't saved? Or was it because his experience, though sincere, simply defied this pattern? At some point, the young Edwards seems to have even argued painfully with his parents about this matter, and perhaps even reached his own conclusion that a more accurate paradigm should be devised. Wilson H. Kimnach senses the tension this may have caused between them:

---

28. See the appendix for a fuller explanation of the Puritan "morphology" of conversion.

29. For the story of Edwards's struggle with his own assurance of salvation, see Marsden, *A Life*, 44–58.

30. Marsden, *A Life*, 57–58.

31. See John Bunyan, *Pilgrim's Progress*, ed. C.J. Lovik (Wheaton, IL: Crossway, 2009), 34–35, and 106.

However intense his son's "inward burnings" may have been, it is unlikely that Timothy Edwards readily accepted them as constituting an authentic conversion if they did not have the prevailing structure. And nothing is more obvious from the evidence of the "Diary" and the "Personal Narrative" than that they did not have the conventional structure. (WJE 10:272)

If in fact Edwards studied the matter and found the traditional pattern unhelpful, then he concluded that it should be "cast away." It should be given due reverence and consideration, yes. But if it positively hindered his trust in Christ alone by unduly worrying his conscience, rather than causing him to look to the Savior, then it should be tossed out.

Ironically, it was this same question that drove Edwards toward literary greatness in his revival writings as a more mature Christian and pastor. In 1740, when the Great Awakening broke out across the colonies (undoubtedly one of the most exciting revival chapters in American history), Edwards played a significant role by writing several important works on how believers could discern whether they had truly experienced saving grace. Most notable was his masterful work, *The Religious Affections*, which we will discuss when we come to the 45th Resolution. For our purposes here, it is probably helpful to think of Edwards's words from that July 4th diary entry: "Then, I thought I could go out of the world, as much assured of my salvation, as I was of Christ's faithfulness, knowing that, if Christ did not fail me, he would save me, who had trusted in him, on his word." It is, after all, the strength of our Savior and not the strength of our faith that saves us.

30. Resolved, to strive to my utmost every week to be brought higher in religion, and to a higher exercise of grace, than I was the week before.

Christians live in the paradox between resting and striving. They *rest* in Christ's finished work on the cross, trusting that they are justified by grace alone. Yet they *strive* because the Christian faith is an arduous pursuit of Jesus in a life of difficult discipleship, harrowing pilgrimage, and exhaustive obedience. Sometimes the Scriptures bid believers to rest (see Matt. 11:28; Heb. 11:4), and sometimes the Scriptures bid believers to strive (see Luke 13:24; Rom. 15:30). We are to rest in such great promises as Christ's love for sinners and God's protective care for his sheep. But we are also to strive to enter by the narrow way and wage spiritual warfare as soldiers. Sometimes the Christian life is more like a peaceful green meadow, and sometimes it is more like a raging battlefield. Both realities are paradoxically true.

Here in the 30th Resolution, Edwards undoubtedly emphasizes the striving aspect of the faith. In fact, some have suggested that the balance of the whole Resolutions/Diary project is skewed far too much toward human striving. Some have suggested that this whole project leans toward a rigorist spirituality, too concerned with human performance and extreme asceticism.

It tends to lack clear statements on grace and leans too heavily on human effort. To a large extent, I agree with that assessment.

For example, in this resolution, Edwards endeavors that "every week" he should "be brought *higher* in religion, and to a *higher* exercise of grace, than [he] was the week before" (italics mine). Is this really possible? Are there any believers for whom their entire spiritual pilgrimage looks like a bull-market line graph: always up, up, and away? Not for me certainly. Probably not for you either. Even an exciting bull-market rally sustains temporary losses in many trading sessions. The real gains are seen only over extended periods of time. Please don't misunderstand: clearly, Christians do grow over time. Over many months and years, we expect all believers to grow in faith, maturity, understanding, and exhibit the fruit of the Spirit (Gal. 5:22–23) in marked ways. But as Edwards wrote this particular resolution out in his own words, he has set himself up only for disappointment. Is this a realistic goal? I don't think so; and for this reason, it seems to me that the 30th Resolution is one of the least sustainable vows the young pastor made to himself.

Now, I have to be as fair as possible here. Edwards certainly emphasized themes of resting, trusting, and justification by grace in his writings. In fact, in September 1723, he presented his *Quaestio* (his master's thesis) publicly on the theme of justification by grace. Edwards wrote his Resolutions and the *Quaestio* just months apart in what I have been calling the early pastoral years. This short treatise is a brilliant defense of justification by faith alone, which is the hallmark doctrine of the Protestant Reformers. The *Quaestio* is one of the lesser studied treatises of Edwards, even though it is just as masterful as many of his later, more mature writings. The thesis of the *Quaestio* is that "a sinner is not justified in the sight of God except through the righteousness of Christ obtained by faith."[32]

In this Latin presentation, the young Edwards asserted before the esteemed Yale College audience the following:

> Accordingly, when it is asserted that a sinner is justified by this faith alone, we mean, of course, that God receives the sinner into his grace and friendship for this reason alone, that his entire soul receives Christ in such a way that righteousness and eternal life are offered in an absolutely gratuitous fashion and are provided only because of his reception of Christ. (WJEO 14:61)

In other words, we become righteous not by our strivings but by our resting (see Phil. 3:9). Note his emphasis here on the "absolutely gratuitous fashion" by which God saves sinners apart from their own contributions. Not even repentance itself, he argues, has saving value as an action of man; it is only "good" insomuch as it receives the grace of Christ. He continues,

---

32. The *Quaestio* is contained in WJEO 14:47–66.

We assert, therefore, that a sinner is justified in the sight of God neither totally nor in part because of the goodness of such obedience, or of any works at all, but only on account of what Christ did and suffered, received by faith. We maintain that Christ is the complete Savior and not merely the partial author of our eternal salvation. Because of these considerations we deny that a sinner is his own redeemer and mediator. (WJEO 14:61)

So, what can we say about Edwards's balance between striving and resting? Well, first, that the Resolutions and the *Quaestio* are mutually informing since Edwards wrote them at about the same time. And second, that while certain Resolutions seem to emphasize human effort too much, we can't go on then to conclude that he didn't yet fully understand the gospel, since the *Quaestio* indicates that he deeply appreciated the meaning of salvation through grace alone. I don't believe Edwards was making the error of confusing justification and sanctification, even if the 30th Resolution seems to suggest that his goals for sanctification were unrealistic.

32. *Resolved, to be strictly and firmly faithful to my trust, that that* [sic] *in Proverbs 20:6, "A faithful man who can find?" may not be partly fulfilled in me.*

In this 32nd Resolution, Edwards stops to ponder the ideal person of faith. Specifically, he hopes to be the very paragon—among the rarest of specimens—of saints. He quotes Proverbs 20:6 from his faithful King James Bible: "Most men will proclaim every one his own goodness: but a faithful man who can find?" In fact, it does seem that more people *claim* to be faithful than actually *are* faithful. The next line in the proverb is instructive as well, "The just man walketh in his integrity." Faithful believers have actions and character that back up their professions and promises. In fact, there is a scriptural motif that God is searching throughout the land for faithful believers, delighting to find them: "For the eyes of the LORD run to and fro throughout the whole earth, to shew himself strong in the behalf of them whose heart is perfect toward him" (2 Chron. 16:9). It's a somewhat vivid anthropomorphism and a mixed metaphor to be sure ("eyes . . . run to and fro"), but it gives the impression that God is constantly searching the landscape for those who stand faithful, while so many can summon no more than words. While the faith of such believers is but a mere pretense, Edwards wanted his to be a reality.

Edwards hoped and prayed that this divine search would be at least partly fulfilled in him—that God would search and find the nineteen-year-old pastor-in-training eminently faithful. The awkward double "that that" is in the original, but he clearly intends to refer and apply the text to himself in full or partial measure. He wills to be a man of confident trust and embody the Christian ideal of patient faithfulness. Indeed, it is more than a little encouraging that God is primarily interested in our faith as opposed to our success, or even our fruit. If God measured us by any standard of quantifiable productivity, then none of us could rest confidently that we meet the standards of Proverbs 20:6. But thankfully, faith is something more like loving and trusting the Father than producing "results" to be sifted and weighed. In "Miscellany 37," one of the earliest of Edwards's theological entries, he considers the meaning of faith and faithfulness and locates it in an extended metaphor of a bride's love for her bridegroom. He defines it like this:

> Now it is *by faith* that the soul is united unto Christ; *faith* is this bride's reception of Christ as a bridegroom. Let us, following this similitude that we may illustrate the nature of faith, a little consider what are those affections and motions of heart that are proper and suitable in a spouse toward her bridegroom.[33]

Throughout his writing career, Edwards came back to this wedding metaphor of the bride, waiting faithfully for her divine Groom. The Song of Solomon, then called Canticles by colonial Puritans, was among his favorites. He returned to this text regularly as a source of devotional inspiration. As he continued to work through this extended analogy in "Miscellany 37" (the faithfulness of the saint is to God, as a bride is to her husband), he added:

> Now it is easy to everyone to know that when marriage is according to nature and God's designation, when a woman is married to an husband she receives him as a guide, as a protector, a safeguard and defense, a shelter from harms and dangers, a reliever from distresses, a comforter in afflictions, a support in discouragements. God has so designed it, and therefore has made man of a more robust [nature], and strong in body and mind, with more wisdom strength and courage, fit to protect and defend; but he has made woman weaker, more soft and tender, more fearful, and more affectionate, as a fit object of generous protection and defense.[34]

It may seem jarring in today's modern egalitarianism for Edwards to describe the coupled wife as physically "weaker, more soft and tender." Such language is certainly unwelcome in many quarters today. But his intention was not to denigrate the female vessel, but rather to locate the very nexus of the believer's faith in the bride's trusting hand, as she holds confidently onto her wedded protector. He concludes,

> Wherefore, the dispositions of soul which Christ looks at in his spouse are a sweet reliance and confidence in him, a humble trust in him as her only rock of defence, whither she may flee. And Christ will not receive those as the objects of his salvation who trust to themselves, their own strength or worthiness, but those alone who entirely rely on him.[35]

---

33. "Miscellany 37," WJE 13:220 (italics mine).
34. "Miscellany 37," WJE 13:220.
35. "Miscellany 37," WJE 13:220.

May that be increasingly true of us as we, too, hope confidently in the Savior's strong and loving hand.

42. Resolved, frequently to renew the dedication of myself to God, which was made at my baptism; which I solemnly renewed, when I was received into the communion of the church; and which I have solemnly re-made this 12th day of January, 1722–23.

We know what Jonathan Edwards was thinking about on the day he wrote this 42nd Resolution because it is the same date as an entry in his diary. On January 12, 1723, he wrote not only these words, but also the 43rd, 44th, and 45th Resolutions. In fact, he wrote three separate times that day in his diary: morning, noon, and night. He had been deeply thinking about the promises made for him when he was baptized as a child, which he had renewed when he joined the church.

> Saturday, Jan. 12, in the morning. I have this day solemnly renewed my baptismal covenant and self-dedication, which I renewed when I was received into communion of the church. I have been before God; and have given myself, all that I am and have to God, so that I am not in any respect my own: I can challenge no right in myself, I can challenge no right in this understanding, this will, these affections that are in me; neither have I any right to this body, or any of its members: no right to this tongue, these hands, nor feet; no right to these senses, these eyes, these ears, this smell or taste. I have given myself clear away, and have not retained anything as my own. I have been to God this morning, and told him that I gave myself wholly to him. (WJE 16:762)

These are certainly profound thoughts, and Edwards was doing something some modern-day evangelicals might easily miss. In the Reformed tradition, the predominant position was paedobaptism, the baptism of infant children. A bit of background is helpful here to understand how this worked. Reformed and Puritan Christians baptized their children, but not because the Roman Catholics did so. In fact, they often despised any correlation with official Roman doctrine. A cursory reading of just a few Puritans shows they did not favorably admire the practices of the Church of Rome! On the contrary, Reformed and Puritan Christians baptized their children because they saw deep biblical warrant for such a practice. The foundational view here is called "covenant theology," which incorporates the idea that God is saving for himself a whole people, and this group includes men, women, and even children. In covenant theology, the children of believers are assumed to be part of the church. In the same way that the Jews of old marked their sons with the covenant sign of circumcision at eight days old (Gen. 17:12) and considered them a part of the true Israel, so also Christians mark their children with baptism and consider them part of the church.

Children of believers are baptized into participation in the church, and as such are treated like probationary members, with many of the duties and privileges of full membership. This includes pastoral care, teaching, admonition, and church discipline. For a young person to come to the Lord's Table, however, they first had to join the church as professing members and give a testimony of saving grace, while evidencing an outwardly pious life. For those of us who practice this form of covenant or infant baptism (I do as a Presbyterian), it is important for maturing believers to eventually take personal responsibility for the promises made on their behalf on that day. The believer then "owns" those promises made by our parents when we officially join the church as full communing members.

It was on these profound vows that Edwards had been meditating. We must admit that his words here are challenging and inspiring. He continues in this rather long entry of that day:

> I have given every power to him; so that for the future I will challenge no right in myself, in any respect. I have expressly promised him, and do now promise almighty God, that by his grace I will not. I have this morning told him, that I did take him for my whole portion and felicity, looking on nothing else as any part of my happiness, nor acting as if it were; and his law for the constant rule of my obedience; and would fight with all my might against the world, the flesh, and the devil, to the end of my life. And did believe in Jesus Christ, and receive him as a prince and a Savior; and would adhere to the faith and obedience of the gospel, how hazardous and difficult soever the profession and practice of it may be. (WJE 16:762)

We are compelled to admit that for any person, young or old, Edwards's view of the all-encompassing demands of the Christian faith are high and lofty. Not all readers will share Edwards's view of covenant/infant baptism. But whether we were baptized as infants, teens, or adults, renewing the promises made at the day of our baptism is an invigorating practice, helpful in wrenching us free from the inertia and lukewarmth of spiritual lethargy.

53. Resolved, to improve every opportunity, when I am in the best and happiest frame of mind, to cast and venture my soul on the Lord Jesus Christ, to trust and confide in him, and consecrate myself wholly to him; that from this I may have assurance of my safety, knowing that I confide in my Redeemer. July 8, 1723.

Something profound was stirring in young Edwards's heart on that date in July. Although there is no corresponding diary entry recorded for that day to spell out for us what it was, he wrote several important Resolutions on that same occasion. We will look at each of them later on in their own place; for now, I think setting them side by side helps to frame some of the deep stirring in his heart that day:

51. Resolved, that I will act so, in every respect, as I think I shall wish I had done, if I should at last be damned.

52. I frequently hear persons in old age say how they would live, if they were to live their lives over again: resolved, that I will live just so as I can think I shall wish I had done, supposing I live to old age.

53. Resolved, to improve every opportunity, when I am in the best and happiest frame of mind, to cast and venture my soul on the Lord Jesus Christ, to trust and confide in him, and consecrate myself wholly to him; that from this I may have assurance of my safety, knowing that I confide in my Redeemer.

55. Resolved, to endeavor to my utmost to act as I can think I should do, if I had already seen the happiness of heaven, and hell torments. (WJE 16:757)

In regard to the resolution before us at the moment, the 53rd Resolution, we can say that it is strikingly beautiful. We can also say this: it's all gospel. If other Resolutions seem to verge on self-reliance, then this one exhibits Edwards's complete trust in Christ. Serene. Dependent. Faithful. He promises himself to "improve every opportunity" (typical Puritan/colonial language for "take advantage," "apply," "make use") in which he is in the "best and happiest frame of mind." Obviously, we are not *always* in the best state of mental clarity to consider spiritual realities. Sometimes life crushes in on us. Sometimes we feel like Atlas, ever carrying the boulder of our daily responsibilities. Sometimes we have to fight just to catch our breath. But then there are those rare moments when the clouds part, the seas still, and all becomes blissfully clear. There are days like July 8, 1723.

In these moments, Edwards felt he must not fail to capture every opportunity "to cast and venture [his] soul on the Lord Jesus Christ." I love the dynamic action of these strong verbs and can make them my own. *Cast* my soul upon him! *Venture* my eternity on him! Let there be no remnant of myself that I have not fully entrusted to his care. And what would be the benefit of such entire trust? "That from this I may have assurance of my *safety*, knowing that I confide in my Redeemer." And that is why this resolution is all gospel. There is not a hint of self-confidence in this Resolution. It is one of entire childlike, trusting dependence.

The words *safe* and *safety* were concepts Edwards dwelled on deeply. At about the time this resolution was written, he preached a sermon at his New York church titled "Christian Safety" from Proverbs 29:25, "But whoso putteth his trust in the Lord shall be safe." Edwards was thinking not only of temporal safety but also the safekeeping of one's soul in the hands of Christ. The doctrinal part was simple enough: "They are safe that trust in God." A message even children could understand, while adults struggle to believe.

The young preacher promised his hearers they were safe from temporal evils, from death, from devils. And most importantly, safe from hell. As he extolled the promises of God in the gospel, he pointed to God's unfailing character in his mercy, goodness, and love. As the young pulpiteer rose to the dynamic conclusion, he encouraged his congregation with the following words:

> Wherefore, let us all be exhorted, immediately to put our confidence in him, to cast our burden upon [him], to commit our way unto him, to dedicate ourselves to him, and deliver up our bodies and souls into his hands; and so go fearless on through this world, neither fearing men, death, nor the devil. Psalms 11:1, "In the Lord put I my trust: how say ye to my soul, flee as a bird to her mountain?" (WJE 10:462)

We mortals never stop being afraid—only our fears change. When we were children, we were scared of shadows under our beds and closets left open. We created imaginary monsters that strangely looked like jackets hanging on doorknobs. When we became adults, our fears merely changed to bills, tuition prices, colonoscopies, and our parents' inevitable aging. But Edwards's simple sermon as a barely-twenty-something reminds us of the ultimate security in the whole universe: In Christ there is no fear that can materialize from the shadows and snatch us away from him. Therefore, we cast and venture our souls upon Christ alone.

64. Resolved, when I find those "groanings which cannot be uttered," of which the Apostle speaks [Romans 8:26], and those "breakings of soul for the longing it hath," of which the Psalmist speaks, Psalms 119:20, that I will promote them to the utmost of my power, and that I will not be weary of earnestly endeavoring to vent my desires, nor of the repetitions of such earnestness. July 23 and Aug. 10, 1723.

The 64th Resolution pertains to the inner prayer life of the saint; specifically earnest, wearying, venting prayers. Prayer is, in a word, exhausting. It requires diligent mental application and spiritual acuity. Paradoxically, it can also be the most freeing and restful experience in the world, as believers place their burdens into the trustworthy hands of Almighty God. In prayer, we consign ourselves as finite creatures to rest and trust in the greater plan of the Sovereign Lord. There are times in which prayer comes upon us suddenly and easily, almost as though we are passive participants. Here, the Spirit of God draws us into communion with himself. But there are certainly times when prayer is a much more difficult task. Paul describes such prayer as "laboring fervently" (Col. 4:12). While on earth, Christ prayed "with strong crying and tears" (Heb. 5:7). We must fight to intercede, labor to supplicate, and strive to really pray (see Rom. 15:30).

In this Resolution, Edwards cites two passages of Scripture that specifically define the kinds of prayer he resolved to offer. Psalm 119:20 is part of the longest psalm in the Bible and focuses relentlessly on the law of God. This particular clause, "My soul breaketh for the longing" (ESV: "is consumed with longing"), describes the psalmist's inner turmoil in response to the beauty and perfection of God's great commandments. Prayer, I might suggest, results in some "wear and tear" on the soul. Prayer pulls on us, placing us in dynamic tension between heaven and earth. The soul in prayer feels stretched, as though it is being pulled in all four different directions from each limb. We desire the kingdom, but we are overwhelmed by the frustrations of the world.

In Edwards's July 23 diary entry, he wrote virtually the same thing as in this 64th Resolution. When he entered into such powerful seasons of prayer—even if they lasted for just a moment—he says he would "humor and promote them to the utmost of my power, and be not weary of earnestly endeavoring to vent my desires, and not to be weary of the repetitions of such earnestness." In other words, he should try to stoke the fire and keep the coals burning. He should not grow tired and quit, even if he found he was somewhat repeating himself. Repetition is only unseemly in prayer if it is "vain" (Matt. 6:7), but Spirit-led perseverance is never vain, even when words run in short supply.

About a month later on August 10, he found his soul laboring in prayer again. He wrote again in his diary, annotating for a second time this same resolution:

> About sunset. As a help against that inward shameful hypocrisy, to confess frankly to myself all that which I find in myself, either infirmity or sin; also to confess to God, and open the whole case to him, when it is what concerns religion, and humbly and earnestly implore of him the help that is needed; not in the least to endeavor to smother over what is in my heart, but to bring it all out to God and my conscience. By this means, I may arrive at a greater knowledge of my own heart. When I find difficulty in finding a subject of religious meditation, in vacancies, to pitch at random on what alights to my thoughts, and to go from that to other things which that shall bring into my mind, and follow this progression as a clue, till I come to what I can meditate on with profit and attention.

Sometimes the burdens of the world are too heavy; too great. Like Frodo the hobbit, we cannot carry this ring alone. Thankfully, the Spirit of God rushes to our aid and fills us with the kinds of prayers that go beyond even human words.

The other text Edwards mentions, Romans 8, describes the help and relief the Holy Spirit brings:

> Likewise the Spirit also helpeth our infirmities: for we know not what we should pray for as we ought: but the Spirit itself maketh intercession for us with groanings which cannot be uttered. And he that searcheth the hearts knoweth what is the mind of the Spirit, because he maketh intercession for the saints according to the will of God. And we know that all things work together for good to them that love God, to them who are the called according to his purpose. (Rom. 8:26–28)

Why do we need divine help when we pray? Because if we didn't have assistance from above, then prayer alone would overwhelm us. In the greater context, the whole natural world itself is groaning, as it exists between the "already" and the "not yet." Certainly, you have felt this: a burden in prayer you cannot quite define in words with sentences and punctuation. What should you even ask for? What do you say? You cannot quite verbalize what you are attempting to convey. No matter—the Spirit of God is present, and an inarticulate groan will do. Holy-Spirit-empowered prayer is the only true prayer that truly relieves the groaning, wearied soul.

❖ Of Heart and Mind
Resolutions 11, 14, 15, 24, 25, 28, 45, 60, 65

Jonathan Edwards was a man of both heart and mind. Love and logic. Thinking and feeling. Doctrine and devotion. Or as he himself phrased it frequently, "heat and light." For some, this is a dilemma, and many choose one over the other. We can all imagine people we know who know the Bible and sound doctrine, but they don't seem to have much love for others. At the same time, we can probably think of a few who have loving, tender hearts but don't seem to be interested in the deeper things of the Lord. Choosing between these two is, of course, a logical and false dilemma. We can have both hearts in love with God and minds that think clearly and precisely. In fact, we are commanded to be such persons. In Mark 12:30, Jesus says, "Thou shalt love the Lord thy God with all thy heart, and with all thy soul, and with all thy mind, and with all thy strength: this is the first commandment." Notice that both heart and mind are mentioned. Neither is excluded. It is freeing to realize that we don't have to choose—nor should we—between having a head full of Scripture, doctrine, and church history versus having a heart full of love for God and the people in our lives. We can have both.

In this next set of Resolutions, we will continue to look at Edwards's Existential Resolutions (our reason for existing) while considering both our heart (the human faculty of loving, affirming, worshiping, treasuring, and adoring) and our mind (the human faculty for thinking, apprehending, analyzing, and computing). Like Edwards, we should resolve to use all that we are made of to love God. This is what Jesus meant by loving God with "all our strength."

11. Resolved, when I think of any theorem in divinity to be solved, immediately to do what I can towards solving it, if circumstances don't hinder.

Jesus once said to a man, "Thou shalt love the Lord thy God with all thy heart, and with all thy soul, *and with all thy mind*" (Matt. 22:37; italics mine). When we speak of the concept of love today, we often correlate that affection most directly to the organ of the heart. The heart is where we "feel," where we "love." But Jesus said that the mind (the brain), too, is to be the organ of expression and reception of divine love. This may come as somewhat of a surprise to us today. How in the world do we love God with our minds?

I would suggest that we love God with our minds when we think pure thoughts, when we think deeply, when we think clearly and logically, and most of all when we think of God himself. The nineteen-year-old Jonathan Edwards knew from his early training from his father, Timothy, and through the example of his grandfather, Solomon Stoddard, that the life of Christian faith incorporates the mind at least as much as any other aspect of devotional piety. For this reason, Timothy Edwards taught young Jonathan to think with his pen (or rather his quill!) always in hand. By writing out his thoughts, Jonathan learned the disciplines of clarity of expression, linear thought, and the freedom to experiment with ideas both new and old.

In the 11th Resolution, Edwards resolved simply to *think*: often, deeply, and reflectively. As he grew into maturity, it became almost impossible for him to think *without* writing his thoughts down. He never let go of the discipline of thinking with words, in ink, on paper. When he came to a perplexity in the Scriptures or theology, he considered them "theorems in divinity." They were like math problems to solve. Geometric shapes to figure out by area. In this resolution, he promised himself that he would not let these puzzles escape him when circumstances prohibited, but to come back to them as soon as reasonably possible. We know of times in which circumstances did hinder his ability to write, especially when he traveled on horseback. During those times, Edwards felt handcuffed for long hours at a stretch since his hands were busy reigning the horse. Even then, he was known to stop from time to time and pin pieces of scrap paper to his winter coat with a simple word or phrase scrawled on it, to remind himself to write down his thoughts once he returned to his study! Once he returned to a place where he could finally sit in peace again, he would remove the scraps of paper from his coat lining and write out his thoughts more fully in his journals.

In Edwards's diary on September 23, 1723, he wrote a brief entry related to the mind. He was afraid that he might allow his cognition to too quickly calcify like certain "old men" he knew. He had seen this happen too often to other people; they simply lost their ability to consider new ideas. He wanted a brain that was free, hungry to learn, and not conformed to standard explanations. In that entry, he wrote,

> Monday, Sept. 23. I observe that old men seldom have any advantage of new discoveries, because they are beside a way of thinking, they have been so long used to. Resolved, if ever I live to years, that I will be impartial to hear the reasons of all pretended discoveries, and receive them if rational, how long so ever I have

been used to another way of thinking. My time is so short, that I have not time to perfect myself in all studies: wherefore resolved, to omit and put off, all but the most important and needful studies.

Along with many others, I share a fear our society is losing the ability to think well. I have noticed in airports or waiting rooms how few people even read actual books anymore. Instead, you see them staring down at the screens of their phones or their laptops. Another problem is that we don't tend to read widely in order to objectively decide what to think. Instead, we end up being spoon-fed by our favorite newspaper, news program, or talk-show host. For years now, new generations having been growing up with the ability to be endlessly entertained by computer games and constant video streaming. All of this has greatly diminished our ability to analyze an argument from an objective point of view. We no longer teach the science of logic in our schools and colleges; and for this reason, we tend to accept "strawman" arguments and other fallacies wholesale.

Perhaps we could learn from Christ and his imperfect and flawed servant Jonathan Edwards how important it is to think clearly. Many of us would benefit from putting our thoughts and observations into words on paper. The very discipline of slowly forming sentences and thinking no faster than the hand can form words forces us to think in linear expressions, building from one idea to the next. Not only that, but we would do well to think on the higher concepts and ideas that draw our minds toward the heavenly throne.

14. Resolved, never to do anything out of revenge.

At just eight words long, the 14th Resolution is the shortest entry of the seventy. It is simple, brief, and powerful. It has neither scriptural citation appended to it nor date affixed beside it in order to pin it definitively to any specific incident. It was included in the first written batch of undated Resolutions, penned sometime before December 19, 1722, but without any other indication of Edwards's mindset. It is impossible to know, then, whether there was a personal antagonist to whom Edwards was internally responding in his heart, or whether he was just reminding himself of an overwhelmingly biblical exhortation.

"Revenge" is a disturbing concept. It has caused nations to go to war. It has caused tribes to seek to snuff out others through violence. It has suddenly ruined marriages that had stood strong for decades. It has caused neighbors on opposite sides of a fence to practically deny one another's existence. It has caused otherwise professional men and women to stoop below their normal, civilized behavior. *Revenge* is a word that has soaked history with blood. It has rattled many a saber and sharpened many a spear. It is a dirty word. A demented idea. Revenge is a deeply un-Christian enterprise, and Edwards vowed to have no part of it. "*Never* to do anything out of revenge." Not just rarely or infrequently. Never.

Defined properly, we might say that revenge takes God's righteous justice into our own hands in order to enact retribution for a perceived injustice. What makes it so horrid is the assumption that we can do God's work for him. Paul exhorts the Romans, "Dearly beloved, avenge not yourselves, but rather give place unto wrath: for it is written, Vengeance is mine; I will repay, saith the Lord" (Rom. 12:19). Most of the time, revenge just cycles itself into the need for more retribution, churning yet more comeuppance after that. This is how gang violence is perpetuated in cities, and lifelong friendships and families are ruined in suburbs. The opposite of revenge, of course, is actually forgiving our enemies, which is often the hardest thing in the world to do. And yet Christ bids his disciples to do the very thing that we loathe: we must forgive (Matt. 6:12; 18:21–35). In fact, Christ demands forgiveness and expects it of his disciples.

Though this Resolution is not tied directly to any known circumstance, there is one paragraph in Edwards's diary that may shed some light on the subject, although it was written half a year later. Still, it gives us some greater insight into Edwards's understanding of the propensities of his own heart:

> Saturday morning, Aug. 24. Have not practiced quite right about revenge; though I have not done anything directly out of revenge, yet, I have perhaps, omitted some things, that I should otherwise have done; or have altered the circumstances and manner of my actions, hoping for a secret sort of revenge thereby. I have felt a little sort of satisfaction, when I thought that such an evil would happen to them by my actions, as would make them repent what they have done. To be satisfied for their repenting, when they repent from a sense of their error, is right. But a satisfaction in their repentance, because of the evil that is brought upon them, is revenge. This is in some measure, a taking the matter out of God's hands when he was about to manage it, who is better able to plead it for me. (WJE 16:779)

What is so insightful about this diary passage and why it is so striking that a man as young as Edwards understood this, is the realization that revenge takes many forms. Some forms of revenge are active (swearing, fighting, shooting, etc.), while other forms are far more passive (silent treatments, cold shoulders, etc.). It is this latter kind he considers in this diary entry. The phrase "though I have not done anything directly out of revenge" indicates that he had not taken any overt actions. He had not thrown punches or used vitriolic language. But that does not put him in the clear. He is concerned that he enjoyed watching others smolder in guilt. He wanted them to know they were wrong and *feel* the sting of repentance. If the other party asked for clemency, then all the better for the glory of God. But he knew he should be more concerned that the other party was right with the Lord than in secretly delighting to watch their consciences squirm.

Later in life, we know Edwards was deeply hurt by the Northampton congregation when they fired him in 1753 over the Communion controversy. But despite the fact that they fired him after twenty-three years of faithful ministry, Edwards dutifully filled the pulpit for them as they sought his replacement. Those Sunday mornings must have been quite awkward for all involved! I can't imagine preaching in a balanced way for a church that just kicked me out! Edwards was able to do it for several months, however, because he had been training himself in the practice of grace for years.

Do *nothing* out of revenge.

24. *Resolved, whenever I do any conspicuously evil action, to trace it back, till I come to the original cause; and then both carefully endeavor to do so no more, and to fight and pray with all my might against the original of it.*

As I have been studying and writing about Jonathan Edwards now for nearly five years, it has occurred to me more than once that I might inadvertently contribute to the literary genre of "hagiography." Hagiography is the lifting up of a person in history so highly that he or she looks nearly angelic to contemporary readers. This amounts to a form of historical fiction in which a person's strengths are magnified, their good deeds are exaggerated, and their rougher edges polished over, if not ignored completely. The result is a "stained-glass" view of church history. While the Roman Catholic Church has from time to time done this on behalf of their formally recognized saints, Protestants have also created marble statues of men like Luther, Spurgeon, and Edwards.

As we think reflectively on the 24th Resolution, let's begin with the rather honest admission on Edwards's part that he was a fallen man. His word of choice is *evil*. That's not my assessment; it is his own. In fact, several of his Resolutions honestly admit that his heart was as corrupt as anyone else's.[36] Biblically, the term "evil" is not a rhetorical flourish on Edwards's part for the sake of humility. Scripture teaches that all people are deeply broken, corrupt at the very heart and root of our spiritual life. As the apostle Paul said,

> There is no one righteous, no, not one: There is none that understandeth, there is none that seeketh after God. . . . Destruction and misery are in their ways; And the way of peace have they not known: There is no fear of God before their eyes. . . . For all have sinned, and come short of the glory of God." (Rom. 3:10–11, 16–18, 23)

Like all men, there were deep places in his heart he could not fully understand. Jeremiah 17:9–10 says, "The heart is deceitful above all things, and desperately wicked: who can know it? I the Lord search the heart, I try the

---

36. See, for example, Resolutions numbered 3, 8, 37, 56, 57, 65, and 68.

reins, even to give every man according to his ways, and according to the fruit of his doings." Although we try to confess our sin before the Lord, there is always something hidden from us. We deceive ourselves, and others are able to see sometimes what we cannot. Even still, there was much that Edwards *could* see. This led him to an honest assessment of his total state before God as a fallen sinner: "evil." In fact, by maintaining a strict, Calvinistic view of the doctrine of total depravity, Edwards swam against the incoming tides of the Enlightenment, Deism, and an age of toleration. In his great works *Freedom of the Will* and *Original Sin*, he argued that mankind's fallen nature had so crippled our race spiritually that it was hopeless for human beings to even attempt to be good on their own.[37] Divine exertion was needed for people to turn to God in repentance and faith. Here, Edwards defended what is known as a "compatibilist" view of human free will. He argued that the Enlightenment philosophers were wrong on many accounts. First, human nature *is* corrupt to the core, as Paul wrote to the Romans. Human nature is not fundamentally good. Second, human beings aren't even able to take the first step toward repairing this fault without divine grace! Not even our "free" will can overcome our sinful nature. Grace is needed to overcome our own nature.

But it was in his 1758 book, *Original Sin*, that Edwards rappelled the deepest into the dark cave of the human heart. In this book, he forcibly argued his defense of the traditional Augustinian/Calvinistic view of the depravity of man. He personally and particularly refuted several recently published works that had suggested that the human heart was not fallen but had retained an essential goodness that made us virtuous, if only prone to bad *choices* from time to time. No, Edwards argued, humankind is like an unfaithful wife. Who would consider a wife "virtuous" who only commits adultery with the household servants once in a while? To change the metaphor, he asked whether or not a ship could be considered a "good" seafaring vessel if it only sunk occasionally? Adam's one sin sunk the whole race. Humanity, he contested, is in desperate need of grace.

While Edwards did not recognize every act of wickedness that he himself committed and could not trace back every fault in his heart, at the very least we can say that he was cognizant of his heart's propensity for darkness and that he sought relief in Christ. Personally, I wish Edwards would have ended this 24th Resolution with a brief recitation of the gospel. Instead, it seems he resolved to "fight" on his own power. It is commendable, of course, to do battle with our sin, whether it be our darkened thoughts, words, or deeds. But as Edwards said better in other places in his writings, that fight cannot be won through the power of the will alone. The help of God's Spirit is necessary to drive us to the cross again and again.

---

37. See WJEO 1 and WJEO 3, which contain *Freedom of the Will* and *Original Sin*, respectively.

25. Resolved, to examine carefully, and constantly, what that one thing in me is, which causes me in the least to doubt of the love of God; and to direct all my forces against it.

The love of God is the surest truth in all of Scripture. It is the reality upon which all other spiritual realities are founded and affixed. In a singular and unique way, Scripture tells us that "God is love" (1 John 4:8, 16). No other attribute is predicated in that express manner. The Scriptures use some of the most powerful words in the biblical languages to show forth God's covenantal faithfulness: ḥesed in the Hebrew and *agape* in the Greek. The former term is often rendered "loving-kindness" in Edwards's King James Version, a word that I wish more modern translations utilized for its beauty and precision. It means God's covenant fidelity and ultimate loyalty. The latter term, *agape*, is the highest and sincerest form of sacrificial love, greater in scope and profundity than *phileo* (brotherly love) or *eros* (romantic love). Not only that, but Scripture also tells us that God's ultimate act that proves and reveals his love is in the giving of his only Son, Jesus Christ. This is the definitive proof of his unyielding favor for his people: "God commendeth his love toward us, in that, while we were yet sinners, Christ died for us" (Rom. 5:8).

Somehow, it is strangely comforting to me to know that the young man who would eventually become one of the greatest theologians of the modern era—probably the definitive Christian thinker in Colonial American history—also struggled with doubts over the love of God. It makes him so much more human! We can relate, can't we? Certainly, there are times when the love of God seems too good to be true—or we feel we're unworthy to be the objects of God's love. Although we may know these things with our minds and we believe them on paper and affirm them in our doctrinal confessions, we struggle to grasp that they could apply personally to us. It would certainly seem that the 25th Resolution indicates that Jonathan Edwards struggled with this basic kind of doubt as well.

So, what did Edwards do when he found himself worrying, fretting, or filling up with anxiety about this? He resolved to do two things. First, he would "examine carefully and constantly" what it was that caused these doubts. He endeavored to search out the source of the matter if he could find it. This is one of six Resolutions that invoke self-examination of some kind. Of course, we can say that all of his Resolutions are a guide to intentional spiritual introspection. Second, once discovered, Edwards would "direct all of his forces against it." If he found a weed of doubt, he pulled it up at the roots. If he found a splinter of unbelief, he took holy tweezers to remove it no matter how much it hurt.

Since the 25th Resolution is part of the early batch of undated Resolutions, its historical context is probably most closely tied to the earliest portions of his Diary. In fact, in his first diary entry, Edwards considered his experience of God's love in some depth and manifested some personal doubts. He observed that the disjunct was not in God's failure to prove his love (he did that on the cross), but rather in his own ability to "feel" it:

> Dec. 18, [1722]. This day made the 35th Resolution. The reason why I, in the least, question my interest in God's love and favor, is, 1. Because I cannot speak so fully to my experience of that preparatory work, of which divines speak; 2. I do not remember that I experienced regeneration, exactly in those steps, in which divines say it is generally wrought; 3. I do not feel the Christian graces sensibly enough, particularly faith. I fear they are only such hypocritical outside affections, which wicked men may feel, as well as others. They do not seem to be sufficiently inward, full, sincere, entire and hearty. They do not seem so substantial, and so wrought into my very nature, as I could wish. (WJE 16:755)

On one hand, we can certainly commend Edwards for being so thoroughly careful and self-aware in his spiritual walk. Probably most of us could use a bit more meditation on the condition of our own hearts. But on the other hand, we might caution young believers against doubting the love of God based on their own experiences and feelings. These are too unreliable. Notice how Edwards complains that he doesn't feel grace "sensibly enough." How much is enough? Would it even be possible to *know* that we feel it enough? If a nineteen-year-old pastor-in-training said these things to me in a counseling session, I would most likely advise him to turn his eyes away from himself, his feelings, and his experiences, and instead look again to that which is verifiable: Christ's death as an accomplished fact. His resurrection is sure history. Christ Jesus died on a particular date, in a particular place, and was seen by a number of named witnesses. In that sense, then, the love of God does not depend on our subjective experience of it, but rather God's objective proof in demonstrating it (Rom. 5:8; John 3:16).

28. Resolved, to study the Scriptures so steadily, constantly and frequently, as that I may find, and plainly perceive myself to grow in the knowledge of the same.

Two men from American Colonial history owned Bibles that were literally cut to pieces and stitched back together again. Their respective Bibles, however, held very different purposes, as their owners had very different views on the nature of Scripture. The first man was Thomas Jefferson. As a deist, he didn't believe the Bible could be trusted as an authoritative sacred and religious text. As an anti-supernaturalist, he held that the Bible's account of such events as miracles, healings, and resurrections could no longer be thought tenable in the modern, enlightened world. For this reason, he physically cut out everything in his New Testament with a razor blade that he no longer held to be plausible: all that Jefferson retained in his highly redacted edition were the ethical and moral imperatives that he thought acceptable for learned and sophisticated men. The Jefferson Bible is still available today as a greatly truncated pocket-sized edition. I have one on my shelf as a reminder of what can happen when people believe that their own insight is a higher authority than God's revealed word. When that happens, we tend to become editors of the word rather than students of the word.

The second man who owned a cut-and-paste Bible was Jonathan Edwards. He acquired this uniquely shaped volume from his brother-in-law, Benjamin Pierpont as a gift.[38] Known today by scholars as the "Blank Bible," it's on display at the Beinecke Manuscript Library at Yale University. It is an old King James Version that had been carefully cut apart and stitched back together again with a full blank sheet of paper for note-taking in between every page of Scripture. Although we don't know who did the original handiwork in putting together this unique volume, it appears to have been done before Edwards took possession of it, because it contains several notes from its previous owner, Benjamin Pierpont. For the rest of his life, Edwards took copious notes in this volume on every book of the Bible. Today, the contents of the "Blank Bible" can be read for free in volume 24 in the online edition of Jonathan Edwards's official works.

Quite the opposite from Jefferson, Edwards held that every word in the sacred text was a divine message from God: unique, authoritative, and infallible. Once he began note-taking in the "Blank Bible," he never stopped. In two columns, opposite the smaller text of Scripture in a corresponding place on the blank sheets, Edwards wrote his observations, sermon illustrations, quotes from other commentators, and other ideas he later imported into his burgeoning collection of treatises and sermon manuscripts. The "Blank Bible" contains around fifty-five hundred handwritten notes in Edwards's tortuous handwriting, crammed into the columns of the uniquely interleaved volume (WJEO 24:1).

As we see in the 28th Resolution, early in his life, Edwards determined to be an avid reader and voracious consumer of the word of God. To him, knowing Scripture was an obsession that couldn't be relegated to the place of a mere hobby. He devoted his whole life to reading, memorizing, and praying through the Bible. Since all of his treaties and written works depended heavily on his understanding Scripture well, this required devoted and sustained effort on his part. His habit of writing in this one-of-a-kind study text allowed Edwards to create his own lifelong system of biblical cataloging. He forged his own compendium of cross-references and created his own running com-

---

38. For a physical description of this book, see WJEO 24:84–89. Because the blank pages were much larger than the King James Version that was spliced into it, it almost appears as if the larger notebook ate the Bible like a python swallowing its prey!

mentary on every biblical book, which he consulted and amplified as he grew in knowledge. To his own observations and insights on the text of the biblical writers, Edwards added copious notes and comments from other writers, such as the esteemed commentator Matthew Henry (WJEO 24:62–64). As Edwards filled the empty spaces between the well-worn leather covers, he created for himself an entire research encyclopedia of biblical knowledge.

Toward the end of his life, Edwards talked about his habits of study in his famous letter to the Trustees of the College of New Jersey (Princeton):

> My method of study, from my first beginning the work of the ministry, has been very much by writing; applying myself in this way, to improve every important hint; pursuing the clue to my utmost, when anything in reading, meditation or conversation, has been suggested to my mind, that seemed to promise light in any weighty point. Thus penning what appeared to me my best thoughts, on innumerable subjects for my own benefit. The longer I prosecuted my studies in this method, the more habitual it became, and the more pleasant and profitable I found it. (WJE 16:762–27)

Edwards's devotion to Scripture as a lifetime obsession harkens back to the passion of the writer of Psalm 119. Here, the anonymous author (perhaps David himself, Ezra the scribe, or another lesser-known believer) tells of his own longing for knowledge in the Holy Scripture: "Open thou mine eyes, that I may behold wondrous things out of thy law. . . . Make me to understand the way of thy precepts; so shall I talk of thy wondrous works" (Ps. 119:18, 27). Let us pray that God would give us today such a love for his word.

45. Resolved, never to allow any pleasure or grief, joy or sorrow, nor any affection at all, nor any degree of affection, nor any circumstance relating to it, but what helps religion. Jan. 12 and 13, 1723.

One of Edwards's greatest literary gifts to the church was his foundational book *The Religious Affections* (1746), a mature evaluation of the Great Awakening in which Edwards carefully analyzed the hallmark signs of true conversion. We recall from our earlier discussion of the 26th Resolution that as a young man Edwards himself agonized over his own spiritual state. He was deeply afflicted by the question of whether or not he was truly saved, because his own conversion didn't fit the expected Puritan "steps" of salvation as taught by William Perkins and his own father Timothy Edwards. In *The Religious Affections*, Edwards presents a completely different paradigm of true salvation from that of Perkins. Rather than looking for chronological or sequential steps, Edwards instead looked inwardly to what he famously called the "affections." (Note the dual use of that soon-to-be-famous term in the 45th Resolution.)

It's helpful to clarify what Edwards means by "religious affections." While some have suggested that they are roughly equivalent to "emotions,"

Edwards means something closer to the deepest inclinations of one's soul. Also, the word *passions* would not have suited Edwards, as the passions were thought to mean primarily the lusts of the flesh, which would hold exclusively negative connotations at that time. As Edwards described, deep within a person's secret heart—within the very will itself—are the cherishing of some things and the repulsion from others, the rejoicing in some objects and the loathing of others. Love, fear, joy, hatred, grief, covetousness—these are the affections. By "affections," Edwards is speaking about the will's own inclinations and dispositions. But above all else, the most fundamental concern in Edwards's mind was to discover how the Christian's converted soul inclined toward the things of God (his holiness, loveliness, righteousness, and glory). Are we drawn devotedly to him? Or are we rather repelled? If God revealed himself to us, would we run to the Lord like David the psalmist or jump into a bush and hide like fallen Adam?

The converted soul inclines to God as its highest good. It desires to praise him and to pour out its life in thanksgiving. The very heart of the believer is drawn in loving affection to the Father. True conversion is necessary to experience these longings for divine intimacy. Contrarily, the soul of the unconverted person is still primarily inclined to the self, one's own pride and glory.

Unfortunately, the work of discerning one's own affections is difficult. How much more to discern the affections of another! It is heart work. Soul-deep work. The problem is that most testimonies, Edwards says repeatedly in *The Religious Affections*, could unfortunately be faked or counterfeited. Almost all external actions could be falsified and did not truly indicate the condition of the heart with its loves, joys, fears, thanks, dreads, and desires. As it turns out, many people are pretty good at mimicking the stories and experiences of others, recounting them artificially as their own. This game was ages old, and the pressure to be able to "prove" one's faith by telling stories of spiritual experiences was overwhelming. Of course, many who professed salvation during the revivals eventually fell away. Time would tell whether these claimants stayed true to the faith or not. Other signs—such as faithful obedience, sincere love toward Christ and others, and perseverance in the faith until life's end—are much harder to fake and therefore more likely to be genuine. These were the affections that Edwards valued most highly in the soul; especially in his own soul.

Because Edwards had gone through such tremendous discernment in studying his own heart, he discovered two spiritual truths that proved greatly helpful in working with the people in his church and surrounding towns during the revivals. First, not everyone's story of conversion is precisely the same. For this very reason, Edwards abandoned the "steps" hypothesis of Perkins and his own father, placing more emphasis on the results of conversion than on the experiences leading to it. Second, a mere profession of faith—even remarkable and dramatic stories of one's inner experiences—was not finally indicative of saving grace. Edwards was far more impressed by a transformed heart, which expressed its true desires in the affections, the long-lasting changes of inclination from the self to the glory of God. This change, Edwards said, evidenced by such deep and transformative restructuring of the heart's desires to love God, rejoice in his presence, hate one's own sin, and lower oneself in meekness and humility, was the real proof that a person had truly been converted by the gospel of God's saving love.

60. Resolved, whenever my feelings begin to appear in the least out of order, when I am conscious of the least uneasiness within, or the least irregularity without, I will then subject myself to the strictest examination. July 4 and 13, 1723.

The 60th Resolution is yet another self-examination vow. Two possible scenarios might trigger this form of internal audit: (1) If Edwards notices that his "feelings begin to appear in the least out of order," or (2) if he observes that he's acting "with the least irregularity without," then he would automatically click into self-review mode. Both of these triggers require self-control and self-awareness.

As for the external actions, "irregularity without," he might for instance be alerted to changes in his tone of voice, or other physical manifestations of stress, anger, or fear. A nervous sweat or a tightening of the throat may indicate that he was beginning to lose self-control. The body gives off subtle signals that stress is rising quickly, and some of those signals may even be observable to others. Just the other day, for instance, I noticed I had slightly raised my voice in a tense conversation with my office staff. Thankfully, I caught myself before I said something regrettable.

By the time we've manifested an obvious "irregularity without," it may already be too late. Perhaps a hurtful, errant comment has slid off our lips, or we slammed a door on the way out. It could be something as subtle as shooting a furrowed brow as a nonverbal poisoned arrow toward a colleague. Indeed, the failure to evidence much self-control in intense moments can be a deep character flaw with potential to do much damage.

Our internal feelings are sometimes harder to monitor, because the very presence of a feeling seems self-evidently justified. Many of us are so incautious with permitting our feelings, the experience of anger, resentment, dread, or jealousy seems like self-confirming proof of their appropriateness. We get angry and we assure ourselves, "Well, I was justifiably upset! I had every reason to lose my cool!" Edwards, however, vowed to be better and to do better than to be led blindly by his feelings alone. Saint Augustine once observed that oars look straight when inside the boat but crooked in the water. We should learn to distrust ourselves, he reasoned, since we are often mistaken in our judgments. In the 60th Resolution, Edwards seems to suggest that our "feelings" can be like bent oars. They are not always to be trusted completely.

This resolution also notes a parallel passage in the diary dated July 4, 1723. Though the wording is similar, an additional line in the diary indicates what possibly caused him to write this particular resolution:

> At night. Whenever things begin to seem in the least out of order, when things begin to feel uneasy within, or irregular without, then to examine myself, by the strictest examination. *Resolved, for the future, to observe rather more of meekness, moderation and temper, in disputes.* (WJE 16:774; italics mine)

So, it seems clear that Edwards had engaged in some sort of verbal fight or "dispute." This may have been with his parents, since earlier in the day he had written in his diary about his anxiety over the condition of his soul and his inability to define the proper "steps" of salvation that his father expected him to experience.[39] In either case, Edwards appears to have lost his temper and subsequently failing to evidence outwardly Christian "meekness" and "moderation."

In my own view, this is where the real Jonathan Edwards comes into view. Here we have a verified genius emerging with an incredible mind, but he is perplexed and disturbed by fights with his parents and arguments at home. Although in these unguarded journal entries he seems easily frazzled, Edwards still managed to demonstrate incredible poise in the pulpit. He often took themes he was wrestling with in his personal life and formed them into stunning pieces of oratory for the pulpit. For instance, in an early sermon (written in the spring of 1723 at the latest) appropriately titled "The Duty of Self-Examination," Edwards created a checklist for more carefully monitoring one's own internal workings, just as he endeavored to do:

> We ought to consider the nature of our thoughts. How are the faculties of our souls chiefly employed; are our thoughts and our affections chiefly exercised upon earthly things, about what we shall eat, what we shall drink, and where-withal we shall be clothed? Are our minds set chiefly on vanities and trifles that are of little profit or advantage? Do we suffer our thoughts to rove to the ends of the earth? Do we give our thoughts the reins to go where they incline, sometimes upon the pleasing objects of concupiscence and the lusts of the flesh; sometimes after the objects of covetousness and the lusts of the eyes; sometimes after the objects of ambitious desires and haughty expectations led and governed by the pride of life, [and] at other times about things of no advantage or importance? Are our thoughts thus employed? (WJE 10:486)

---

39. See the appendix for a fuller explanation of the Puritan "morphology" of conversion.

This paragraph demonstrates an impressive rhetorical power in which we see how the budding genius could simultaneously preach world-class exhortations to a small congregation in New York City, even as he argued with his parents about his personal life. Like the rest of us, Jonathan Edwards was all too mortal.

65. Resolved, very much to exercise myself in this all my life long, viz. with the greatest openness I am capable of, to declare my ways to God, and lay open my soul to him: all my sins, temptations, difficulties, sorrows, fears, hopes, desires, and everything, and every circumstance; according to Dr. Manton's 27th sermon on the 119th Psalm. July 26 and Aug. 10, 1723.

Knowing God's omniscient knowledge of his own heart and soul, Edwards promised to "lay open [his] soul to him." He would hide nothing from the divine, all-seeing Lord. How could he escape even if he wanted to? Rather than close off any area from God's view, like Adam covering himself with leaves, Edwards determined to lay open all his "sins, temptations, difficulties, sorrows, fears, hopes, desires, and everything." Though none of us can truly conceal our hearts from God's piercing gaze (Ps. 139:1–16), Edwards would rather cooperate than run, opening the shutters of his heart so the light could shine in.

Like all true Christians, Edwards wrestled with the paradox between who he really was in his heart of hearts and who he knew he wanted to become. He was trying to work out the tension between being justified yet not fully sanctified, but he knew he needed divine help to grow stronger. On July 27, the day after he jotted down this Resolution, he wrote in his Diary,

> When I am violently beset with temptation, or cannot rid myself of evil thoughts, to do some sum of arithmetic, or geometry, or some other study, which necessarily engages all of my thoughts, and unavoidably keeps them from wandering. (WJE 16:776)

George Marsden, Edwards's most precise modern-day biographer, hypothesizes that he was probably fighting off strong sexual urges and temptations during this period. Given our shared human nature, Marsden's suggestion is a likely possibility. If Marsden is correct and sexual temptation was an acute concern for this single adolescent male, Edwards never recorded that battle specifically in any of his personal writings.[40] Perhaps he had a hard time even putting such words into his notebooks. Yet he would resolve to still confess these things in his heart before God, who would understand, love him, and accept him unconditionally.

In the 65th Resolution, Edwards refers to the twenty-seventh sermon of Dr. Thomas Manton, which Edwards drew from Manton's book *One Hundred*

---

40. Marsden, *A Life*, 56.

and Ninety Sermons on the Hundred and Nineteenth Psalm (London 1681). This reference, then, is not from a sermon Edwards heard, but rather one that he found in an old book. Manton (1620–77), a renowned divine, was a Presbyterian who took part in the Westminster Assembly (WJEO 24.66). Apparently, Manton was ejected from the pulpit and even imprisoned for his Presbyterian views following the Act of Uniformity in 1662. This would only have increased his admiration from colonial Puritans such as Edwards, who seems to have discovered these writings early in his career, which he then used in his own works. On a number of occasions throughout his writing career, Edwards drew material from Manton, using his commentaries on Scripture to supplement his own studies and sprinkling Manton's notes copiously throughout his own "Blank Bible" study system.

The sermon to which Edwards refers is one of Manton's nearly two hundred sermons from Psalm 119, the longest chapter in the Bible. This old, printed exhortation greatly affected Edwards's soul to a deep level, and he noted its provocation upon him in this resolution to be recalled regularly. The sermon focused primarily on 119:26, which reads, "I have declared my ways, and thou heardest me: teach me thy statutes" (WJE 16.758). It was a powerful piece of Puritan oratory, somewhat complex in structure, though clear in its main thrust. Manton, the long-dead Presbyterian pulpiteer, pleaded with his hearers to "go to God with clearness and openness, revealing your whole state, tell him what are your temptations and conflicts, and how your heart works." A true Christian, Manton argued, would "distinctly and without hypocrisy, lay open the state of the heart, and the course of his affairs to Thee . . . as a sick patient will tell the physician how it is with him, so should we deal with God if we would find mercy."

By purposefully opening up our hearts to God and admitting to him even the things that no other mortal might know, we prepare ourselves for forgiveness, cut off Satan's attempts to accuse us at the pass, and prepare our hearts to be "filled up with grace."[41] Edwards referred back again to the penetrating power of this sermon in his diary at least one more time, writing two weeks later on August 10, 1723:

> As a help against that inward shameful hypocrisy, to confess frankly to myself all that which I find in myself, either infirmity or sin; also to confess to God, and open the whole case to him, when it is what concerns religion, and humbly and earnestly implore of him the help that is needed; not in the least to endeavor to smother over what is in my heart, but to bring it all out to God and my conscience. By this means, I may arrive at a greater knowledge of my own heart. (WJE 16:778)

---

41. Thomas Manton, *One Hundred Ninety Sermons on the One Hundred Nineteenth Psalm*, 3 vols. (London: William Brown, 1845), 224–35.

As we have seen throughout the Existential Resolutions, this minister-in-training was eminently concerned, even preoccupied, with the condition of his own heart. In large part, we can view Jonathan Edwards as a man willing to confront his known sin and obvious personality defects, being honest about his shortcomings before Almighty God, while asking the Lord for divine help to overcome his struggles along the way. Whereas Saint Augustine by way of contrast also struggled mightily in his heart and mind with his sinful nature, the difference between the two great thinkers could not be starker: Augustine struggled for years with lust, which spilled out into full-blown sexual immorality, fornication, and other sins of the depraved nature before he was finally given victory in his life through his conversion. In contrast, Edwards likely struggled with the same human tendencies but, by all accounts, was able to maintain his purity as he waited for marriage through the power of the Holy Spirit. There is no record or even a hint that Edwards was anything less than a faithful husband to his wife and a chaste follower of Jesus Christ.

As we conclude our study together through this first large grouping of Existential Resolutions, it should have become clear that the young Jonathan Edwards, not yet even fully ordained to ministry but still in the preparatory stages of his career, went through many of the same trials and tribulations we all go through. He argued with his parents, doubted his own conversion, struggled with indwelling sin, and through it all sought refuge in Christ. By the end of his teenage years, he had figured out what life is all about to an incredibly accurate degree, narrowly and exhaustively pursuing Christ in heart, mind, and Christian vocation. Now we move on to consider his Ethical Resolutions related to self-control, speech, duty, service, and action.

2

ETHICAL RESOLUTIONS:
HOW THEN SHALL WE LIVE?

❖ Peace, Relationships, and Self-Control
Resolutions 15, 20, 21, 33, 39, 40, 46, 56, 58, 59, 69

Ethics is a place of overlap between philosophy and theology. Both sciences have a large place in their field of knowledge for a discussion on what constitutes the good life, or the virtuous life. Both philosophy and religion also have a basic foundational assumption that some actions are virtuous (good) and others are vice (evil). Even non-Christians, like Aristotle for instance, considered the concept of the virtuous life in great depth.[1] Technically, there is a difference between ethics and morality, though they are often used interchangeably. Reformed theologian R. C. Sproul wrote that ethics is concerned with what "ought" to be done, and morality is concerned with what "is" done.[2] Ethics is that to which we should aspire, or what is essentially right; while morality describes the basic behaviors and patterns of a given society. Ethics, therefore, is the loftier goal.

As Christians, of course, we should be highly concerned with leading the kind of life that is pleasing to God. Even though we cannot save ourselves through our actions and deeds, the way we live our lives after our conversion is not at all inconsequential. Our lives matter greatly! As Francis Schaeffer posed the question a generation ago, if Christ is our Lord and Savior, "How should we then live?" How should my Christian life be different from that of an unbeliever who is not fundamentally motivated by the glory of God?

Like Benjamin Franklin and George Washington who also wrote resolutions in their day, Edwards here likewise takes up that task of defining for himself what kind of life should be pursued as the virtuous (or ethical)

---

1. See, for instance, Aristotle's *Nicomachean Ethics*.
2. R. C. Sproul, "The Difference between Ethics and Morality," https://www.ligonier.org/blog/difference-between-ethics-and-morality/.

life. Even if society chooses its own set of "morals" (from the word *mores*, meaning patterns of accepted behavior), Christians are motivated to live for a higher goal and more glorious ideal, given that we have been purchased by the precious blood of Christ!

Of course, a large portion of Christian ethics centers around the complexity of human-to-human relationships. Relationships are often frustratingly hard. To pursue the ethical life is to set a course toward healthy and God-honoring interactions with other people, who are likewise made in the image of God. In this first section, we will consider primarily those resolutions that have to do with peace, relationships with other human beings, and self-control, which is, after all, one species of the fruit of the Spirit (Gal. 5:22–23). Here, we look at the resolutions numbered 15, 20, 21, 33, 39, 40, 46, 56, 58, 59, and 69. We will notice how Edwards had a great desire to honor and please those around him, including his parents and elders, especially in a society given to hierarchical functions and expected norms and patterns of comportment.

Also considered in this main section will be Resolutions on speech (resolutions numbered 16, 31, 34, 36, 38, 66, and 70). The Bible has much to say about our manner of using words to harm or to heal (e.g., Prov. 12:18; James 3:3–12). Scripture commends bold preaching at some times and silence at other times. Rounding out this section, we will also consider resolutions on duty, service, and action (Resolutions numbered 13, 35, 41, 54, 57, 61, and 62). Just as there are times when we should take up the pulpit, the megaphone, or pen and *say something*, so also there are times when direct action is required and we must *do something*.

15. Resolved, never to suffer the least motions of anger towards irrational beings.

I'm sure that all of us have allowed ourselves to become frustrated with nonhuman objects. You've probably pounded the keys of a computer that wouldn't load fast enough or muttered an imprecation at the corner bedpost that clobbered your toe in the dark of the night. And though your dog is certainly a sentient being, you may have chastised her for doing something most responsible humans would consider "irrational" (like chewing up the dryer sheets as my dog did this morning). We all lose our cool at times with the things in our lives that frustrate us. When we lash out in anger against such irrational beings, we are acting as Jonathan Edwards vowed never to do in this 15th Resolution. Though these objects of our ire may receive our scorn for not obeying our direct orders, they cannot do otherwise; they are "irrational," or non-thinking things. When I punch the passenger seat in my car when the engine doesn't start, I'm simply venting empty rage, screaming into the abyss. My car has no sensitivity whatsoever to my "motions of anger," and no amount of scolding will prompt it to change its own battery in the cold of winter.

The focus of this vow, and much of this larger section of Ethical Resolutions now under consideration, is what Galatians 5:23 calls "meekness" or "temperance." In this important text, Paul is contrasting how life under the influence of the Holy Spirit differs from life directed and controlled by the sinful nature alone, or our flesh. (The Greek word for flesh in 5:17 and 19 is *sarx*, from whence we get the word *sarcastic*.) The positive term "self-control" is technically somewhat of a misnomer, because when left to the control and influence of our own emotions, we end up being directed by that remnant of Adam's nature that leads us deeper into sin. Rightly understood, biblical "self-control" is something closer to Holy Spirit control: being steered by the help, comfort, and consolation of the very Spirit of God himself.

In Numbers 22:27, Balaam lost control of his temper when his donkey veered out of the way of the angel of the Lord, crushing Balaam's foot against a wall. The prophet lashed out in anger, striking the otherwise obedient animal with a cruel blow. Then, in one of the more humorous moments of the Old Testament, the donkey spoke in human language to defend itself. The irony here is that the donkey was thinking and acting more rationally than Balaam!

So, in an Edwardsean exercise of self-examination, let's trace this bad habit back to the source and ask ourselves why we sometimes curse, scream, or even strike out at our car, laptop, or lawnmower when we lose our temper. Obviously, the first reason is that the fruit of self-control (Spirit-control) has not yet fully ripened into maturity in our lives.

Think of the most mature believers you know. Have you ever seen them smash a phone or send a video game controller into a wall? Probably not. The reason you regard them as mature is likely because they have developed the fruit of a greater calm in their lives. But perhaps the root of the issue goes deeper still and our frustrations are only the symptoms of a greater disease. Perhaps we expect our tools, gadgets, and possessions to obey our every command because deep down we too want to be sovereign. We want to be little "lords" of our own little worlds. Instead of obeying our commands, however, the very objects we expect to perform our lordly decrees rebel against us. Our phones freeze. Our watch stops on a busy day. The ax handle splinters and breaks. The bus is late. The faucet won't stop dripping. Indeed, we're furious, but our fury has no ability to convince the irrational object to do otherwise. It is dumb. Inert. Lifeless. Irrational.

In fact, we can trace this frustration all the way back to the Garden of Eden when God placed a curse on the serpent, the woman Eve, and the gardener Adam. God warned Adam that his work would no longer be joyfully fulfilling, and instead that he would experience the frustration of a stony ground, thorns, and thistles, and work attended by the "sweat of your face" (Gen. 3:17–19). So, the next time you're frustrated by an animal that won't obey you, or a gadget that breaks down on the day you need it, or a Lego you painfully step on in the middle of the night—relax, repent of your known sin, and ask God to help you remain under his benevolent direction. Instead of lashing out, ask him for the privilege of bearing greater measures of the fruit of self-control.

20. Resolved, to maintain the strictest temperance in eating and drinking.

When God created human beings, he breathed into the dust of the ground and humanity took on life (Gen. 2:7). Herein is a great mystery: we are both physical creatures and living souls. The first part is comprised of muscle, bone, and blood; the latter part of knowledge, the will, and the affections. The body requires physical nourishment of food and drink; the soul the spiritual nourishment of the word of God. Of course, there are two equal and opposite errors we can make in this regard. One grave error is to forget that we have an eternal soul dwelling within our bodies and focus exclusively on physical fitness, diet, appearance, and overall health. In this error, we neglect the soul. The opposite error, however, is to neglect the body's health through the extremes of ascetic or gluttonous practices (cf. Prov. 23:20; Col. 2:18). We've all met believers who are otherwise mature in their faith but have ignored their bodily health to great detriment.

Edwards seems to be keen to avoid this either/or error. Though most of the Resolutions address spiritual insights, there are a couple that address physical health, especially diet. Here, as in the 40th Resolution, Edwards is concerned about the effect food has on the body. It has been well reported that Edwards was preoccupied with food intake, especially since eating too much made him lethargic—which as a highly productive thinker and writer, he desperately wanted to avoid. For instance, he writes in his Diary:

> Saturday night, Feb. 15. I find that when eating, I cannot be convinced in the time of it, that if I should eat more, I should exceed the bounds of strict temperance, though I have had the experience of two years of the like; and yet, as soon as I have done, in three minutes I am convinced of it. But yet, when I eat again, and remember it, still, while eating, I am fully convinced that I have not eaten what is but for nature, nor can I be convinced that my appetite and feeling is as it was before. It seems to me that I shall be somewhat faint if I leave off then; but when I have finished, I am convinced again, and so it is from time to time. (WJE 16:784–85)

This is counterproductive as it causes the body to want to go into shut-down mode and inhibits clear thinking and writing. In another similar entry during his time at Yale College as a tutor, he wrote,

Tuesday, Sept. 2. By a sparingness in diet, and eating, as much as may be, what is light and easy of digestion, I shall doubtless be able to think clearer, and shall gain time. 1st, by lengthening out my life. 2dly, shall need less time for digestion after meals. 3dly, shall be able to study closer without wrong to my health. 4thly, shall need less time to sleep. 5thly, shall seldomer be troubled with the headache. (WJE 16:786)

Unfortunately, while these measures to control his caloric intake may have enabled him to work longer hours, they didn't necessarily pay long-term dividends as he aged. Edwards's biographer Douglas Sweeney points out that such a lifestyle probably was detrimental to his overall health. Pushing themselves too hard for too long with heavily starchy and salted diets often caused colonial pastors to suffer a host of physical effects often described generally as "the ague": weakness, lack of energy, bodily pain, and chills. Sweeney says that Edwards "suffered all his life from these and other such infirmities. . . . [H]is spindly body broke down frequently under stress."[3]

Nevertheless, while Edwards seems to have again veered toward a "rigorist spirituality," often pushing himself too hard he does however show us a good model for receiving our food with gladness and thankfulness, as he preached in one sermon:

We ought frequently to consider what are our obligations to our duty, and to meditate on the reasonableness of it: to think what an absolute right God has to our service; how great and excellent a being he is, and what he deserves of us upon that account; to consider that he has made us, and how just it is we should obey him upon that account; to consider what we receive from him, and what is due from us to him on that account. *We ought not to eat and drink like beasts, never considering whence these good things come.* Nay, we ought not to breathe like beasts, without considering who it is that gives us our breath, without considering the God in whose hand our breath is; for every breath we draw is a mercy of God that we do not deserve. (WJE 10:485; italics mine)

In other words, even our daily food and breath are to be received as good gifts from God. One of the primary factors that separate mankind from the beasts is not so much our ability to gorge ourselves with vast amounts of food as quickly as possible (anyone who owns a dog can testify how astounding this feat can be!), but in that we return thanks for our food when we receive it as gifts from the hands of a benevolent Lord.

21. Resolved, never to do anything, which if I should see in another, I should count a just occasion to despise him for, or to think any way the more meanly of him.

---

3. Douglas Sweeney, *Jonathan Edwards and the Ministry of the Word: A Model of Faith and Thought* (Downers Grove, IL: InterVarsity Press, 2009), 50–51.

Genesis 16 tells the somewhat sordid story of Abraham, Sarah, and their unfortunate handmaid Hagar. When Abraham temporarily lost faith in God's covenant promises to multiply nations through his lineage, Sarah suggested that Abraham consort with Hagar. When Abraham did just that, Sarah began to "despise" Hagar (Gen. 16:4–5), to hate her in her heart. After that, Sarah "dealt hardly with her" (ESV says "harshly"). We cannot help but feel for the manipulated Hagar, whom God comforts with his grace later in the chapter. To "despise" another individual is to think lowly of them, to regard them as of lesser quality, of second tier or an inferior caste. When we despise others, we raise ourselves up as if we're living on a higher plain of society. We exhibit toxic levels of interpersonal arrogance. Scripture gives serious warnings to those who make a habit of despising others in their hearts (cf. Prov. 14:21; James 2:5–6).

Edwards recognized this tendency in himself, even though he lived in a day and time in which society functioned somewhat more hierarchically than it does today. Elite landowners, clergymen, and the well-educated thought of themselves as more beneficial to society than slaves or laborers, and treated each other accordingly. The "despising" Edwards refers to here in this resolution, however, is not based on class or privilege, but on the more apparent failures of moral character that happen on occasion in all societies and in all communities.

In his 21st Resolution, Edwards acknowledges that there are "just occasions" to despise another man's deeds and ethical failures. Indeed, what some people do is truly "despicable." For his own part, Edwards resolved not to then do the same. To think or act in the same way as the morally reprehensible— even as he judged them in his own heart—would be the height of hypocrisy. Instead, he vowed to note their transgression and to avoid what brought them down. Edwards also cautioned himself against the temptation toward thinking "the more meanly of him," since the very temptations that caused him to fall so visibly were likewise present in him. He's right here, isn't he? We often think less of people who gossip, lose control of their temper, get caught in a lie, or go through a public moral failure, even as we ourselves nourish the same temptations in our hearts, although less conspicuously!

But sometimes this "despising" of others works the other way around too. Sometimes we are the despised ones, while others whisper and murmur about our more conspicuous flaws. When this would inevitably be the case for him, Edwards determined to make the best practical use of these occasions. In his Diary, he records some thoughts on improving these embarrassing moments so they wouldn't be to the detriment of his character over the long haul:

Sabbath day, Nov. 22. Considering that bystanders always espy some faults which we don't see ourselves, or at least are not so fully sensible of; there are many secret workings of corruption which escape our sight, and others only are sensible of: resolved therefore, that I will, if I can by any convenient means, learn what faults others find in me, or what things they see in me, that appear any way blameworthy, unlovely or unbecoming. (WJE 16.787)

What Edwards is talking about here are the "blind spots" that follow us around. Just as when we are driving in a vehicle, there is an angle in which we cannot see the danger in either the mirrors or our peripheral vision, so also are there minor (or major!) defects in our character that are apparent to others but we ourselves can't see. For many of us, it's painful to hear what others identify as our blind spots. For Edwards, however, he saw this as an opportunity to grow in maturity and in the faith: "I will, if I can by any convenient means, learn what faults others find in me, or what things they see in me, that appear any way blameworthy, unlovely or unbecoming." These "convenient means" might include difficult conversations with his parents, a colleague, pastor, or a mentor. He would have to learn about these faults somehow, which most likely came through the agency of another's rebuke or public observation.

But when he learned of these blind spots, instead of defending himself or denying that they exist (as most of us would), he would rather own them, admit and confess them, and then work toward their repair and improvement. Recognizing our own faults, even when others point out what we cannot see ourselves, is in fact a sure characteristic of Christian maturity.

33. Resolved, always to do what I can towards making, maintaining, and establishing peace, when it can be without over-balancing detriment in other respects. Dec. 26, 1722.

Edwards wrote this 33rd Resolution while suffering from a debilitating headache. It was the day after Christmas, though the colonial Puritans didn't hold the Christian calendar holidays very highly, if at all.[4] Though his head pounded, he hoped to make considerable progress in his studies during the usable daylight hours. He wrote in his journal,

Wednesday, Dec. 26. Early in the morning yesterday, was hindered by the headache all day; though I hope I did not lose much. Made an addition to the 37th Resolution, concerning weeks, months and years. At night; made the 33rd Resolution. (WJE 16:760)

Perhaps he had been hindered by not only the physical ailment of a headache but also by the emotional pain of a strained relationship. These too can make working, writing, reading, and even *thinking* all that more difficult.

---

4. Christmas, Easter, Advent, and Lent were thought to be too Anglican—or worse—Roman Catholic!

No doubt we've all experienced the strain of a relationship left in a tangled mess: a conversation ended with roughhewn words rather than apologies and a fond embrace; the dreaded anticipation you might see your adversary unexpectedly at the market or, more painfully still, in the church narthex on the Lord's Day. One of the worst parts of all is the awkward waiting period while both parties test each other's patience to see who apologizes first. The longer it goes without resolution, the worse it is. It is for this reason that Paul pleads with Christians to "let not the sun go down upon your wrath" (Eph. 4:26).

Relationships that have run afoul and begun to disintegrate can be not only a great distraction from our daily life and errands, but they also place us in the uncomfortable zone of being askance with the Lord as well. Jesus warns several times that hindered relationships with a brother inhibits one's walk with God:

> Whosoever is angry with his brother without a cause shall be in danger of the judgment: and whosoever shall say to his brother, Raca, shall be in danger of the council: but whosoever shall say, Thou fool, shall be in danger of hell fire. Therefore if thou bring thy gift to the altar, and there rememberest that thy brother hath ought against thee; Leave there thy gift before the altar, and go thy way; first be reconciled to thy brother, and then come and offer thy gift. Agree with thine adversary quickly. (Matt. 5:22–25)

Matthew 18:15–17 likewise provides a prescription for reconciliation with a brother. Though the process involves the hardest step in the world—going directly to the offended brother rather than hiding or gossiping about him—Jesus' prescribed path is the surest route to reconciliation. Interestingly, in Matthew 5 it is the offender who is to take initiative, while in Matthew 18, it is the offended one who takes the first step. When these passages are put together, we clearly see Jesus' point: the tenderhearted and conscientious Christian is to be the one to make a reconciliatory move in either case. There can be no waiting game.

Several years after Edwards wrote this insightful resolution, he nudged himself to keep up his relationships. This is part of "maintaining peace." The young scholar-pastor recognized his propensity to ignore the proper upkeep of healthy relationships, while sinking too deeply into his own writing projects:

> One thing wherein I have erred, as I would be complete in all social duties, is, in neglecting to write letters to friends. And I would be forewarned of the danger of neglecting to visit my friends and relations, when we are parted. (WJE 16:788)

So, despite the setback of a daylong headache, just after Christmas in 1722, Edwards put pen to notebook and wrote his 33rd Resolution, which is essentially a gloss of Romans 12:18 where Paul says, "If it be possible, as much as lieth in you, live peaceably with all men." In this resolution, Edwards made a mature decision: volunteering to be brave enough to place relationships above being "right." He would be the one to offer the healing salve of apology and forgiveness to an aggrieved party.

Notice that this Resolution has two parts. The first part says, "Always to do *what I can* towards making, maintaining and establishing peace" (italics mine). The phrase "what I can" is important, because it's not always possible to resolve all interpersonal conflicts in this life. In my own ministry, I have noticed that some people lack the emotional wherewithal to apologize properly much less say the hard words of "I forgive you." They are simply unable. In those cases, we must be content to allow the possibility that some people simply don't desire to be restored. They love to hate. Their torture is self-imposed. They have swallowed the key to their own prisons.

The second line Edwards adds is also instructive: "When it can be without over-balancing detriment in other respects." This means he would not be willing to compromise his integrity, even in the process of restoration. He would not participate in manipulative games. He would not grovel or demean himself or the other party. He would not involve third parties inappropriately, unless according to the instructions of Matthew 18. In other words, he would not add sin to sin as he took bold steps toward establishing and restoring peace.

39. Resolved, never to do anything that I so much question the lawfulness of, as that I intend, at the same time, to consider and examine afterwards, whether it be lawful or no: except I as much question the lawfulness of the omission.

I wonder how often in history such a gifted mind has been paired with such a tender heart! Though many of Edwards's writings reveal his incredible intellect, the "Resolutions" are such a valuable contribution to his corpus of writings because they reveal the sensitivity of his inward conscience. Here in the 39th Resolution, Edwards considers the matter of the actions that are morally questionable. We might consider them "gray areas," or as my mother used to call them, "iffy." Though the Bible is clear in many areas of life about what is good and what is evil—consider for instance the stark clarity of the Ten Commandments—its general overarching principles don't speak to every possible moral conundrum into which we allow ourselves to become entangled.

The key term in these lines is "lawfulness." Edwards says here that he should never do anything that seems to be unlawful at first blush, especially if he would later have to agonize over it by way of self-examination all over again—wrestling with whether he had somehow inadvertently transgressed God's holy law. He imposes a policy of caution or restraint upon himself. *If it's "iffy," don't do it! If it's gray, back away.* The only exception to this rule is the possibility that failing to do that very thing would put him in danger of having committed a sin of omission (cf. the 27th Resolution). In these difficult cases in which it wasn't precisely clear what action might lead toward the greatest good, Edwards decided to take whatever course would result in the least disturbed conscience when it was all over. For him, it was better to always act in a way that enabled him to live with himself later.

Interestingly, Edwards doesn't often use the words *lawful* and *lawfulness* in his earliest writings, although one conspicuous place is in his "Miscellany 12," where he uses it negatively (i.e., *unlawful*) six times in brief succession:

> If any ceremonies in divine worship are in any wise *unlawful* for this reason, because they are ceremonies of human invention, then human invention is a thing that makes ceremonies *unlawful* in the worship of God; and if so, then the ceremonies of the Church of England are *unlawful*. But if no ceremonies are *unlawful* because they are of human invention, then none of the ceremonies of the Church of Rome, nor all of them together, are *unlawful* upon this account, viz. because they are of human invention. But if it is said that the ceremonies of the Church of Rome are not *unlawful* upon that account, but because of their insignificancy or ill tendency; I say, who is to be judge in that case? Surely their legislators, as much as the legislators in England about the English ceremonies. (WJE 13:206; my italics)

Through complex reasoning, Edwards is once again agonizing over what would most glorify God, in this context, in holy worship on the Lord's Day. The controversy here is with regard to the so-called regulative principle of worship, in which Puritan and Reformed believers permitted only those actions in gathered worship that are expressly *commanded* by God and not contrived or invented by men (as apparently in Anglican and Roman Catholic worship). Once again, we see Edwards's policy of caution in his conclusion: It is better not to perform an act—even in worship—if there is any possibility it offends the Living God.

The term "lawfulness" comes up around thirty times in the KJV New Testament, whereas it is used only nine times in the Old Testament. This is because the New Testament characters struggle with moral dilemmas, prompting consideration of the applicability of the law to real-life situations. The preponderance of the usage of this term is related to the controversies between Jesus and the Pharisees in the Gospels. The Pharisees often pose a challenge to Jesus regarding the "lawfulness" of a certain action—such as healing on the Sabbath, divorcing one's wife, or paying taxes to Caesar—to which the Lord Jesus responds with his wisdom, grace, and power. One of the key elements of these stories is that Jesus *always* exemplifies a servant of God who obeys the fully revealed law of the Old Testament to the letter, while simultaneously living purposefully and brilliantly for the glory of God.

This idea of living most wholly to the glory of God was the emphasis most Puritan and Reformed theologians of Edwards's day placed on the law. Since the time of Luther and Calvin, Reformed theology has taught that the law has three "uses" (or purposes) for Christian believers: (1) to turn our hearts toward repentance and faith in Christ as we realize our guilt before a holy God, (2) to better order society in ways that accord most fully to the good of all persons in the community, and (3) to encourage believers to live the highest, most noble life we can, being truly pleasing in the eyes of our Heavenly Father. While Martin Luther placed more emphasis on the "First Use," Calvin and his followers (including the Puritans and Pilgrims) emphasized the "Third Use." We see that emphasis here in Edwards's 39th Resolution: Never do that which does not clearly glorify God, but never fail to boldly do what does bring him the utmost honor.

40. Resolved, to inquire every night, before I go to bed, whether I have acted in the best way I possibly could, with respect to eating and drinking. Jan. 7, 1723.

There are a great many reasons why you may choose to alter or restrict your diet. Perhaps your doctor recently told you must significantly change your caloric intake and monitor your cholesterol or risk further physical compromise. Perhaps an allergy has come on you in your adult life. Or maybe a conviction has developed in your conscience about the propriety of certain kinds of meat. Most commonly, adult Americans make dietary changes simply to lose weight, look better, and be more physically attractive. I don't think any of these motivations are wrong in and of themselves. But these are not the factors Edwards weighed. There does not seem to be a hint of personal vanity, for instance, in either the 20th or 40th Resolution, which both touch on the theme of food and drink.

The idea that food had a direct impact on Edwards's ability to think, write, and serve God in his calling and vocation as a pastor has been noted by many commentators who have worked through the material from his early pastoral years. For instance, George S. Claghorn, who wrote the introduction to *The Personal Writings* (Yale Works of Edwards, vol. 16), comments on these kinds of passages:

> Several themes run through the entries. One of them is the danger of temptation. Edwards felt the allure of riches and luxury. He had to train himself to resist a life of ease and procrastination, which was most attractive, especially when compared with the demands of study and the weariness of physical labor. Another source of peril was the body's need for sustenance and rest. If the dinner call came while Edwards was in the middle of a project, the meal would be forfeited. He viewed sleeping as a potential waste of time, to be cut to a minimum; consequently, he attempted to push the limits of his constitution. A further snare for the socially awkward Edwards was silence. His natural reticence often restrained

him from speaking to people about spiritual matters, even when he felt the need to do so. (WJE 16:743–44)

Notice how Claghorn ties together the ideas of temptation and diet in the above observations on Edwards's concerns as a young man. It almost seems that Edwards combines these two streams of thought (fending off temptation and guarding his diet carefully). True enough, fasting in Scripture is at times tied directly to resisting temptation, since the believer submits their whole self to carefully guarding what enters the heart, the mind, and even the body. The Lord Jesus Christ himself is probably the most obvious example of combining fasting with resistance to the spiritual assaults of Satan. Jesus' temptation in the wilderness (Matt. 4:1–11; Mark 1:12–13; Luke 4:1–13) was preceded by an astonishing forty-day fast. A number of other scriptural texts combine fasting with prayer, spiritual power, significant moments in the church, or personal sanctification (Mark 9:29; Acts 10:30; 13:1–3; 1 Cor. 7:5).

In one sense, we might suggest that Edwards was attempting to hold a sort of extended, perpetual fast. Because he recognized the beauty and brevity of life, he thought of his mortal pilgrimage as a spiritual vigil of prayer, devotion, and sanctification. Unlike the Anglicans and Roman Catholics—who devoted certain times and seasons to fasting (such as Lent)—Edwards, the Puritan Calvinist, considered his entire life as one decades-long fast in view of his full devotion before God. Consider this 1724 Diary entry in which he describes feasting and more-than-usual sumptuous meals:

Sabbath day, Feb. 23 When I am at a feast, or a meal, that very well pleases my appetite, I must not merely take care to leave off with as much of an appetite as at ordinary meals; for when there is a great variety of dishes, I may do that, after I have eaten twice as much as at other meals, is sufficient. If I act according to my resolution, I shall desire riches no otherwise than as they are helpful to religion. But this I determine, as what is really evident from many parts of Scripture, that to fallen man they have a greater tendency to hurt religion. (WJE 16:785)

Even on these occasions of family celebrations and reunions, while most present dined and celebrated in an unguarded manner, Edwards would separate himself from such common practices, concerned about what might be happening in his soul. As the Diary selection above shows, he knew he must not allow these occasions to "hurt religion"—that is, to impede his walk with the Lord.

Now that I think of it, I cannot think of one passage in all of Jonathan Edwards's writings where he appears the least concerned about the vanities of physical appearance or relative attractiveness to the opposite sex. No, the entire thrust of Edwards's life seems to be that his heart and life were beautiful to the Living and True God. For Edwards, this purity must extend even to what he would take on his plate and fork. This, I think, is an admirable aim for us, provided we don't lose sight of grace. Just as we guard our diet, we should also be careful to avoid swallowing the error that God is pleased with our austerity and religiosity, when in actuality we are justified in his sight only by grace through faith in Christ.

46. Resolved, never to allow the least measure of any fretting uneasiness at my father or mother. Resolved to suffer no effects of it, so much as in the least alteration of speech, or motion of my eye: and to be especially careful of it, with respect to any of our family.

By the close of April 1723, the most delightful and sublime period of Edwards's Christian experience to that point came to an end. His short pastorate in New York City was now over. A bitter departing from Madam and John Smith's house—a spiritual haven and joyful refuge during his interim pastorate—was followed by a disappointing and anticlimactic return to his parent's oversight. I am sure we can all relate. Edwards records glibly the pain of parting in his Diary: "Wednesday, May 1. Forenoon. Last night I came home, after my melancholy parting from New York." Not only had this spiritual mountaintop-experience in the small Presbyterian church come to a close, but Edwards had to again submit to the rulership of his father's home.

Tensions between the blossoming prodigy and his dutiful parents soon began to rise, however, prompting the younger Edwards to make a stern resolution to guard his heart against violating the fifth commandment to honor his parents. This friction likely centered around two or three discussion points. First, we recall that Edwards's own conversion experience didn't match his father's more traditional paradigm of conversion. Wilson H. Kimnach explains:

> However intense his son's "inward burnings" may have been, it is unlikely that Timothy Edwards readily accepted them as constituting an authentic conversion if they did not have the prevailing structure. And nothing is more obvious from the evidence of the "Diary" and the "Personal Narrative" than that they did not have the conventional structure.
>
> Neither document ("Diary" nor "Personal Narrative") breathes a hint of filial joy upon the return of the young minister to the bosom of his family. And during the succeeding months at home, the only references to his family are in self-admonitions. (WJE 10:272)

Second, the return home meant his father's resumption of control over his future career. While Jonathan busily prepared to deliver his master's thesis (in Latin) to the faculty of Yale in September 1723, Timothy Edwards was arranging for him to serve in a congregation (with his protective oversight of course) in Bolton, Connecticut, starting that November. All indications show that Timothy was far more excited about this possibility than his son. The pastorate at Bolton never really got off the ground, however, and after just a few months, it floundered for reasons not fully understood by modern scholars.[5]

Most likely, Edwards was becoming his own man and began to resent his father constantly questioning his faith and micromanaging his career. Edwards struggled between his own desires and aspirations and his humility in still wanting badly to please his parents. In mid-May, he wrote with remorse in his Diary:

> I now plainly perceive what great obligations I am under to love and honor my parents. I have great reason to believe, that their counsel and education have been my making; notwithstanding, in the time of it, it seemed to do me so little good. I have good reason to hope that their prayers for me, have been in many things very powerful and prevalent; that God has in many things, taken me under his care and guidance, provision and direction, in answer to their prayers for me. I was never made so sensible of it as now. (WJE 16:770)

In a similar Diary entry in July, however, Edwards encouraged himself to endure their verbal provocations as a servant suffering wrongly, although patiently, reminding himself of the promises of passages like 1 Peter 2:18–20.[6] Nevertheless, tensions continued to persist with his doting parents, and he resolved in another Diary entry to both repent of his attitude and reload with better arguments to buttress his positions the next time they quarreled. In this telling entry from later that summer, Edwards wrote,

> Tuesday morning, Aug. 13 1723. Have sinned, in not being careful enough to please my parents. Afternoon. I find it would be very much to advantage, to be thoroughly acquainted with the Scriptures. When I am reading doctrinal books or books of controversy, I can proceed with abundantly more confidence; can see upon what footing and foundation I stand. (WJE 16:779)

So then, in this important and highly personal 46th Resolution, we see Edwards's steely resolve to walk carefully between defending his own viewpoints from Scripture and personal conviction against the formidable interlocutors of his parents and simultaneously submitting to God and the properly ordained authorities in his life. This resolution would have to be so thoroughly heartfelt that it would not be betrayed even by "so much as in the least alteration of speech, or motion of my eye."

---

5. Murray, *Jonathan Edwards: A New Biography*, 55.
6. "Diary" July 19.23. "Friday afternoon, July 19. 1 Peter 2:18, "Servants, be subject to your masters, with all fear; not only to the good and gentle, but also to the froward." How then, ought children to honor their parents. This verse, together with the two following, viz. "For this is thankworthy, if a man, for conscience toward God, endure grief, suffering wrongfully; for what glory is it, if, when ye be buffeted for your faults, ye shall take it patiently; but if, when ye do well and suffer for it, ye take it patiently, this is acceptable with God" (WJE 16:774).

56. Resolved, never to give over, nor in the least to slacken my fight with my corruptions, however unsuccessful I may be.

The concept of holiness is largely lost on many Western Christians. Ever since John Dewey's philosophy of pragmatism swept through our society's thinking, our preoccupation has focused more on "what works." We see this in much preaching in evangelical churches, where short sermon series are organized around topics such as "Six Steps toward Being a Better [fill in the blank!]" Whereas previous generations engaged in a battle to preserve their heart and life in purity toward God, many of our churches and ministries have settled for aiming merely at practical application instead.

Edwards was one such man who desperately sought holiness. We see this reflected clearly in the 56th Resolution in which he utilizes war imagery to describe the Christian experience with sin. It is a "fight," as he describes it, to preserve one's life as holy (the Hebrew term literally means "set apart") for the Lord. In using combat language, Edwards picks up another theme from the Westminster Confession of Faith. Defining the term "sanctification" in chapter 13, the Divines described the process as "a continual and irreconcilable war, the flesh lusting against the Spirit, and the Spirit against the flesh." Notice that the confession describes this battle as both *continual*—the fight rages in the life of the believer until death—and *irreconcilable* as there can't be any compromise between the renewed spirit of the believer and the "old man" (cf. Rom. 6:6).

This July 1723 resolution reflects a larger theme present in Edwards's extant writings during his early pastoral years. Besides this resolution, two specific writings address his preoccupation with personal holiness around this time.

"Miscellany a" is the first foray in his decades-long collection of journaling that essentially served as his scrapbook. This first entry, however, is unusual in that the writing style isn't typical of the rest of the collection. "Miscellany a" is flowery, poetic, sublime, and written in a manner of high artifice. The theme, of course, is personal holiness, and Edwards describes this attribute of the believer without the technical language of typical Reformed dogmatics. Here is a small sample:

> Holiness is a most beautiful and lovely thing. . . . 'Tis the highest beauty and amiableness, vastly above all other beauties. 'Tis a divine beauty, makes the soul heavenly and far purer than anything here on earth; this world is like mire and filth and defilement to that soul which is sanctified. 'Tis of a sweet, pleasant, charming, lovely, amiable, delightful, serene, calm and still nature. 'Tis almost too high a beauty for any creatures to be adorned with; it makes the soul a little, sweet and delightful image of the blessed Jehovah. (WJE 13:164)

Absent from this entry is the confessional language of fighting, warring, or doing battle with the flesh. Instead, Edwards uses the images of beauty, gar-

dens, flowers, and music to describe the amiable character of the individual
who loves Jesus. The writing of Edwards that most closely resembles this piece
in style is his early love poem for his future wife Sarah.[7] Edwards's goal in this
miscellany is to show how beautiful holiness is in the sight of God as he sees
and approves of his saints, sanctified in the grace of Christ.

The other relevant piece on holiness from this time is his spring 1723
sermon, "The Way of Holiness." This sermon actually lifts and incorporates
several lines and paragraphs directly from "Miscellany a," which shows us an
early example of how Edwards would come to use his Miscellanies notebooks
as rough drafts for other projects. At the same time, he brilliantly blends in
his more poetic descriptions of the holy life with some of his fiercer language
of "striving":

> III. [Use of] Exh. Exhort all to holiness. You have heard what holiness is and of
> the necessity of it, the absolute necessity in order to escaping hell; what we must
> have or die forever, must be forever forsaken. Now, nothing is so necessary to us
> as holiness; other things may be necessary to discover this life, and things that
> are necessary men will strive for with all their might, if there is a probability of
> obtaining of them. How much more is that to be sought after, without which we
> shall [fare] infinitely worse than die ten thousand deaths! (WJE 10:478)

Taken together, these contemporary pieces on the theme of Christian
holy living and the pursuit of sanctification depict a life that paradoxically
is both beautiful to the Lord as well as a desperate fight for one's soul in the
midst of a thousand dangers. Unlike in many modern churches then, Edwards saw holiness not as a bare practicality but as a toilsome striving for an
experience "of a more bright and pure nature, more serene, calm, peaceful,
and delightsome" (WJE 10:479).

*58. Resolved, not only to refrain from an air of dislike, fretfulness, and anger
in conversation, but to exhibit an air of love, cheerfulness and benignity. May
27 and July 13, 1723.*

The 58th Resolution is difficult to the modern reader in containing two
somewhat outdated expressions. The word *benign* is most commonly used
today in reference to the categorization of a tumor or mass discovered in a
body. If it is malignant, it is lethal; left untreated it will kill you. If it is benign, it is not lethal, but it still may need to be removed. Of course, the word
benign actually means something far more positive than simply "not quite
deadly." To be benign is to be blessed, gracious, wholesome, kindhearted, and
magnanimous in nature.

Additionally, the word *air* is here used in a somewhat antiquated fashion.
I remember hearing my mother and grandmother describing people unfavor-

---

7. See "On Sarah Pierpont" in WJE 16:789–90.

ably as "putting on airs." Nowadays, we more commonly call someone two-
faced or simply *fake* when we mean that they're trying to present themselves
as someone or something they're not. But in the early 1700s, having an "air"
about you could be positive or negative—either way, you left people with a
stark impression they couldn't easily forget.

This resolution also contains two dated annotations, meaning that Edwards pondered his wording here meaningfully at least twice, lingering over
his desire to be shaped by his own words (cf. the 59th Resolution). In his May
27, 1723 Diary entry, Edwards clarifies in list form what exactly he meant by
"an air of dislike." This included social attributes such as "diffidence, discon-
tent, uneasiness, and a complaining temper, self-opinion, self-confidence,
melancholy, moroseness, slight, antipathy, privacy, indolence, and want of
resolution—to beware of anything, in discourse or conversation, that savors
of these" (WJE 16:771). If he manifested any of these attributes in the presence
of others, it would leave behind a foul stench. The "air quality," to make a pun,
would be nasty and offensive.

Nearly two years later in the winter of 1725, Edwards was still concerned
with the lasting impression he left with people. He wrote in his Diary using
the same terminology, "Tuesday, Feb. 16. A virtue, which I need in a higher
degree, to give a beauty and luster to my behavior, is gentleness. If I had more
of an air of gentleness, I should be much mended" (WJE 16:787). He sought
to be a favorable and kindhearted man among others. History is somewhat
mixed as to whether Edwards was successful in his stated goal to give off a benign fragrance. Some considered Edwards among the more gracious people
of the day. Others, including a few from the Northampton Church that fired
him in 1750, described him as aloof, intimidating, reserved, and overly stern.

But if Edwards failed in this degree, his Savior did not. In "Miscellany
108," Edwards writes a somewhat extended contemplation of the glory of
Jesus Christ. This endearing passage may be of some interest to us since:
(1) Edwards returns to the language of "benignity" that he used above in the
58th Resolution, and (2) this description of Jesus Christ also entails the idea
of the scent or aroma of the Lord. As you read this passage below, look carefully here for language that evokes these themes:

> When we are delighted with flowery meadows and gentle breezes of wind, we
> may consider that we only see the emanations of the sweet benevolence of Jesus
> Christ; when we behold the fragrant rose and lily, we see his love and purity. So
> the green trees and fields, and singing of birds, are the emanations of his infinite
> joy and benignity; the easiness and naturalness of trees and vines [are] shadows
> of his infinite beauty and loveliness; the crystal rivers and murmuring streams
> have the footsteps of his sweet grace and bounty. When we behold the light and
> brightness of the sun, the golden edges of an evening cloud, or the beauteous
> bow, we behold the adumbrations of his glory and goodness; and the blue skies,
> of his mildness and gentleness. . . . That beauteous light with which the world is

filled in a clear day is a lively shadow of his spotless holiness and happiness, and delight in communicating himself. (WJE 13:279)

Even if Edwards was not personally able to evoke the air of genuine benignity he hoped to carry forth in his personal comportment—and in fact he did tend toward a somewhat reclusive and occasionally abrasive personality—we can say at least two things in his favor. First, he seems to have been aware of this fault and took strides toward correcting it. As you know, many people aren't even aware of their obvious faults and cannot even begin to pray about them. Second, while Edwards was at times unable to evince the cheerfulness he hoped to when in public, there are few people in the history of the church who have been able to describe the goodness and glory of Christ nearly so well. Praise God that our Lord and Savior is benign when we are unable to be so!

59. Resolved, when I am most conscious of provocations to ill-nature and anger, that I will strive most to feel and act good-naturedly; yea, at such times, to manifest good nature, though I think that in other respects it would be disadvantageous, and so as would be imprudent at other times. May 12, July 11, and July 13.

The 59th Resolution is very much tied to what we just read above in the 58th Resolution. As in the previous one, Edwards here displays a self-awareness that he has a disposition toward grumpiness that causes him to act in ways that all too clearly expose the displeasure he was feeling in his heart. Some people call this "wearing your emotions on your sleeves." Indeed, it can be hard to control our outward appearance, countenance, or even posture when we're feeling disgruntled. Recognizing this in himself, Edwards resolved to continue to "strive" toward something better during those moments.

What is most interesting in this resolution, however, is that Edwards vows to strive to control not only his outward mannerisms but also the way he feels—his emotions: "I will strive to *feel* and act good-naturedly." Is this even possible? Most of the time, it seems we think of emotions as something like choppy waves in a sea we can't control. Sadness, anger, jealousy, and so on, rise up within us and we assume we can't do anything about it. We have no choice but to be tossed around helplessly by our feelings as we ride those emotional waves. We think we can't help feeling a certain way, so we just go with it.

But is this biblical? Does Scripture support the idea that we're responsible for our actions but not for controlling our inward emotions? I don't think so. Scripture says we are responsible even for our emotions, even telling us *how* we should *feel*. For instance, the Bible sometimes implores us to rejoice, as when Paul says to the Philippians, "Rejoice in the Lord always: and again I say, Rejoice" (4:4). Similarly, Psalm 32:11 admonishes us to "be glad in the Lord, and rejoice, ye righteous: and shout for joy, all ye that are upright in heart." Interestingly, Psalm 2:11 tells us to feel a complex mix of both terror and gladness, "Serve the Lord with fear, and rejoice with trembling." In Luke 7:13, Jesus commanded the widow of Nain to cease sobbing: "And when the Lord saw her, he had compassion on her, and said unto her, Weep not." Contrariwise, Paul instructs the Roman Christians to "weep with them that weep" (12:15). James also warns his audience to mind their inward expressions: "Be afflicted, and mourn, and weep: let your laughter be turned to mourning, and your joy to heaviness" (4:9). All of these biblical admonitions are in the imperative aspect, meaning that they are commanded. So, we conclude, we do have some sway over the raging sea of our emotions. We are not tossed around helplessly by our inward feelings.

Is Edwards, then, simply trying to "will" himself into a better, more cheerful mood at all times? Not exactly. Notice that in the latter lines of this resolution, he acknowledges that there are times when acting good-naturedly is not appropriate and even (to use his own word) "imprudent." As the Teacher in Ecclesiastes 3 writes:

> To every thing there is a season, and a time to every purpose under the heaven: . . .
> A time to weep, and a time to laugh; a time to mourn, and a time to dance; . . .
> A time to keep silence, and a time to speak;
> A time to love, and a time to hate.

As the Teacher says, there are times to weep, and doing anything else would indeed be inappropriate. Likewise, there are times when it's entirely appropriate to feel righteous anger; even our Lord Christ himself displayed this zeal (cf. John 2:13–22). When we see gross injustice and evil in the world, we ought to be rightly provoked. In Act 17:16, the apostle Paul experienced this in-filling of ire when he saw the proliferous idolatry in the city of Athens.

So, the controlling idea or the main point of this resolution is twofold. First, that we don't need to let our feelings dominate our inward or outward comportment. In fact, Scripture commands that we maintain a proper inward disposition, just as it commands us to act outwardly in ways that are consistently Christian. Second, however, we should not pretend to be chipper and happy-go-lucky at all times either. There are true evils and lamentations in this world, and to respond to them in any way other than appropriately would be wrong.

To sum up, then, we should constantly tune our hearts to the heart of the Lord himself. On May 12, the date annotated to his Diary in this Resolution, Edwards leaves himself this piece of advice:

I think I find in my heart to be glad from the hopes I have that my eternity is to be spent in spiritual and holy joys, arising from the manifestation of God's love, and the exercise of holiness and a burning love to him. (WJE 16:770)

This, I suggest, is wise counsel indeed.

69. Resolved, always to do that, which I shall wish I had done when I see others do it. Aug. 11, 1723.

There was one time when I wish I had acted with the alacrity Edwards resolved to have. I was waiting to board one of those smaller jets where passengers climb a stair ramp (an "airstair") from the tarmac to the cabin. I was standing there, twiddling the nametag on my bag, when someone suddenly pushed me out of the way, almost knocking me down. Offended, I looked up to see what was happening. Immediately it all became clear: an elderly woman had fallen and a man with greater awareness had pushed me aside to jump to her rescue. He helped her sit up and administered first aid, while I just stood there. In that moment, I thought: *Why couldn't I have been quicker to act! That could have been me helping care for this aged woman, rather than looking on as a spectator.*

Edwards seemed to be struggling here with what we might call "analysis paralysis." That is, he tended to overthink certain situations before finally taking action. When he saw others quickly taking initiative to perform the same action he had been contemplating, it became obvious to him that he should have acted right away rather than just considering the various ramifications of that action.

Suppose you see something you know is wrong happening right before your eyes. Alarm bells tell you to do *something*. Say *something*. Intervene *somehow*. But you don't. Instead, you just stand there, as if you had been turned to stone while someone else jumps in to intervene. Isn't it true that you immediately chide yourself for failing to act, having afterward been inspired by the other person's courage?

Like many of the resolutions we've covered so far, and several we haven't yet touched on, we find fuller context on the 69th Resolution in Edwards's Diary entry of the same date.:

Sabbath day, after meeting, Aug. 11. Resolved always to do that which I shall wish I had done, when I see others do it. As for instance, sometimes I argue with myself, that such an act of good nature, kindness, forbearance, or forgiveness, etc. is not my duty, because it will have such and such consequences: yet, when I see others do it, then it appears amiable to me, and I wish I had done it; and I see that none of those feared inconveniencies follow. (WJE 16:779)

In his Diary, he mentions several specific examples, including acts of kindness, forgiveness, and so on. The fact that this entry contains a notation that he contemplated this on the Lord's Day following a church meeting suggests something may have been said or done that day in church he wished he would have been brave enough to act on. Perhaps it was to confront a bully. Perhaps it was to witness to an unbeliever. Perhaps it was to invite a traveler into his home for a meal following morning worship. Maybe it was to give alms to a pauper in desperate need of help. Whatever it was, Edwards balked while another stepped up. Next time, he vowed, he would act instead of just think about it.

In this Diary entry, we also notice that he brings up the idea of "duty," which we will more fully consider in the next section of the Resolutions. For this moment, however, we should appreciate that it is the very idea of "duty" that appeared to be holding him back from sudden, gracious, and spontaneous action. He seems to be reasoning with himself that it wasn't his place to act or speak, thus rationalizing his inactivity. Frozen in inertia, he allows his brain to "buy time" in the matter by pontificating whether it was even his duty to speak up or to step forward.

I'm sure we've all had moments where we experienced tension with another believer. For example, talking ourselves out of apologizing: *They should be the one to apologize. It wouldn't be appropriate for me to speak out of turn in this situation anyway.* Yet, supposed that other person does in fact offer a gracious apology or display an act of contrition, how quickly do we move from "duty" to shame for not having the courage to speak first. "No!" we assure the other. "It was my fault all along! I should be apologizing to you!" Their act of moral courage has inspired us to act likewise in returned kindness and graciousness.

Like Edwards, we should remind ourselves that sometimes acting first and fast—without letting too much deliberation delay us—is the most appropriate and beautiful action of all.

❖ Speech
Resolutions 16, 31, 34, 36, 38, 66, 70

Speech is one of the things that sets us apart from almost all other things God has made—both animate and inanimate—with the exception of the angels and perhaps Balaam's donkey (Num. 22:22–41)! While it does seem to be true to the best of our knowledge that other many intelligent animals such as primates, whales, and dolphins have their own sort of vocalized communication, fully developed speech and refined language is one of the gifts humans have been given to reflect the image of God (Gen. 1:26–27).

In Genesis 1:3, God spoke creation into being, and then gave humans the gift of speech so they might praise and thank their God. Praise is a gift to man, to return blessing and honor to God. Interestingly, the first human words recorded in Scripture before the fall belong to Adam, as he declares a Hebrew love poem, perhaps even a song, over his beautiful newly created wife Eve (Gen. 2:23).

The fall indicates that speech can also be used to twist truth and to manipulate, as Satan and Eve discussed the technicalities of God's command about the tree of the knowledge of good and evil (Gen. 3:1–5). Soon after the flood narrative, God confused the human languages at the tower of Babel because speech had become a tool and a weapon to be wielded by the ungodly for evil (Gen. 11:1–9). Thankfully, at Pentecost (Acts 2), God reversed the curse of Babel and united the nations again through miraculous powers of speech, even as they together declared the wonderful works of God (Acts 2:11, 22).

The apostle James warns fellow believers that words can be used to praise God, but also to destroy others with curses, taunts, and mockery. He says that when believers use their words in such ways, they become like a fresh spring tainted and ruined by salt water (James 3:9–11). In this next section of the Resolutions, Edwards vows to be the kind of person that uses his God-given ability of speech to glorify the Creator and not as a vehicle of harm to others. Here we will consider Resolutions numbered 16, 31, 34, 36, 38, 66, and 70.

16. Resolved, never to speak evil of anyone, so that it shall tend to his dishonor, more or less, upon no account except for some real good.

Edwards once made a valuable comparison between men and wild beasts:

> We (humans) are all reasonable creatures. 'Tis the part of beasts, of wolves, tigers, dogs and the beasts of the forest to bite and devour one another. 'Tis exceeding hateful amongst creatures that have reason and understanding, and of such a noble make.[8]

The point of contrast is fair enough, I think, and his point is well taken too. While the ferocious animals in the wild bark, snarl, and growl at one another—often with vicious intent—human beings were created to use their mouths not to ruin one another or to tear each other to shreds, but to build one another up in love. When we do the opposite, Edwards avers, we err in two ways. First, we lower ourselves to the activity of the very beasts themselves, when we have been created of a more "noble make," or higher order and purpose. Second, and this is the real issue in the 16th Resolution, we contribute toward the "dishonor" of the brother or neighbor.

Today, the word *honor* has practically lost all meaning. We use it to describe a student's success (she graduated with honors) or perhaps to rec-

8. Marsden, *A Life*, 97.

ognize a military distinction (he was given the honor of the purple heart). But in Edwards's day, as well as in Scripture, your honor was the worth of your personal reputation in the church or community and from which you lived on the higher plane of integrity, character, and moral fidelity. When we "speak evil," whether that evil is careless gossip or more direct character assassination, we besmirch someone's reputation and denigrate their honor. The problem with this is that our words don't even have to be *true* to contribute to this erosion of their honor. Sometimes the evil we speak is quite deserved, but other times it is not. In both cases, we speak evil when our words have the ability to cut our neighbors down rather than to redeem, repair, and to recognize them as creatures bearing the very image of God (Gen. 1:27).

Although the word *of* is only two letters, it bears a great weight when considering the moral weight in this resolution. Notice that Edwards mentions speaking evil "of" someone rather than speaking evil "to" someone. Of course, both can be hurtful and often are, but in the former kind of speech, people are not present to defend their own honor and reputation. It's one thing to throw a verbal jab at a person in their presence, which they can dodge, parry, or reply in kind. It's another thing to strike a person with words who can't see the punch coming, leaving them unable to block or counter the blow.

I have actually heard people say terrible things about other people outside of their presence, and then justify their speech on the basis that both Jesus and Paul occasionally spoke severely. True enough, in Matthew 23, Jesus called the Pharisees "hypocrites" at least five times (vv. 13, 15, 23, 25, 29). Added to that, in the same context, Jesus called them "blind fools," "child(ren) of hell," and "whitewashed tombs." But notice that in this context, Jesus didn't say these things "of" the Pharisees, but rather "to" them. We can't help noticing the repetition of the phrase "Woe unto you" seven times. This is no gossip session; this is a direct confrontation with the desire to save men who were literally in danger of hell (see 23:33). So also, the apostle Paul called Elymas the magician, "O full of all subtilty and all mischief, thou child of the devil, thou enemy of all righteousness" (Acts 13:10). But remember Scripture says that Paul was also filled with the Holy Spirit and "looked intently at him" as he spoke. Again, this was a spiritual confrontation, not a salacious backstabbing.

Edwards closes his 16th Resolution with the words, "except for some real good." He does leave room for the possibility that harsh and even piercing words could serve some possibility of genuine good. What kind of good? Well, in the cases of the Pharisees and Elymas, the possibility was that their conviction might lead to repentance and salvation. Some hearts are so hard they must meet the blunt end of the gospel hammer to be softened. Another possibility is that we bring someone to legal justice. It's not gossip to point out a murder suspect to the police or a courtroom jury. In that case, stating the truth about someone's actions draw evil into the light and bring about temporal justice. Sadly though, preaching the gospel to an unconverted person or giving testimony in a proper court is usually not the occasion in which we emit the most ferocious barks and growls Edwards warned about. Too often, we reserve those base sentiments for our family, friends, colleagues, and church members. When we let loose such snarls with teeth bearing, we show ourselves to be little better than the animals.

31. Resolved, never to say anything at all against anybody, but when it is perfectly agreeable to the highest degree of Christian honor, and of love to mankind, agreeable to the lowest humility, and sense of my own faults and failings, and agreeable to the Golden Rule; often, when I have said anything against anyone, to bring it to, and try it strictly by the test of this Resolution.

This Resolution builds on and advances the general guidance Edwards left for himself in the 16th Resolution, which (we recall from the previous section) summons our consideration of the honor of others as it pertains to our speech. Though he repeats himself to some extent here in the 31st Resolution, he does add several other significant guardrails to help keep his speech honorable and uplifting. These additional guardrails are: (1) that his speech would be generally toward the love of all mankind, (2) that it would evidence his own humility, (3) that it would call to mind his own "faults and failings," and (4) that it would be tested by the Golden Rule.

Among the most quintessentially important teachings of Jesus' overall ethic, the Golden Rule states: "Therefore all things whatsoever ye would that men should do to you, do ye even so to them: for this is the law and the prophets" (Matt. 7:12). In one sense, this statement is a summary of Jesus' entire Sermon on the Mount's teaching on the horizontal morality of the Christian regarding our neighbor; and Jesus himself declares that this is the gravitational center of the Law and the Prophets. Interestingly, the Golden Rule falls in a particularly poignant place in the Sermon on the Mount, immediately preceding three concluding sections related to fruit bearing (Matt. 7:15–20), the judgment (7:21–23), and the final testing of the strength of the foundation of a man's life (7:27).

In both the Golden Rule and in Edwards's 31st Resolution, we are to go far beyond our grade school teachers' sage advice, "If you don't have anything nice to say, don't say anything at all." True neighborly love insights the *positive* use of the mouth and human speech to love, to edify, and to build up. Silence alone can't do what "I love you" can.

But as we all know through experience, controlling our tongues is difficult, which the apostle James acknowledges:

> We put bits in the horses' mouths, that they may obey us; and we turn about their whole body. Behold also the ships, which though they be so great, and are driven of fierce winds, yet are they turned about with a very small helm. (James 3:3–4)

Indeed, rudders are a fraction of the size of the vessel, just as the tongue is to the body. Yet in all these cases, they contribute over-proportionally to the entire direction of the whole. The apostle concludes with a warning: "Even so the tongue is a little member, and boasteth great things. Behold, how great a matter a little fire kindleth!" (3:5).

In Edwards's November 26 Diary entry, we find one key to controlling our speech in a moment of passion. Here, he counsels himself to discipline the mind far before the opportunity ever presents itself to disparage one's rival. Contemplating the ways in which the mind stews itself into boiling turmoil—much like a volatile volcano builds pressure under the earth— Edwards wisely counsels himself to refuse his heart and mind access to the destructive dialogues that only renew one's pain and aggravation:

> Tuesday forenoon, Nov. 26. 'Tis a most evil and pernicious practice in meditations on afflictions, to sit ruminating on the aggravations of the affliction, and reckoning up the evil, dark circumstances thereof, and dwelling long on the dark side; it doubles and trebles the affliction. And so when speaking of them to others, to make them as bad as we can, and use our eloquence to set forth our own troubles, and are all the while making new trouble, and feeding and pampering the old; whereas the contrary practice would starve our afflictions. If we dwelt on the light side of things in our thoughts, and extenuated them all that possibly we could, when speaking of them, we should think little of them ourselves; and the affliction would really, in a great measure, vanish away. (WJE 16:782)

Oh, how often we do just that regretful thing! We meditate day and night on the words of the person who hurt us, reciting arguments and counterarguments in our minds, preparing for the day when we might have an opportunity to launch a revengeful assault with words. We sharpen the daggers that we can use to stab our opponent in the back. We ruminate on a better retort, a sharper comeback, a punchier riposte. All the while, we only deepen the anger and widen the resentment we have been building. The magma pressurizes under such contemplations, and we prepare to spew out red-hot hatred. No, says Edwards, he would not "pamper" and "feed" such interpersonal histories, even with those who have hurt him most, so that he is not tempted to use his tongue to ignite yet another forest fire that will burn many.

34. Resolved, in narrations never to speak anything but the pure and simple verity.

In a court of law, when a person takes an oath to give testimony before a judge, jury, or magistrate, they swear to tell "the truth, the whole truth, and nothing but the truth." Even if we have not been a part of a legal proceeding before, we are familiar with this famous line through television and movies. Both in real courtrooms and on the silver screen, we have all seen people raise their right hand, place the other on a Bible, and give this oath to truth-telling.

And yet for Christian believers, we should not need such formalities in order to encourage us to speak forth the truth at all times.

In Matthew 5:37, Jesus says, "But let your communication be, Yea, yea; Nay, nay: for whatsoever is more than these cometh of evil." This does not mean that believers are forbidden to swear oaths in any situation, and there are certainly times in which we are called to give proper testimony (see Deut. 10:20; Rom. 1:9; 2 Cor. 1:23; Heb. 6:16). But we should speak at all times and in all situations what Edwards calls in the 34th Resolution "pure and simple verity." Both adjectives are instructive. "Pure" means that what we speak is unadulterated by falsehood, lies, purposeful omissions, or misstatements meant to deceive. "Simple" means that our statements should not be encumbered with unnecessary exaggeration, superfluous details, ornate language meant to impress, or other ostentatious descriptions to allure the listener with persuasive rhetoric.

The word *verity* was precious to Edwards, coming from the word *veritas* ("truth") in the Latin. In his Diary, Edwards reminded himself multiple times to continue to speak mere verity, especially in "narrations"; that is, the recounting of certain events in the presence of others. He writes,

> Feb. 23, 1724. Sabbath day, Feb. 23. I must be contented, where I have anything strange or remarkable to tell, not to make it appear so remarkable as it is indeed; lest through the fear of this, and the desire of making a thing appear very remarkable, I should exceed the bounds of simple verity. (WJE 13:785)

Edwards demanded pure and simple verity of himself, especially when the story was "strange or remarkable." This could include stories of heroism, rescue, battle, danger, or spiritual encounters. A couple months later, he would again remind himself: "Aug 24, 1723. Remember to examine all narrations, I can call to mind; whether they are exactly according to verity" (WJE 13:780). When I read these mature words from such a young man, I have to admit I find this honorable, and the intention to state facts plainly and humbly admirable and worthy of imitation. A little under a year later, Edwards once again posted a note-to-self to continue his prior pledge:

> Wednesday, May 22, 1724. In the morning. Memorandum. To take special care of these following things: evil speaking, fretting, eating, drinking and sleeping, speaking simple verity, joining in prayer, slightiness in secret prayer, listlessness and negligence, and thoughts that cherish sin. (WJE 13:771)

Though this is important for all believers, it is especially true for preachers and pastors. This is so because they among all people bear special responsibility to speak gospel truth from the pulpit. When telling a story or illustration (Edwards did not tell stories in his sermons), modern pastors should take special guard to avoid sensationalizing their personal accounts to make themselves look holier, bolder, more faithful, or more courageous. Neither should the spiritual results of a meeting or revival service be exaggerated. The Holy Spirit needs no assistance in his divine word from preachers who stretch the truth to make their churches, mission trips, or outreach events seem more extraordinary. Even developing a holy intonation of the voice should be avoided when preaching. Consider "Miscellany w," where Edwards addresses what we might call using a "preacher voice" from the pulpit:

> A tone is to be avoided in public, either in prayer or preaching, because it generally is distasteful; and a whining tone, that some use, [is] truly very ridiculous. But a melancholy musical tone doth really help in private, whether in private prayer, reading, or soliloquy; not because religion is a melancholy thing (for it is far from it), but because it stills the animal spirits and calms the mind and fits it for the most sedate thought, the clearest ideas, brightest apprehensions and strongest reasonings, which are inconsistent with an unsteady motion of the animal spirits. Wherefore, this may be a rational account why a melancholy air doth really help religious thoughts; because the mind is not fit for such high, refined and exalted contemplations, except it be first reduced to the utmost calmness. (WJE 13:175)

In Psalm 15, the psalmist asks what kind of a person is able to approach the Lord and then answers his own question, "Who shall dwell in thy holy hill? He that walketh uprightly, and worketh righteousness, and speaketh the truth in his heart. . . . He that sweareth to his own hurt, and changeth not" (vv. 1–2, 4b). Indeed, God is greatly pleased by the man, woman, or child who can confidently state the truth—without fabrication or equivocation—even when it hurts most to do so.

36. Resolved, never to speak evil of any, except I have some particular good call for it. Dec. 19, 1722.

Edwards began writing his Diary on the day he wrote his 35th Resolution (December 18); and then the very next day, he wrote this 36th Resolution. As Edwards continues here to struggle with the speech that spills off his lips, I would like to jump ahead to two other dates that come later in his life: one the next spring and the other a few months before his death.

Just a few months after Edwards wrote this Resolution, we have an interesting Diary entry in which his ongoing battle with controlling his speech comes up directly. Having just returned from a brief trip, Edwards received a letter from John Smith, which likely a great delight to Jonathan. Smith, as you recall, was among his bosom friends while in New York. Edwards had stayed with John and his mother during his short ministry at the Presbyterian church. In the letter, there was some counsel related to speech that Smith had given to our Jonathan, as he had apparently trusted his friend deeply enough to share the innermost turbulence of his heart, which prompted Edwards to write this entry:

Saturday night, May 18, 1723. This day returned, and received a letter, from my dear friend, Mr. John Smith. The last Wednesday, took up a resolution, to refrain from all manner of evil speaking, for one week, to try it, and see the effect of it: hoping, if that evil speaking, which I used to allow myself in, and to account lawful, agreeably to the resolutions I have formed concerning it, were not lawful, or best, I should hereby discover it, and get the advantage of temptations to it, and so deceive myself, into a strict adherence to my duty, respecting that matter; that corruption, which I cannot conquer by main strength, I may get the victory of by stratagem. I find the effect of it already to be, to make me apt to take it for granted, that what I have resolved on this week, is a duty to be observed forever. (WJE 16:777)

Although it is not clear exactly what Smith had advised Edwards, it seems as if the one young believer had recommended to the other that he needed to play chess against his temptations. He ought to counter the sin he felt welling up inside him by making parries and advances, anticipating the movements of the greatest temptations, plotting escape routes, while planning three moves ahead when necessary. Most of all, he would absolutely refrain from anything remotely resembling evil speech for at least one week, to determine if the results were better than that of those battles of conscience in which he questioned whether he should have said anything at all. His conclusion, after one week of trying out Smith's war games suggestions, was that he should adopt this strategy for the rest of his life.

Now we jump ahead to 1757, just months before Edwards died in 1758. Here, we read a snippet from one of the most important personal letters he ever wrote: his reply to the College of New Jersey (now Princeton University) in having invited him to take the mantle of the presidency of the school.

Although Edwards felt honored and truly humbled to receive such a call, his response was not altogether enthusiastic. In this letter, Edwards lists several reasons why they should discontinue his consideration! Here, instead of a résumé, Edwards gives sort of an anti-résumé, listing all the reasons he should be disqualified. In part, the letter reads,

The chief difficulty in my mind, in the way of accepting this important and arduous office, are these two: first my own defects, unfitting me for such an undertaking, many of which are generally known; besides other, which my own heart is conscious to. I have a constitution in many respects peculiar unhappy, attended with flaccid solids, vapid, sizy and scarce fluids, and a low tide of spirits; often occasioning a kind of childish weakness and *contemptibleness of speech*, presence, and demeanor; with a disagreeable dullness and stiffness, much unfitting me for conversation, but more especially for the government of a college. (WJE 16:726; italics mine)

In other words, there were both physical and emotional reasons he might not make the best president. As to the physical, he admitted being weak, frail, and generally not in good health. But emotionally, he was often of "low tide of spirits," could act "childish," and here it is: prone to "contemptibleness of speech, presence, and demeanor" rendering him "unfitting . . . for the government of a college." Eventually he took the job, but sadly he died after holding it for only a few months.

We learn two important things here in this letter about speech: first, a warning and then an encouragement. Both should be heeded by all serious Christians. Edwards never fully won the battle over his own speech, nor did he entirely eradicate hurtful speech from his lips. Yet even just months before his death, he was *still fighting* his archenemy of sin by confessing and admitting his faults.

38. Resolved, never to speak anything that is ridiculous, or matter of laughter on the Lord's day. Sabbath evening, Dec. 23, 1722.

Of the Seventy Resolutions, several of these short, personal goals may come across as shocking, unsettling, or perhaps even totally irrelevant to modern readers. This 38th Resolution, written just two days before his nineteenth Christmas, will surely be seen by many as the strangest of the seventy.

Why in the world would this pious teenager resolve never to *laugh* on Sundays? Is that so wrong? Does the Lord forbid us to have *fun*? Is it a sin to *chuckle* or *giggle*? It's hard to believe that this is the same author who wrote the 22nd Resolution we read earlier on obtaining "as much joy as possible." No wonder the Puritans and the Early American Colonial Christians are viewed as dour. Killjoys! Right? But to truly understand this resolution, we must do two things. First, we should quickly survey our own modern, evangelical views of the Lord's Day. And then, second, we should compare it to that of the Puritans.

Today, if we are honest, Sunday is not much different from any other day of the week. At many of our churches, we expect our services to be light. Perhaps the pastor opens with several jokes, and the praise band plays in a style similar to popular rock bands. We check our email, schedule our meetings, and place phone calls just like any other day. More and more, community events like soccer tournaments, volleyball games, and travel baseball use up the whole weekend. We likely spend a large part of our Sunday in some form of leisure. Perhaps we watch hours of TV on the couch if we find any time to sit down at all (NFL football anyone?).

Truth be told, our cell phones and the ubiquitous availability of Wi-Fi connectivity allow most of us to actually work seven days per week. We've nearly lost the traditional vocabulary of the "Lord's Day," and the term "Sabbath" is viewed as belonging almost exclusively to our Jewish and Adventist friends. At the same time, we often complain that our lives are too hectic, that we are constantly exhausted, and that we don't have any "free time" to catch up. In short, the Lord's Day has become for us just any other day—part of the grind.

Colonial Christians, and the English Puritans from whom they descended, had a very different view of the Lord's Day.[9] For one thing, they viewed the Sabbath as a continuing ordinance, held over from the Old Testament, though it changed from the seventh day of the week (Exod. 20:8–11) to the first day after the resurrection of Jesus Christ (John 20:1, 19; Acts 20:7; 1 Cor. 16:2). In this way, they sincerely believed they were obeying the heart of the fourth commandment. Colonial Christians viewed the entire day as different from the other six: it was sanctified, set apart, and unique. As an agrarian society, probably more like the times of the Old Testament than many of us will experience in our own lives, their bodies were tired and physically worn down by the end of the week. They longed for one day in seven to completely cease from all labor, and they used the Lord's Day as a complete, twenty-four-hour period of rest and worship.

The colonial Sabbath consisted of riding or walking to church, taking in a several-hours-long service, in which the Psalms were sung, prayers were offered, and sermons given that were double or triple the acceptable length today. They often fellowshipped over a meal as a congregation or retired for Sunday dinner to their own homes. While resting, Puritan families discussed the sermon, and children were expected to recite the main points of the minister's oration. Later, the families of the town gathered again for a Sabbath evening service. In this way, they devoted the whole day to worship and rest.

In Edwards's heart, the Lord's Day was a day to consecrate oneself to the Lord. The Puritan people believed they were renewing their covenant with the Lord God Almighty every time they gathered to receive Communion as a congregation. In this way, jocularity, frivolity, entertainment, and sportiveness were viewed as unwelcome intruders. Edwards did not want to become a distraction to himself or others who came to the meetinghouse, hoping for a spiritual rest that could provide some remittance from a hard life where death, disease, war, and other existential threats loomed heavy over every colonial village.

Perhaps Edwards went too far in restraining himself from even humor on the Lord's Day. Each reader can decide that on their own. On the other hand, perhaps it is we who have gone too far in making this day too much like every other.

66. Resolved, that I will endeavor always to keep a benign aspect, and air of acting and speaking in all places, and in all companies, except it should so happen that duty requires otherwise.

70. Let there be something of benevolence, in all that I speak. Aug. 17, 1723.

---

9. See, for instance, the Westminster Confession of Faith, chapter 21, on "Religious Worship and the Sabbath Day."

In Puritan and colonial society, the sting of "correcting and reproving" one another was simply a part of life (2 Tim. 3:16). Parents reproved children, and teachers rebuked their students. Magistrates corrected their citizens, and ministers occasionally upbraided their flock. For a pastor who was already inclined toward a more serious and stoic nature, Edwards had to often remind himself to also be as affirming and kind as possible. The 66th and 70th Resolutions are Edwards's "notes to self" to be as gracious as he could when performing this duty. Since his personality was naturally bent toward sternness, he needed to constantly remind himself to also consciously speak words of benevolence at every opportunity. He should never tear down with a hammer what he would not repair and rebuild with a trowel. He should never lash anyone with words without simultaneously offering a salve and tonic to heal.

One person who seems to have always appreciated Edwards's affirmation and guidance is his adult daughter, Esther Edwards Burr (see JEE 78–79). She was his third-oldest child and possibly one of his greatest admirers. Having married a Presbyterian pastor herself, Reverend Aaron Burr (the father of Aaron Burr, the third U.S. vice president), Esther knew more than others what struggles pastors and their families have. Esther, the daughter and then wife of a minister, Esther knew full well how the best disciplinary efforts of well-intentioned clergymen could be misunderstood. Where others perhaps saw a stern, flint-faced preacher—not especially given to social graces and chit-chat—Esther grew to appreciate her father as a warm sage, both a gentle guide and a trustworthy counselor.

In one place, Esther comments in her own journal,

> Last eve I had some free discourse with My Father on the great things that concern my best interest. . . . He gave me some excellent directions to be observed in secret that tend to keep the soul near to God, as well as others to be observed in a more publick way—What a mercy that I have such a Father! Such a Guide![10]

In this journal entry, we see a hint of what others would testify to throughout his life: whereas Edwards never quite grew out of his fear of saying the wrong thing publicly—which manifested in what many interpreted as standoffishness—he was far more suited to small, intimate gatherings and one-on-one counseling situations. In such contexts, as one young minister wrote, he could be positively "pleasant and edifying."[11]

Kenneth P. Minkema, one of the foremost experts on Jonathan Edwards studies says,

---

10. Kenneth P. Minkema, "Personal Writings" in *The Cambridge Companion to Jonathan Edwards*, ed. Stephen J. Stein (Cambridge: Cambridge University Press, 2007), 54.

11. Minkema, "Personal Writings," 46.

Edwards knew that he was thought to be stiff and opinionated; his "Diary" entries also exhibited concerns over his introversion. He visited parishioners rarely and reproached himself for neglecting "social duties."[12]

Yet in certain situations, Edwards could more than shine in conversation. Among trusted friends and colleagues, he could even be the center and heart of the conversation. In a 1754 letter from Esther to her friend Sally Prince in Boston, the famed preacher's daughter imagined that she too was among the gathered guests in a small fireside setting at Prince's home:

> I imagine now this eve Mr. Burr is at your house. Father is there and some others. You all set in the Middleroom, Father has the *talk*, and Mr. Burr has the *Laugh*, Mr. Prince gets room to stick in a word once in a while. The rest of you set and see, and hear, and make observations to yourselves.[13]

This snippet from a letter is endearing and takes us inside the walls of a setting where Edwards must have melted away the frozen impression given his countenance in the famous oil painting depicting his typical Puritan frown. He could be warm, thoroughly engaging, and even fill the room with charisma. Esther paints a picture of a scene that probably occurred hundreds of times throughout the years: Edwards with his wig off, sitting comfortably among close friends, engaged in the most earnest of spiritual conversation. We too can imagine the scene that Esther sketches: The fireplace is crackling, Pastor Burr's uproarious laugh occasionally rippling through the house, several interested sets of ears listening—even occasionally daring to chime in—all the while Edwards doles out incredibly deep thoughts for all gathered to collect and to ruminate. For those who could keep up with his genius, he must have been absolutely captivating. For those given to superficiality and banality, however, he must have been impossibly mysterious and intimidating.

The 70th Resolution, as you know, was the last Edwards wrote. On August 17, 1723, he completed his list of personal guidelines, eight months after he began writing them. It is fitting, then, that in his last and final Resolution, he once again prodded himself toward holiness and benevolence in his greatest struggle, using words. The paradox is startling: he, who could write volumes of prose so freely and meaningfully with his pen when alone, always struggled to say the right thing among others.

❖ Duty, Service, and Action
Resolutions 13, 35, 41, 54, 57, 61, 62

Duty seems like such an outdated word. We often think of it in terms of the military or law enforcement operations. If you ask any soldier why they

---

12. Minkema, "Personal Writings," 46.
13. Minkema, "Personal Writings," 46.

acted with valor in a dangerous situation, they will most likely say that duty was a primary motivating factor that enabled them to act with such courage. Similarly, when emergency responders are either injured or killed while on the job, it will be said that it happened "in the line of duty." Duty may first of all, then, be defined as "service in action."

Aside from civil or patriotic acts, the term can also be used of faithful worship and service to God. The Westminster Shorter Catechism, which Edwards doubtlessly learned as a child and taught his own children as they grew up, speaks of "duty" in Q&A no. 3: "What do the Scriptures principally teach? The Scriptures principally teach what man is to believe concerning God, and what *duty* God requires of man" (italics mine). Here, the word *duty* is used as a summary of the entire Christian life. Rendering to God what he deserves is our duty, which includes everything related to right worship, service, helping, loving, and obedience.

In the King James Version that Jonathan Edwards used throughout his life, the word *duty* appears only eight times total: six times in the Old Testament and two times in the New Testament. In most of the Old Testament references, duty refers to the regular assignments of priests, Levites, or on occasion, family members. In the two New Testament uses, the primary idea is Christian service to God and man, which is expected or owed as a consequence of our redemption. Perhaps the usage of the term that best comports with Edwards's own use of it is found in the philosophical book of Ecclesiastes: "Let us hear the conclusion of the whole matter: Fear God, and keep his commandments: for this is the whole duty of man" (12:13). In this last set of Ethical Resolutions, we will consider Resolutions numbered 13, 35, 41, 54, 57, 61, and 62.

13. Resolved, to be endeavoring to find out fit objects of charity and liberality.

Many readers of the King James Version will already be aware that the Greek word translated as "charity" in earlier times signifies what we mean today by the word *love*. This is a real loss to the modern English language, since we now have to use the same word to describe our feelings for pizza, our grandparents, and our spouse! It has become all too commonplace. Indeed, the word *love* has lost some of its power. But in the Christian Bible, love or charity (from the Greek word *agape*) is the most sublime and beautiful of affections. Charity spills out from the affection of the heart to the actions in one's life. Perhaps the most famous definition of charity is the famous "love chapter" in 1 Corinthians 13, most commonly read at weddings today. In this incomparable passage, Paul writes the following to that frustrating Corinthian congregation:

> Though I bestow all my goods to feed the poor, and though I give my body to be burned, and have not charity, it profiteth me nothing. Charity suffereth long,

and is kind; charity envieth not; charity vaunteth not itself, is not puffed up, Doth not behave itself unseemly, seeketh not her own, is not easily provoked, thinketh no evil; Rejoiceth not in iniquity, but rejoiceth in the truth; Beareth all things, believeth all things, hopeth all things, endureth all things. (vv. 3–7)

Unfortunately, when we hear the word charity today, we think almost exclusively of giving to causes like the Salvation Army or Goodwill. The expression "giving to charity" has become something cheap; something we give away all too casually. We drop a few quarters in the red kettle at Christmas, or put our discarded used clothes in the pickup station to be sold at a second-hand store. But for Jonathan Edwards, as for his KJV Bible, the word *charity* is so much more. Infinitely more.

Notice in this 13th Resolution that Edwards vows to *endeavor* "to find out fit objects of charity and liberality." He won't just sit back and wait for something to happen; he will go out looking for it. If we wait passively for someone to come along who happens to need our help, we may be waiting for a rather long time. Love is proactive. It seeks. It hunts. It searches. In Luke 19:10, Jesus says, "For the Son of man is come to *seek* and to save that which was lost" (italics mine). When Christ walked the hills of Galilee, he found innumerable people to love, heal, and care for because he sought them. In this way, he encountered outcast women, tax collectors, lepers, Roman soldiers, religious hypocrites, patriotic zealots, uneducated fishermen, and more. When he found them, he loved them. When he loved them, he transformed them.

Like charity, the word *liberality* in the 13th Resolution has also lost much of its potency. In contemporary usage, "liberal" is almost always political. Ideas are viewed on a spectrum from conservative (the Right) to liberal (the Left), with ideologies and identifiable party platforms in tow. But in Edwards's day, liberality meant free, profuse, in abundance. Edwards's vow therefore means that he would not only find people to love, but when he did, he would love them abundantly and with little constraint. In his early Diary entry of May 18, 1723, Edwards rebuked himself for not doing enough for the good of mankind,

> At night. Concluded to add to my inquiries, as to the spending of time–at the beginning of the day, or the period, what can I do for the good of men? and, at the end, what have I done for their good? (WJE 16:771)

Edwards's early biographer, Samuel Hopkins, states that though Edwards never boasted publicly about his concern for the poor, he consistently lived out the goals described in this early resolution. Edwards had "uncommon regard" for the poor, weak, ill, and marginalized. As a pastor, he often exhorted others to do likewise, and he feared too many believers were "greatly deficient in this duty." Edwards often exhorted that every "Church ought by frequent and liberal contributions to maintain a publick Stock [food pantry], that it

might be ready" to care immediately and directly for its "poor and neces-
sitous Members." When Edwards did help the poor of his own contribution,
Hopkins says that Edwards "took great care to conceal his deeds."[14] In this
way, Matthew 6:3 would be fulfilled in his life and his actions would not be
seen as ostentatious, conspicuous, or merely for show.

Edwards's late-night meditation on May 18 is a noble one that is still
helpful to us today. He asked himself if he was *really* helping anyone, if his
life was making much of a difference, was he just living for himself to advance
his own goals and career objectives, or was there some sense in which he was
truly caring for the hurting people in this world. It's fairly obvious that there's
enough pain and suffering in this world to exhaust a thousand lifetimes of
compassionate charity. But are *we* doing anything about it? It is a powerful
question, and one worthy of our ardent consideration.

*35. Resolved, whenever I so much question whether I have done my duty, as
that my quiet and calm is thereby disturbed, to set it down, and also how the
question was resolved. Dec. 18, 1722.*

The 35th Resolution is important because it contains the earliest date
noted among all Seventy Resolutions. This place marker helps scholars to
approximate the commencement of this project, given that we can pin with
certainty the front end of the entire project to the tail end of the calendar
year of 1722. Careful readers may wonder why the 8th and 33rd Resolutions
come before the 35th Resolution but have dates after December 18. This is
because Edwards occasionally postdated some of his resolutions as he reread
them later and was again convicted by his own promises, especially as he
cross-referenced them with his Diary, which he also began during this winter
(WJE 16:759).

In substance, the 35th Resolution is primarily preoccupied with the idea
of "duty." Here, Edwards is discussing the correlation between his duty and
his conscience. The former stirring or calming the latter, as the case may be.
Edwards thought that the closer he adhered to his duty, the more his conscience would be at peace. To fail to discharge one's duty, however, would stir
the conscience and deny peace and tranquility of soul to the mindful believer.
Edwards uses the terms "quiet," "calm," and "disturbed" to convey the changing surface of the conscience, varying from placid to turbulent.

Since he speaks about it several times in his early writings, Edwards appears to have been both perturbed and provoked by this idea of duty. He seems
especially concerned that the idea of duty had been secularized, stripped of
spiritual connotations, and reduced to mere civility by the Enlightenment

---

14. The above quotations are taken from Samuel Hopkins' *Life and Character of
the Late Rev. Edwards*, quoted in Sweeney, *Ministry of the Word*, 65–66.

thinkers. He gives two notable treatments of "duty" in his early works, one in a sermon, and the other in one of his private "Miscellanies."

In "Miscellany tt" titled "Devotion," Edwards argues against the idea that duty is primarily a secular vocation, as though our highest ends and deepest purposes were merely toward community, society, and nation. Though all men should obviously contribute toward the good of the whole, like a gear smoothly functioning in a greater machine, the *machine itself* has no purpose if its purpose is merely to "function." If, he says, "the highest end of every part of a clock is only mutually to assist the other parts in their motions, that clock is good for nothing at all." Paying your taxes, reporting for military duty, returning library books on time, or cleaning up your garbage at the beach are all important and necessary. But Edwards argues that duty rises higher than mere civic responsibility. Duty done mindlessly or heartlessly is mere empty performance. Rather, duty ought to rise beyond the civil realm and the duty-bound person should burn with inward spiritual devotion.

In his 1723 sermon, "The Duty of Self-Examination," Edwards likewise defines duty, particularly with respect to the Creator/creature relationship. As in "Miscellany tt," this "oughtness" is primarily oriented toward God:

> We ought to consider what our ways ought [to be]. It ought to be our greatest inquiry: What ought I do? That question in Acts 9:6 ought to be the grand question: "Lord, what wouldst thou have me to do?" This is a thing woefully neglected by most of this wicked generation. They never consider what they ought to do, care not what is their duty, nor what is contrary to their duty. Their care is what will get them the most money and the most bodily pleasure. Nothing so much concerns us as to know our duty, that we may do it; for we must be miserable if we don't do it. (WJE 10:484–85)

Notice above how Edwards warns that misery will befall those who are negligent of their duties to God. Their consciences will find them out and deny them rest. If we wonder how we can know what our duty is, Edwards points us to the word of God itself:

> And God has been so gracious to us as to reveal our duty to us, so that we may know it if we will, only at [the] cheap rate of reading and considering. Our privileges in this respect [are] above most of the world's, and yet for all this many never consider what is their duty. We ought to be diligent to know what those things are which God has commanded, seeing he has commanded them. (WJE 10:484–85)

By way of application, the young preacher stirred his congregation to meditate deeply on what it is that we each owe to God, especially as it relates to our devotion and worship. Though we often confuse duty with drudgery—things that we would rather not do but feel we must for the sake of some higher obligation—Edwards would say that duty is much closer to worshipful and obedient devotion. Duty is performing the actions we ought to perform, *because God is worthy of our highest praise.* Do your duty and God will be glorified, your conscience will be at rest, your family will be strong, and yes, your civic community will also be all the better.

41. Resolved, to ask myself at the end of every day, week, month and year, wherein I could possibly in any respect have done better. Jan. 11, 1723.

There is a slight discrepancy in the records as to the dating of this Resolution, not that it matters terribly much. The note added by Edwards in the resolutions, as edited by Dwight and Hopkins (recall that their editions differ slightly), indicate that he wrote it on January 11, but Edwards's Diary states that he wrote this goal for himself the day earlier, after the sun went down on January 10. He had been feeling particularly strong that night, having felt the vivification of his new dietary experiments, and likely that success in monitoring his calories resulted in some parallel spiritual enthusiasm.

> I think I find myself much more sprightly and healthy, both in body and mind, for my self-denial in eating, drinking, and sleeping. I think it would be advantageous every morning to consider my business and temptations; and what sins I shall be exposed to that day: and to make a resolution how to improve the day, and to avoid those sins. And so at the beginning of every week, month and year. . . . At night made the 41st Resolution. (WJE 10:761–62)

A couple of things are salient here: notice how in both the Diary and the 41st Resolution, Edwards vows to monitor the state of his soul in a regular pattern: daily, monthly, and yearly. He saw each fresh calendar page as a new challenge to take on and a new set of obstacles to overcome. One interesting difference is that in the Diary entry, he counsels himself to take stock of his position at the *beginning* of the day; while in this resolution, to do so at the *end* of every day. Twice? And just as in the initial briefing, he vowed to make himself aware of possible temptations and trials to come, so also in the debriefing he asked himself in review how he "could possibly in any respect have done better." By any account, this is a lot of soul searching.

We have seen this sort of exhaustive rigor before in church history, particularly in the case of Martin Luther, whose incessant soul searching led him to the brink of spiritual collapse. Luther's designated confessor, Johann von Staupitz, was so tired of hearing his self-analysis that he virtually bade him to let up until he committed a sin *worth* confessing! Thankfully, Luther discovered the powerful, healing message of the gospel of grace. Just as he felt the breaking weight of his own sin, which ultimately led him to the rejuvenating discovery of the doctrine of justification by faith, likewise there were signs that Edwards also was being beaten down by the oppressive nature of his own inability to live up to self-imposed standards. When Edwards put pen to paper again, just about ten days later in his Diary, these stress fractures were clearly showing:

Jan. 20, sabbath day. At night. The last week I was sunk so low, that I fear it will be a long time, 'ere I shall be recovered. I fell exceedingly low in the weekly account. I find my heart so deceitful, that I am almost discouraged from making any more resolutions. Wherein have I been negligent in the week past; and how could I have done better, to help the dreadful, low estate in which I am sunk? (WJE 10:765)

How long could Edwards bear this burden? How long can one man ruminate on his own sin? At what point is it too overwhelming to the soul to continually ask himself—or rather, *demand* from himself!—that he should have "possibly in any respect have done better"? In his Sermon on the Mount, it is true that Jesus demands perfection (Matt. 5:48), warning his hearers that unless their righteousness "exceed the righteousness of the Scribes and Pharisees, [they] shall in no case enter into the Kingdom of God" (Matt. 5:20); but these warnings serve primarily to drive us to the hope of the gospel by despairing in ourselves.

Yet, for the time being, Edwards pressed on with his spiritual rigor, preaching publicly to the New York Presbyterian congregation that they should likewise do the same:

We ought frequently to consider whether our ways have been in all respects as they ought to be, whether they could not have been better, and to be nice and critical in searching for faults in our behavior. Some men stifle and muzzle their consciences when [they are] about to tell them of their past actions, which is a certain sign that they are very bad; but conscience ought not to be [by] any means to be restrained, but to have full liberty to tell us of all our faults, and set the heinousness of them before us. Yea, we ought instead of stifling it to assist it; for conscience is our best friend in this world when its rebukes are severest. (WJE 10:485)

Though his counsel seems wise to the small church he oversaw as a twenty-year-old pastor, it also seems evident that this was too much for even Edwards himself. The fact that the pressure drove him to abandon the Resolutions experiment altogether will be considered more fully in the conclusion of this book. For the moment, however, let's dwell together on the goodness of the gospel: When we cannot be "better," Christ is best on our behalf. When we cannot be perfect, we trust in Christ's manifest perfection. Should we take stock of our failures each day, week, and month, let these heart inspections drive us deeper and deeper into grace and to the cross where Jesus died.

54. Whenever I hear anything spoken in commendation of any person, if I think it would be praiseworthy in me, resolved to endeavor to imitate it. July 8, 1723.

In Galatians 5:26, Paul wrote, "Let us not be desirous of vain glory, provoking one another, envying one another." Yet one of the most difficult temptations of our sinful flesh to resist is that of jealousy. As often as we see something excellent in another person, perhaps a talent we don't have, we tend to wish it were our own. It's a difficult urge to repress, this envy. It rises up in our hearts even when we know we shouldn't let it. Like an unmannered dog that can't help jumping up on guests, our jealousies are often difficult to control within us.

There can be no doubt that Jonathan Edwards was a talented and gifted person. What would we give to have a mind as sharp as his? To have a place in history as important as his? To be near the center of America's greatest revival as he was? To write even *one* important work, much less dozens? And yet in writing this 54th Resolution, the young Edwards admitted that his heart veered toward jealousy and envy, just as it does in every one of us.

The bare fact that he wrote the words of this resolution indicates that envy could have been a problem for him at times. Why else would he bother to write this resolution at all? His goal in writing the Resolutions wasn't to highlight his strengths and successes, but rather to be able to mark, understand, and confess his faults. Instead of envy, Edwards resolved to incorporate *imitation* into his life as a better expression of devotion to Christ. Imitation is appropriate, of course, given that the trait under consideration is "praiseworthy" (1 Cor. 4:16; 11:1).

One event, occurring seventeen years after the teenage Edwards wrote this Resolution, best illustrates his attempt to incorporate godly imitation into his life. In 1740, the great evangelist George Whitefield rode through the colonies on his preaching tour. This exhibition was, in reality, the central event of the Great Awakening. Whitefield was by most accounts the most famous man on earth at this time, having almost unimaginable celebrity. He was a tremendous preacher, wielding a once-in-a-generation voice and a powerful command of his audience. The stories of his large crowds were legendary, with none else than Benjamin Franklin himself attending, just to measure the crowd attendance and the approximate range of Whitefield's voice.

There is no doubt that the Northampton pastor heard much about Whitefield's power and flair long before they finally met in person. Whitefield's style of preaching was almost the exact opposite of Edwards's. Whitefield was dramatic; Edwards rather restrained. Whitefield was a storyteller; Edwards a theologian. Whitefield spoke with booming voice and tear-filled eyes; Edwards with precision and calm logic. When Edwards did actually hear him preach, he wept throughout most of the sermon. He, too, was among the throngs of people deeply moved by the oratory.

And yet, rather than allow a jealousy for Whitefield's gifting and skill to rise up in his heart, Edwards attempted to put into place the sentiment of his 54th Resolution. Starving envy, he endeavored instead to *imitate* Whitefield's style, at least as much as his slender frame would allow. After 1740, many of his extant sermon manuscripts change form markedly. Rather than writing out every word, we see more occasions of Edwards writing in outline form, essentially forcing himself to be more extemporaneous from the pulpit.

Edwards had seen the power of Whitefield's freer delivery method and sought to imitate it.[15] Rather than resent the itinerant evangelist for his novel manner of preaching "from the heart" (Whitefield's homiletics were highly controversial in his day), Edwards actually sought to *emulate* him as much as he could. Whether or not his congregation at Northampton appreciated his efforts—or even noticed the changes—we may never fully know. We do know, however, that Edwards sought to continually improve his preaching ability, even as he had already gained some fame for himself as the revival's greatest thinker.

It may be the case that Edwards continued to improve his preaching throughout his whole life. His Stockbridge sermons to the Mahican tribe may actually be the best sermons he ever preached. After Edwards was fired from Northampton, he ended up preaching many of his sermons over again to the lesser-literate First Nations people. Here, the manuscript evidence shows his sermons were even briefer in outline form and were likely delivered far more extemporaneously, and with much less concern for critique.[16]

Believers, whenever we see something praiseworthy in another person, let us endeavor to imitate it rather than envy another person's gracious gifts from God.

57. Resolved, when I fear misfortunes and adversities, to examine whether I have done my duty, and resolve to do it; and let it be just as providence orders it, I will as far as I can, be concerned about nothing but my duty and my sin. June 9 and July 13, 1723.

In my opinion, this is a brilliant and helpful Resolution and one of the most practical insights contained in Edwards's early writings. Here, the young pastor-in-training evidences wisdom far beyond his nineteen years. In one fell swoop, Edwards acknowledges the presence of his inward fears and anxieties, counsels himself to trust more fully in the sovereignty and goodness of God (cf. Rom. 8:28), and attempts to narrow his mental energy primarily toward those things that he can control, specifically his own reactions to "misfortunes and adversities." It is the latter phrase that is often the hardest part for many of us. In one sense, anxiety is simply the mind restlessly attempting to bring order to the chaos of dangers both actual and imagined. The only thing Edwards admits that he can control when adversity arises is his *response* to such misfortunes. These responses can result in either acts of fidelity that fortify his trust and obedience, or acts of worry that exacerbate doubt and mistrust, which only debilitate him further.

---

15. Toby K. Easley, *Jonathan Edwards: Beyond the Manuscripts* (Fort Worth, TX: Feder Ink, 2016), 63–80.
16. Easley, 102–9.

This Resolution is unique among the seventy in that it seems to be the promise that Edwards returned to more often than any other. Only two dates are affixed to this resolution, June 9 and July 13, 1723. But on July 23, he came back to it again in the Diary, counseling himself to consider afflictions of all kinds as "an opportunity of rending my heart off from the world, and setting it upon heaven alone" (WJE 16:786). This is a good word. Anything that weans us from our dependency on temporary things, which rust and moth destroy, is ultimately for our good (Matt. 6:19–20). Later that same week, he returned to the same words he had written earlier, serving as his own pastoral counselor by advising his inward parishioner "to be particularly careful to keep up inviolable a trust and reliance, ease and entire rest in God in all conditions, according to the 57th Resolution; for this I have found to be wonderfully advantageous to me" (WJE 16:776). In a somewhat curious and enigmatic entry the very next month, he similarly wrote:

> With respect to the important business which I have now on hand, resolved, to do whatever I think to be duty, prudence and diligence in the matter, and to avoid ostentation; and if I succeed not, and how many disappointments soever I meet with, to be entirely easy; only to take occasion to acknowledge my unworthiness; and if it should actually not succeed, and should not find acceptance, as I expected, yet not to afflict myself about it, according to the 57th Resolution. (WJE 16:778)

We might wonder what this "important business" that Edwards referred to was exactly. Apparently, it seems it was a matter that could result in clear failure or defined success. Given that this Diary entry was written just a month prior to delivering his master's thesis in Latin to the Yale faculty, it seems likely that he was busily finalizing his draft of the work. At the same time, his father Timothy was intervening actively, trying to arrange a pastoral call in Bolton, Connecticut. Meanwhile Edwards's belly churned with the familiar anxiety of hypothetical failures and unanticipated misfortunes.

One more time, this 57th Resolution stilled his unsteady heart. On October 4, the day after his birthday and several weeks after he successfully delivered his Latin oration, he was still fretting about the future. So again, he returned to the sage words of this resolution, stating clearly:

> This day fixed and established it, that Christ Jesus has promised me faithfully, that, if I will do what is my duty, and according to the best of my prudence in the matter, that my condition in this world, shall be better for me than any other condition whatever, and more to my welfare, to all eternity. (WJE 16:781)

Another possibility for his "important business" is that Edwards had been eagerly preparing a written essay of natural philosophy (science) on the activity of arachnids. Edwards had hoped to have it published by the Royal Society in London. He sent it to one Judge Paul Dudley, a connection of his father's, on October 31 of that year (WJE 16:41–48). Having such a piece published when he was so young would have been a tremendous advance in his scholarly career, setting him on a trajectory for further successes. Sadly, that did not happen.

Edwards passed the final Latin academic exercise capably and received his master's degree, but he failed to publish the spider piece. The Bolton call didn't work out well and turned out to be a minor incident in his noteworthy life. It seems his father wanted this to go through far more than Jonathan did.

All of this proves once again that sometimes we fail miserably, sometimes things just don't work out generally, and sometimes our worries never materialize at all and we simply move on to stressing about the next event in our lives. How much better then, to live in simple, childlike trust, confident in the good graces of the God of providence!

61. Resolved, that I will not give way to that listlessness which I find unbends and relaxes my mind from being fully and fixedly set on religion, whatever excuse I may have for it—that what my listlessness inclines me to do, is best to be done, etc. May 21 and July 13, 1723.

The word *listless* comes from the Middle English root word *liste*, which originally meant joy, delight, or pleasure. Ironically, it is related to the modern English word *lust*, which took on the far more negative connotations of improper or inordinate desire. But the idea of longing or yearning is common to both terms. To be listless, then, as Edwards uses the term here, means to lack heart or drive, to have waning zeal or passion. Sailors often describe a ship that's stalled in the water for lack of wind in its sails as listless. Today, when we feel dispirited, we commonly use the words *lethargic, sluggish,* or *apathetic* to describe such moods. And mark this: *We are all subject to such times of apathy.* Perhaps this is because we are either overwhelmed, worn out, or simply bored. Life seems to lack thrill. The heart feels dull, and we are barely moved by either motivation of fear or reward. It's that "I-can't-get-out-of-bed" feeling.

Edwards was aware that our souls are prone to this pattern at times; otherwise, he wouldn't have warned himself about it. No one is driven and empowered for high-energy output all of the time. Even those few who are strangely wired for nearly perpetual motion and productivity can often be unexpectedly and inexplicably beset by the heavy gravity of lethargy. Such states of indifference can come upon us without much notice and rob us of both our love for God and his beautiful world.

Scripture has much to say on this topic, usually related to the biblical antonym of "listlessness" called "fervency" or "zeal." God himself is described as zealous (Isa. 9:7; 37:32; 59:17), and it was zeal that caused the Lord Jesus to upend the tables in the temple (John 2:17). Paul reminds Titus that Christ "gave himself for us, that he might redeem us from all iniquity, and purify unto himself a peculiar people, zealous of good works" (Titus 2:14). In the book of Colossians, Paul mentions one Epaphras who is "always labouring fervently for you in prayers. . . . For I bear him record, that he hath a great zeal for you" (Col. 4:12–13). Likewise, Christ reminds the lukewarm church of Laodicea, "As many as I love, I rebuke and chasten: be zealous therefore, and repent" (Rev. 3:19).

Summing up the biblical data on the terms "zeal" and "fervency," we are to be compelled with holy yearning for the glory of God above all things, as well as serving him, defending his honor, obeying his law, loving his people, and sharing the gospel with the lost. Internally, we are to be impelled to God through dependent prayer and heart-filled repentance from sin. Of these great matters, we ought not be indifferent. We cannot remain blasé. These are matters of eternal significance. Edwards recognized early, however, that we don't always feel these things as deeply as we should. We sink into what Bunyan called the "Slough of Despond."[17]

Notice how Edwards describes this experience both in mechanical and anatomical terms. Mechanically, he uses the term "unbends" to describe the straightening of a spring, which would normally convert potential energy to kinetic energy in a machine. During times of listlessness, though, there is little energy to convert. A straightened spring has lost its purpose. He also says that the mind "relaxes" or falls into a state of low attention or potency. I find it interesting that he locates this problem primarily *in the mind*, which he thinks ought to be "fully and fixedly set on religion."

Again, we need to consider whether his goals were realistic. Such a state is perhaps out of the reach of possibility for most saints; can anyone maintain such a devoted gaze for long? There is no question that such states of lethargy can manifest in the body, and Edwards's resolutions on the diet recognize this (see the 20th and 40th Resolutions). But the fact that Edwards locates his own personal struggles with listlessness *in the mind* seems to suggest that we can remedy such apathy to some extent by remembering, meditating, and reevaluating the things of glory and eternity in stark relief with the duller, plainer, and transient things of this world. When we come to the Resolutions numbered 7, 9, 10, 18, and 55, we will see how Edwards often "shocks" himself awake from spiritual slumber by meditating on themes of death, martyrdom, heaven, and hell, putting these two worlds in loud and alerting contrast.

Here in the 61st Resolution, Edwards resolves not to prevent the onset of listlessness entirely, which I don't think is possible for anyone in this life. Rather, he more wisely resolves not to "give way" to it; if he did, he would rob himself of the higher joys and greater delights of knowing God and serving

---

17. Bunyan, *Pilgrim's Progress*, 26–28.

him to the everlasting glory of his name. Listlessness must not ultimately win out: life is too short, the world is too beautiful, heaven is too rich, hell is too hot, and God is too good to remain mired in apathy.

62. *Resolved, never to do anything but duty; and then according to Ephesians 6:6–8, do it willingly and cheerfully "as unto the Lord, and not to man; knowing that whatever good thing any man doth, the same shall he receive of the Lord." June 25 and July 13, 1723.*

The apostle Paul wrote to the Ephesians that the servants among them should be obedient to their masters,

> Not with eyeservice, as menpleasers; but as the servants of Christ, doing the will of God from the heart; With good will doing service, as to the Lord, and not to men: Knowing that whatsoever good thing any man doeth, the same shall he receive of the Lord, whether he be bond or free. (Eph. 6:6–8)

In similar terms—almost the same exact wording even—Paul also bid Colossian household servants among the believing congregation to likewise offer the same willing, cheerful service to their earthly masters as though they were serving the Lord Jesus Christ himself instead (Col. 3:22–23).

The English word *eyeservice* used in Edwards's King James Version is a strange word in modern English, but makes more sense with a bit of etymological context. In the Greek of Paul's day, the word was *opthalmodoulian*, the root word from which we probably recognize the term "ophthalmologist," the eye doctor we visit when we need the prescription in our glasses adjusted. The rest of the term, derived from the Greek *doulos*, is a common word meaning "servant" or even the lowly "slave." If we put these ideas together into one long Greek word, we get the vivid picture of a lazy servant who works hard only when the master is watching! When the master draws within view, that servant is the hardest worker in the whole crew; but when the boss passes out of the sightline, he does as little as possible.

In this 62nd Resolution, the last of our larger section on ethics, Edwards takes these passages from the Pauline letters and applies them directly to himself: he, too, is a slave of Christ and should serve the Lord cheerfully and willingly, for there is no time in which the Master does not have his eye on his redeemed servants. This reflects the relatively humble and submissive posture of Edwards, the pastor-in-training, and is probably suggestive of a settled resignation under his parents' authority, since he had just that day returned to his childhood home in East Windsor, Connecticut.

He had come home from the New York Presbyterian Church in May of that year and done a bit of travel, including a trip to Boston, the major metropolis of the area. The rest of Edwards's future was still very much up in the air at that point. He couldn't have foreseen how short his time in Bolton would be, or that he would return to Yale to serve as a tutor, or his eventual call to serve alongside the revered Solomon Stoddard at Northampton, Massachusetts.

After being out on his own, returning to his parents' home had to be seen as a disappointment (as it would probably for many of us). In the best frame of mind, however, he resolved to serve his parents again "willingly and cheerfully." In a Diary entry from July 19, 1723, he quotes 1 Peter 2:18 (a verse quite similar to those in Ephesians and Colossians) and then states, "How then, ought children to honor their parents!" (WJE 16:774). Imagine one of the greatest minds America has ever produced doing simple household chores like milking cows, sweeping barns, and cutting the grass with the scythe. But no one is so gifted that they exceed the basest duties of the common household. Edwards would have to put his scholastic aspirations aside for the moment and do his chores while he studied for his Latin *Quaestio* exam the next month.[18]

Personally, I find this kind of simple humility from Edwards refreshing. We live in a day and age when many of our young people sincerely believe the world owes them something for nothing. They want the world given to them on a silver platter, and they want it now. They want the same health care, reliable transportation, and college education for which their parents had labored years, but without the hard work required to earn it. In our society today, we see a growing resentment of traditional skilled trades like plumbing and welding, an unwillingness to work with one's hands. At the same time, it seems that many young people seek to be heard or an influencer in popular social media. And yet in this Resolution and parallel Diary entries, we see one of the all-time great thinkers reminding himself to clean the chicken coops more cheerfully and gather the potatoes more willingly as the Lord watches from heaven and his parents watched from the house.

John Calvin, the great sixteenth-century French Reformer—whom Edwards no doubt studied during his time at Yale[19]—took as his family crest the image of a heart held upward towards the heavens by a servant's hand, graced with the motto, "Promptly and Sincerely." Calvin willed to serve the Lord immediately and with a compliant spirit, no matter what hardship or difficulty God asked him to endure. Many generations later, God would also use Edwards in a similarly dynamic way, most likely because Calvin and Edwards both shared that tender, willing, humble, gracious spirit of servanthood that God requires of his most useful instruments.

---

18. The *Quaestio* is contained in WJEO 14:47–66.
19. See WJEO 26:47.

3

ESCHATOLOGICAL RESOLUTIONS: THE BREVITY OF THIS LIFE AND THE ETERNAL WORLD TO COME

❖ Life: Its Brevity and Beauty
Resolutions 5, 6, 7, 17, 19, 52, 67

In this third and final section of our study of Jonathan Edwards's Seventy Resolutions, we will now consider what I'm calling his "Eschatological Resolutions." "Eschatology" is a term often used in systematic theology and other studies of Christian doctrine to designate the "last things" (the Greek word *eschatos* means "last" or "final"). So, eschatology is usually concerned with things related to death and the afterworld, including heaven and hell.

Quite often, the study of eschatology in systematic theology courses and textbooks is further subdivided into two parts: historical eschatology and personal eschatology. Historical eschatology considers things on a larger, global scale such as the signs of the times, the coming of the antichrist, the tribulation, the nature of the millennium, the return of Christ, and the judgment. While Edwards had much to say on these issues—all of which is very interesting—historical eschatology is outside of the scope of our study here as we work through his resolutions.[1] Edwards does, however, also have quite a bit to say about personal eschatology, which is closer to our subject matter at hand as we study his 1722/23 charter for personal formation. This second subdivision focuses more on the end of one's individual life, preparing for death, and considering the condition of one's eternal state in either heaven or hell.

First, we will consider the brevity of life and the inevitability of death (resolutions numbered 5, 6, 7, 17, 19, 52, and 67). Unlike many modern people who push off the very thought of death as long as possible, the Puritans and

---

1. Edwards talks about many of these items, particularly the millennium, in his "Miscellanies." See WJEO 5:15–29. See also "Millenarianism" in JEE 378–9.

the colonialists were comfortable thinking and speaking about death quite readily. They knew death was a stark reality, and they preferred to deal with it openly. Death often confronted the Puritans quickly and brutally. Perhaps it was because their lives were marked by suffering and difficulty that the thought of death was not at all off-topic or unwelcome. It was even a subject commonly brought to the attention of children, which may come as a surprise to many parents today who try to shade their children's eyes from thinking about their own mortality. As a pastor, I have heard of several parents who don't allow their children to attend or participate in a funeral, for fear it will scar their impressionable minds.

In this set of resolutions, we will look at how Edwards seems to dwell on, perhaps even obsess over, his own inevitable demise. After that, we will look at a set of Resolutions on confession and renewal (8, 12, 29, 37, 47, 48, 49, and 68). It may seem slightly out of place to consider them so late in our study, and I'm certainly not suggesting that confession should be held off until the very end of one's life! No, the whole of the Christian life should be one of repentance, as Martin Luther said in the first of his famous Ninety-Five Theses. But as we consider the reality of death, and our final confrontation with the living and true God, we do well to make sure we're as ready for that great meeting as much as possible. We should continue to repent—and all the more often as that day of reckoning hastens on! So, here we will look at what Edwards says about confession, repentance, forgiveness, and finding a resting place for our troubled conscience in the mercies of God's amazing grace.

Finally, in the last set of Resolutions in our study, we will consider those provoking thoughts of the young pastor that focus on the joys of heaven and the torments of hell (Resolutions numbered 9, 10, 18, 22, 50, 51, and 55). I think we will be surprised to see how, rather than being confined to theoretical or fantastical thoughts, Edwards's reflections on the eternal destiny of humanity has a wonderfully relevant and transformative influence on our present lives. True enough, thinking on the joys of heaven and the horrors of hell should be both revolutionary and practical as we consider what kind of people we ought to strive to become.

5. Resolved, never to lose one moment of time; but improve it the most profitable way I possibly can.

Our lives are fleeting. The past cannot be undone (though it can be forgiven), the present lasts for a fraction of an instant before it eludes us and dissolves, and the number of our future days are completely unknown. If our lives are like sands in an hourglass, then the past has already fallen to the bottom, never to be gathered up again. The present is the moment in which we live, swiftly passing through the narrow channel of time. The number of future grains of sand yet to fall is known only to God. Life is brief, and then we pass into eternity. Scripture gives a number of vivid images to impress this reality on us from the arching of the sun over our heads, hastening to the opposite horizon (Eccl. 1:5), to the wispy image of the morning mist or vapor that soon ebbs away (James 4:14), to the lengthening evening shadow that soon descends into darkness (Ps. 144:4).

The young Edwards knew this and did everything in his power to capture each moment for the glory of God. Early in his life, he learned of the precious nature of time and resolved to live in that consciousness. George Claghorn, writing of this urgency in Edwards, remarks,

> Time management was a major concern to Edwards. His aim was to rise early, work late, and fill every moment with constructive activity. At first, he even begrudged time for recreation, although he came to realize the need for exercise and the profit of sociability. Eventually, he followed the custom of giving a half-hour a day to chopping wood. (WJE 16:744)

Jesus asks, "And which of you by being anxious can add a single hour to his span of life?" (Matt. 6:27 ESV). No mortal is able to slow the inevitable, unthwartable progress of history for even a moment. Multiple times in his Diary, we see Edwards agonizing over this possibility:

> Sabbath day, Jan. 6, at night. Much concerned about the improvement of precious time. Intend to live in continual mortification, without ceasing, and even to weary myself thereby, as long as I am in this world, and never to expect or desire any worldly ease or pleasure. (WJE 16:761)

And again,

> Saturday night, May 11. I have been to blame, the month past, in not laying violence enough to my inclination, to force myself to a better improvement of time. (WJE 16:769)

If there was an impulse toward sloth in his veins, he determined to slay it by "laying violence to my inclination." Edwards chastised himself when hours fell through the cracks. His goal was to be an entirely efficient scholar, prizing time as a gift of God for the primary use of contemplating God's excellencies through his word. In order to do better, Edwards contrived ways to waste less time. When traveling on horseback or carriage, he made a memorandum to himself to obtain a small chalkboard on which he could hastily write notes to himself for later, fuller articulation in his notebooks.

> Wednesday night, Aug. 28. When I want books to read; yea, when I have not very good books, not to spend time in reading them, but in reading the Scriptures, in perusing Resolutions, Reflections, etc., in writing on types of the Scripture, and other things, in studying the languages, and in spending more time in private duties. To do this, when there is a prospect of wanting time for the purpose.

Remember as soon as I can, to get a piece of slate, or something, whereon I can make short memorandums while traveling. (WJE 16:780)

The wasting of time seems to be a particular vice of character that Edwards sought to remove from not only his own life but also from the hearts of his congregation. In December 1734, he preached a sermon from Ephesians 5:16 titled "The Preciousness of Time." The scriptural text read simply, "Redeeming the Time." He considered it one of his best pieces or oratory and re-preached this message more often than any other sermon we know of (WJEO 19:245). In my view, it is a devastating sermon to modern readers. Edwards uses a number of vivid images to show the precious nature of time: it is like morsels of bread in the bag of a pilgrim traveler, lest he run out before the journey be done; it is more rare than worldly goods, which if lost in business can be regained by other means; it is a waning sun streaking toward the horizon, never to rise again; to squander time is as reckless as making a sword from precious metal, only to stab oneself with it!

Edwards strikes to the hearts of both young and old alike: the young because they are now wasting the prime of their lives, which God gives to them to passionately seek his presence and favor; and the old because they are utterly unprepared for eternity as they try to cling on to any last vestige of their vitality. As a reader of Jonathan Edwards and a student of Scripture, I too have been particularly impressed with the precious nature of time and exasperated by the fact that it seeps through my fingers like oil in the hand. Though we hold it tight, we cannot retain it. Best then to heed the words of the Preacher of Ecclesiastes and enjoy God for whatever duration we have before the dawn of eternity breaks (Eccl. 5:18; 6:12; 8:15).

6. Resolved, to live with all my might, while I do live.

Life is short.

When we were children, it seemed like ages from one birthday to the next. We marked our lives by six-month increments because years were too long to comprehend. We boasted, "I'm five *and a half*!" Now, into my fifth decade, I'm convinced that the passage of time increases in velocity relative to the age of the observer! I can't seem to slow down my life, even when I try. Birthdays seem to come every fortnight rather than every year. The past and future seem as vast as the sea, but the present is as thin as a razor blade. Grain after grain slips through the hourglass, and no one can slow it down or cling to even one moment.

The teenage Jonathan Edwards—not yet famous or influential—realized his time on this earth was going to go by fast. "While I do live," he resolved, "[I should] live with all my might." I take this expression as a determination to face life head-on, intentionally and purposefully, rather than carelessly and matter-of-factly. The brevity of our lives only seems to increase the urgency of living them purposefully. Though short, our lives are deep, beautiful, and meaningful if we view them as means to glorify the eternal God. According to Edwards, life is to be seized and apprehended *actively*, rather than allowing ourselves to be carried along *passively* like corks bobbing on the water.

James, the brother of our Lord, acknowledged the fleeting nature of time when he wrote,

> For what is your life? It is even a vapour, that appeareth for a little time, and then vanisheth away. For that ye ought to say, If the Lord will, we shall live, and do this, or that. But now ye rejoice in your boastings: all such rejoicing is evil. Therefore to him that knoweth to do good, and doeth it not, to him it is sin. (James 4:13–17)

In this text, James warns those who greedily collect goods and riches in this present life rather than live faithfully and obediently, with the dawning of eternity in full view. He scolds those who merely view life as an exercise in unbridled materialism, fattening themselves to no good spiritual end. He chides those who view time as something that can be *possessed*. Grasped. Manipulated. In using the imagery of the "mist" or "vapor," James employs an age-old prophetic metaphor to capture the rapidity of passing time (cf. Ps. 102:3; Job 7:7). The mist of life is here and then gone as soon as the morning sun rises over the tree line.

Along with the brevity of life, Edwards's 6th Resolution also seems to accept life's inevitable end: death. Notice: "while I do live." Just a teenager, Edwards had already experienced several of his relatives dying in the prime of life or coming close to sudden death. In 1704, a year after his birth, his uncle John Stoddard was in Deerfield, Massachusetts, when French and Indians attacked on February 29, killing forty-seven of the town's three hundred residents and taking captive one hundred and twelve (only sixty survived to be ransomed later by their families or community). Somehow, Stoddard escaped.[2] Young Puritans in the colonial era were raised to accept death as a matter of fact alongside its corollary: the preciousness of life. *The New England Primer*, studied by all children in Edwards's time, stated memorably for the letter *T*, "Time cuts down all, both great and small." For the letter *Y* it read, "Youth forward slips, Death soonest nips."[3]

But the brevity of life does not in any way diminish the importance and significance of being alive while we do live. That's what Edwards intoned with his phrase "all my might." This line is no doubt a reference to the Greatest Commandment in Matthew 22:37.[4] Having read the Bible since childhood,

---

2. Marsden, *A Life*, 14–115.
3. Marsden, *A Life*, 27.
4. See also Eccles. 9:10, "Whatsoever thy hand findeth to do, do it with thy might; for there is no work, nor device, nor knowledge, nor wisdom, in the grave, whither thou goest."

Jonathan would have also been familiar with the sentiments of the apostle Paul, who likewise spoke in such ways. In Philippians 1:21–23, Paul wrote,

> For to me to live is Christ, and to die is gain. But if I live in the flesh, this is the fruit of my labour: yet what I shall choose I wot not. For I am in a strait betwixt two, having a desire to depart, and to be with Christ; which is far better.

And in Acts 20:24, he said,

> But none of these things move me, neither count I my life dear unto myself, so that I might finish my course with joy, and the ministry, which I have received of the Lord Jesus, to testify the gospel of the grace of God.

Even at the young age of nineteen, Edwards sensed that life—though short—can be used for great ends. The eternal, ever-living God can be glorified through the finite, mortal lives of his people. Edwards longed for such a meaningful life and mightily determined to pursue it.

7. Resolved, never to do anything, which I should be afraid to do, if it were the last hour of my life.

Edwards's most famous sermon, "Sinners in the Hands of an Angry God," pleads with his hearers to consider the fragility and mortality of human life.[5] In vivid and shocking images, "Sinners" jolts both original listeners and modern readers awake to the possibility that death may be closer than we dare imagine. But this line of thought was something Edwards had been musing on long before 1741. Since his late teenage years, he thought deeply about how close death might be to him at any moment. Nearly twenty earlier, he wrote something similar in his 1721/22 sermon "The Importance of the Future State." He may have shocked his New York congregation when he said, "We know not how near we may be to the end of our lives, and to the brink of an endless eternity, and if we han't our eyes about us, we are in danger of dropping into the bottomless pit every moment" (WJE 10:371). In another early sermon, he likewise preached that all men "work upon the very edge of a dreadful precipice" (WJE 10:288).

In this 7th Resolution, Edwards vowed to live as though his entire life was on the very edge of an eternal canyon. Below his feet—at least for that moment—stood what seemed to be the sure footing of our mortal life. But he knew that the edge of eternity was always perilously close. At no point can our grounding on the "here and now" be thought entirely secure nor should we take it for granted. In fact, both history and reason point in the opposite direction: myriads of men, women, and children have fallen unexpectedly

---

5. The sermon "Sinners in the Hands of an Angry God" can be found in WJEO 22:404–18.

into eternity on account of the unsure footing of sudden death. Not many in the history of the world can know beforehand the exact time and particular circumstances of their own death—only condemned criminals, the terminally ill, and the suicidal. For the vast majority of human beings, death can come upon us at an unexpected time. It pounces like a predator from the shadows of anticipation.

In his "Spider" sermon, Edwards used this kind of jolting and shocking language to throw cold water in the faces of his sleepy congregation, startling them to a state of awareness:

> Consider the great uncertainty of life: what assurance have you that you shall live till that time comes in which you propose to begin to be religious? Have you made an agreement with death, or a covenant with the grave, or have God and you made a bargain that he shall not cut you down before such a time? Don't you believe that multitudes in the world die every day, that intended as you do, before the time they proposed comes: don't you believe that hundreds of thousands are now in hell that were as full of good intentions as you are? What assurance have you, that you shall live five or six years longer? Supposing death should come by some disease and tumble you into your grave, or some accident should suddenly throw you out of the world: what a miserable condition you would be in! Where, then, would be your spider's web of projections and fair intentions; what, then, would become of your hopes of long life? (WJE 10:448)

With this in mind, Edwards vowed to live in a constant state of readiness. What else can a mortal do? If he should be afraid to act in some way an hour before death when he might imminently meet his Maker and Judge, then why should he dare act that same way at any point in his life? What kind of fool lives with the audacity of pretending he is immortal, when death, eternity, and the judgment to come might overtake him suddenly? Man's life is a shadow. A mist. A setting sun. His days are "vain" (Hebrew: like a vapor) and "few" (1 Chron. 29:15; Eccles. 5:12; James 4:13).

Modern readers might think these ideas as entirely too morbid. We can't bring ourselves to entertain such dark and depressing thoughts regarding the proximity and circumstances of our own death. But for Edwards (and the reaction he hoped to elicit in these sermons), the very acknowledgment of certain death is freeing. It serves as a sort of vantage point from which we can view the beauty and transiency of our lives. The point is clear: Life is too short and eternity too long to waste with frivolous and sinful pursuits. More than that, life is also too beautiful and precious to fill with lesser passions and superficial obsessions.

Personally, I find this line of thought in the 7th Resolution to be liberating rather than emotionally encumbering. The certainty of my own death helps me to delineate the difference between what really matters and what has no eternal value. My wife, children, and church all matter. Caring for the hurting, lonely, and lost matters. Worship among the believing people of God matters—eternally! But death also brings baser ends and lesser purposes into stark clarity and relief. Would I want to waste my last hours surfing the internet or scrolling social media? Would I dare leave home without kissing my family and reminding them of my love? Should I allow bitterness and resentment to go on for another year without resolving these interpersonal conflicts? Am I ready to go into eternity in the present state and condition of my soul? The 7th Resolution—if taken seriously—won't allow me to let my one and only mortal life be poured down the drain of such an unreflective and meager existence.

17. Resolved, that I will live so as I shall wish I had done when I come to die.

One day—as impossible as it may be to imagine now—you might find yourself lying on a hospice bed. You will have already taken your last steps. Your strength will be sapped. Your vigor evaporated; your body wrinkly, gray, and tired. Perhaps your family will surround you in those moments, singing hymns, praying, and reading the Scriptures to bring you spiritual comfort. Or perhaps you may find yourself lying there alone with your thoughts. As I picture this scenario, I imagine it will be in those moments when our reflections on the significance of our lives will be the most acute and intense.

Of course, it's also possible that our death is much more sudden, entirely unexpected. This, too, is an Edwardsean thought, as we have already seen above in our considerations of the 7th Resolution. Of those who go through surprise near-death experiences, some 71 percent say they experienced what is called an L.R.E. or "life review experience."[6] This is the proverbial "my life flashed before my eyes" moment, an intense brain-event in which synapses fire rapidly and memories flood to the fore of the conscience. Either way, whether our death comes slowly or leaps upon us suddenly, we'll want to have confidence—total confidence—that we lived altogether for the glory of God.

Edwards's 17th Resolution is as powerful as it is short and clear: Live now so that when the moment comes in which you're brought into eternity through the inevitable corridor of death, you'll have no regrets. One of the saddest deaths of the Old Testament is the unmourned death of King Jehoram in 2 Chronicles 21:19–20.

His people made no burning for him, like the burning of his fathers. Thirty and two years old was he when he began to reign, and he reigned in Jerusalem eight

6. Laura Donnelly, "Your Life Really Does Flash Before Your Eyes," *London Telegraph*, January 29, 2017, https://www.telegraph.co.uk/news/2017/01/29/life-really-does-flash-eyes-die-study-suggests/#:~:text=Every%20person%20in%20the%20study,medial%20temporal%2C%20and%20parietal%20cortices.

years, and departed without being desired. Howbeit they buried him in the city of David, but not in the sepulchers of the kings.

The ESV renders verse 20, "And he departed with no one's regret." No one would miss him. No one would mourn him. No fire would be built. He was not worthy to be buried with the other kings. His life was mostly an exercise in futility.

One of Edwards's earliest sermons is his 1722/23 sermon "The Nakedness of Job," which he preached while he was crafting his resolutions. In brief, it is a meditation on death. The sermon itself rings hauntingly like a funeral bell, summoning mourners. His text on that Lord's Day morning was simply, "Naked came I out of my mother's womb, and naked shall I return thither" (Job 1:21). Edwards called his congregation that day to imagine their own death:

> They very seldom think where, and how, and what their bodies will be a few years hence. They are now in life and health, stirring and moving about the world amongst the rest of the crowd of mankind; but they little think how, in a little time, they must lie buried in the ground, in the dark, still, and silent grave, rotting and putrifying, loathsome and filthy, by degrees turning to dust, and none taking notice of them, their flesh by degrees rotting off from their bones, leaving nothing but the ghastly skeleton. (WJE 10:411)

As disturbing as this image is, though, the nineteen-year-old preacher argued before his stunned-silent hearers that there is a fate worse still than death. It is dying without Christ. Dying and going into eternity unprepared is a miserable fate indeed. He concluded the sermon with an exhortation that became a penetrating question:

> Let all be exhorted to apply themselves immediately to the preparations for eternity. Set about it with the greatest seriousness and diligence, with the utmost vigor and most fixed resolution, for such things as concern eternal happiness or eternal misery are not to be trifled with, nor to be trusted to a mere peradventure; *for what shall it profit you, if you gain the whole world, and lose your own soul?* (WJE 10:412; italics mine)

If this short meditation is alarming to the reader, and I can't see how it wouldn't be, perhaps it would be best to consider Edwards's own prescription to himself when he too was beset with these alarming thoughts. In the summer of 1723, he recorded the following entry in his journal:

> Friday morning, July 5. Last night, when thinking what I should wish I had done, that I had not done, if I was then to die [almost a direct quotation of the 17th Resolution]. . . . I thought I should wish, that I had been more importunate with God, to fit me for death, and lead me into all truth, and that I might not be deceived, about the state of my soul. (WJE 10:774)

Indeed, it is both fitting and wise to ask God to prepare us for that moment—be it in a few days from now or many decades hence—so that our death will be a joyful celebration and reception into the hands of God and his gathered saints, rather than a dreadful regret of the past and terror of what is to come.

19. Resolved, never to do anything, which I should be afraid to do, if I expected it would not be above an hour, before I should hear the last trump.

"The last trump" to which Edwards refers in this 19th Resolution is, of course, that great trumpet blast Scripture describes as immediately preceding the personal and triumphant return of our Lord Jesus Christ (Matt. 24:31; 1 Cor. 15:52; 1 Thess. 4:16). The two Greek words most commonly used in the New Testament to describe the return of Christ are his *ephiphania* and his *parousia*. *Epiphania* (from which derives the name of the church season of Epiphany) comes from *epi*, which is an intensifying prefix, and the root word *phaneroo*, which means "appearing" or "manifestation." The main point here: His manifestation will be intense indeed! The latter word *parousia* was drawn from the grand Greco-Roman military parades in which a conquering king or emperor returned home victoriously after battle. Edwards himself described this *parousia*—this vivid and colorful scene of a returning king—as a joyful and gladdening march, in which the great hero arrives

> in triumph in a most joyful manner, as the Roman guards when they had been forth on any expedition and had obtained any remarkable victory, when they returned to the city of Rome whence they were sent forth by the supreme authority of that city, used to enter the gates of the city in triumph. The authority of the Roman state gladly opening the gates to 'em and all the Roman people receiving them with shouting and the sound of the trumpet and such like manifestations of joy, with many attendants and their enemies that they had conquered led in triumph at their chariot wheels. (WJE 10:219)

Coinciding with this spectacular parade, Scripture draws the concept of the "last trumpet" as ringing out accolades just moments before the victorious hero bursts through the gates in pomp and splendor. In point of fact, Scripture places a strong emphasis on the spiritual and moral condition of our hearts and lives *at the precise time* of Christ's return; that is, as he emerges through the very gates. There is a rather urgent exhortation toward holiness from the witness of the apostolic writers of the New Testament for believers to live in constant awareness of the inevitability of the return of Christ—in the sense of both a warning against sin and an encouragement to remain faithful—up to the last hour preceding his coming.

The prevailing language in these *parousia* and *epiphania* texts indicates that when the Lord appears in glory, his believers would be "found" faithful in that moment. Consider as examples the following Scripture verses:

That the trial of your faith, being much more precious than of gold that per-
isheth, though it be tried with fire, might be *found* unto praise and honour and
glory at the appearing of Jesus Christ. (1 Pet. 1:7; italics mine)

Wherefore, beloved, seeing that ye look for such things, be diligent that ye may
be *found* of him in peace, without spot, and blameless. (2 Pet. 3:14; italics mine)

Believers are to maintain their pursuit of purity and holiness until the last days,
never once growing weary or letting their guard down. Paul writes to Timothy,

I give thee charge in the sight of God, who quickeneth all things, and before
Christ Jesus, who before Pontius Pilate witnessed a good confession; That thou
keep this commandment without spot, unrebukable, until the appearing of our
Lord Jesus Christ. (1 Tim. 6:13–14)

Likewise, Paul instructs Titus,

Teaching us that, denying ungodliness and worldly lusts, we should live soberly,
righteously, and godly, in this present world; Looking for that blessed hope, and the
glorious appearing of the great God and our Saviour Jesus Christ. (Titus 2:12–13)

The apostles often reminded believers that they should be mortified by the
possibility that they might be found to be acting duplicitously or scandalously
as Christ bursts unexpectedly through the gates of time and history to gather
his elect people from the ends of the earth.

But what if someone were to try to game the system? What if someone
tried to do like the protagonist in Dr. Seuss's classic story *The Cat in the Hat*
and clean up their lives just moments before the denouement, when "Mother
comes home"? Sure, she found a clean house when she walked in the door,
but that tidy living room certainly did not present the full report of the go-
ings on while Thing One and Thing Two recklessly ran through the halls! No,
Edwards says in his 19th Resolution, believers should will to live their whole
lives as if Christ could return at any moment (because he could!). Edwards
resolves to live *expecting* that Christ may return at any time. He vowed to
never do anything he would be afraid to do in the last hour. If we're terrified
to be caught with our proverbial "hand in the cookie jar" the instant Christ
appears in the heavens when the final trumpet signal blasts, then we should
be all the more wary of daily faltering before that time, since "of that day and
hour knoweth no man" (Matt. 24:36).

*52. I frequently hear persons in old age say how they would live, if they were to
live their lives over again: resolved, that I will live just so as I can think I shall
wish I had done, supposing I live to old age. July 8, 1723.*

In 2 King 20, there is a remarkable story about King Hezekiah to whom
God gave an extra fifteen years to his life. When Hezekiah fell ill, the prophet

Isaiah told him he would not recover and warned him to put his household in order before he died. Hearing this, Hezekiah pleaded with tears to the Lord for extra life, and God graciously granted his request, confirming it with a supernatural sign (vv. 10–11). With his renewed vitality and the confidence of God's promise, Hezekiah foolishly invited a Babylonian envoy into Jerusalem, inadvertently exposing the city's intelligence to what would become a hostile enemy for Judah in the very near future. Hezekiah gained fifteen years for his own enjoyment but hurt his own people's cause (vv. 16–18).

This story poses an interesting question: What would *you* do if the Lord granted you an additional decade or more to live? Supposing God granted you a dozen or more years of preternatural long life, how would you use the time for his glory? Over and over, Scripture reminds us of the brevity of human life, and such reminders weigh heavy, even for those whose lives are longer than average (Eccles. 6:12; Ps. 90:10; James 4:13). Whether we are young or old, the question still remains a potent wakeup call: *How will you live the remaining years of this mortal life?*

Edwards noticed that Hezekiah's story is repeated in the lives of many, even those given what appears to be "extra time" (though perhaps not supernaturally like Hezekiah). He notes the following in his Diary,

> Monday, Sept. 23, 1723. I observe that old men seldom have any advantage of new discoveries, because they are beside a way of thinking, they have been so long used to. Resolved, if ever I live to years, that I will be impartial to hear the reasons of all pretended discoveries, and receive them if rational, how long so ever I have been used to another way of thinking. My time is so short, that I have not time to perfect myself in all studies: wherefore resolved, to omit and put off, all but the most important and needful studies. (WJE 16:781)

Here, Edwards promises that he will always think like a young person, even as both body and mind begin to show wear. He vows to receive new information and insight, weighing it carefully before rejecting it out of hand. He wills to see the world with new eyes and a humility to learn, thinking freely and weighing the evidence. He resolves to guard himself against believing the lie that he already knows everything.

Later the next year, Edwards was still warning himself against the possibility of calcified thinking, perhaps all the more being disappointed in some of the elder men and women to whom he had referred in his journal above, or perhaps even more perplexed having seen this same pattern carried over in others who had likewise fallen into the same bad habit of predictable thought patterns.

> Saturday, Feb. 22. I observe that there are some evil habits, which do increase and grow stronger, even in some good people, as they grow older; habits that much obscure the beauty of Christianity: some things which are according to their natural tempers, which, in some measure, prevails when they are young

in Christ, and the evil disposition, having an unobserved control, the habit at last grows very strong, and commonly regulates the practice until death. By this means, old Christians are very commonly, in some respects, more unreasonable than those who are young. I am afraid of contracting such habits, particularly of grudging to give, and to do, and of procrastinating. (WJE 16:785)

In this second journal entry, he goes further, even calling these habits "evil," since this failure to consider new insight has the negative aspect of "obscuring the beauty of Christianity." These refusals to think with an open mind end up causing older persons to be "unreasonable" and selfish ("grudging to give"), ironically fostering procrastination, and squandering the very thing that's most precious toward the end of one's natural life: time.

This seems to be a perennial problem even today—both older and younger people tend to think the other group "just doesn't get it." But I do believe Edwards was onto something important in the 52nd Resolution. Whether younger or older people think more wisely, we should all agree that no Christian believers should *ever* come to the end of their life wishing they had spent their time more wisely. No Christian believers should ever reach the end of this mortal journey dreading the end because they had not prepared their souls adequately for death's inevitability. Whether or not we have another fifteen years like Hezekiah, we should ask God to make us wise, humble, and tender as we walk with him over many decades. Likewise, we should endeavor to live with an optimistic boldness, taking risks and daring to live faithfully even *now*—the very present moment—so that we don't regret the way we lived *then*.

67. Resolved, after afflictions, to inquire, what I am the better for them, what good I have got by them, and what I might have got by them.

Like all colonials in the pre-Revolutionary period of American history, life was hard for the Edwards family. Though he had the benefit of a strong family structure, the fellowship of congregational life among the saints, and the incomparable advantage of the era's best education, Edwards was no stranger to suffering. For one, the threat of war was constant. The French and Indians cast a looming shadow of fear that one's village or town could be attacked at any time (as with Deerfield in 1704). More than that, surgery was crude and primitive, medicine was experimental at best, and sudden death was common.

Although I could select any number of sufferings the Edwards family endured as we look at his 67th Resolution on affliction, I will focus on an event in his life to which most of us can unfortunately relate: Jonathan Edwards was fired from his job.

In 1750, the renowned pastor came to loggerheads with his congregation and most of its leaders and members. The confrontation had been building for some time, with ill will going back to the 1744 "Bad Book Case."[7] Then, Edwards had made a questionable leadership decision in a case of church discipline regarding several of the town's young men (when he had caught them reading a "bad book"). Now, six years later, the congregation and their pastor were at odds with one another regarding Communion. Edwards had sought to roll back his grandfather's position on the Lord's Supper, a long-accepted compromise in the Northampton Church, to return to a stricter and more conservative position. In so doing, Edwards wanted to tighten up the restrictions on who could—and who could not—receive the Lord's Supper. In short, Edwards wanted the church to move to what he felt to be a more biblical position. The church, he argued, had the obligation to "fence the table" more cautiously.

Through a series of writings and sermons, Edwards sought to defend his more conservative position against the moderate position of his grandfather, Solomon Stoddard. By and large, the church members by were not interested in his explanations.[8] The lines had been drawn all too clearly, and now the church was ready to vote on their pastor's continued calling and employment at the church. When the votes were tallied, Edwards was soundly defeated and almost unanimously cast out of the pulpit.

The pastor for some twenty-three years, Edwards was now out of a job.[9] America's greatest scholar, and arguably the most famous pastor-theologian of the age, was unemployed. With such a large family of children, finding another job wasn't an easy problem to solve. He couldn't just start a new church or move to another congregation on the other side of town. It simply didn't work that way back then.

Edwards had only a few options, including taking a call in Scotland, but he eventually settled on moving his family out farther, to the edges of civilization at an Indian outpost in Stockbridge, Massachusetts. This fringe outpost on the skirts of organized society consisted of a small English-speaking congregation and the opportunity to serve the Mahican Indians as a missionary-teacher. It also put his family in further risk of attack. They moved the family in stages, with Jonathan going first and Sarah to follow.

Yet his youthful 67th Resolution had called for thoughtful analysis of his afflictions, accepting them as God's designed molds for character, spiritual

---

7. For more on this unfortunate event, see Marsden, *A Life*, 292–302.

8. See especially Edwards's treatise, "An Humble Inquiry into the Rules of the Word of God, Concerning the Qualifications Requisite to a Complete Standing and Full Communion in the Visible Christian Church," in WJEO 12:167–348.

9. There is an excellent chapter on Edwards's dismissal from the Northampton Church titled "How Jonathan Edwards Got Fired and Why It Is Important for Us Today," by Mark Dever in *God Entranced Vision of All Things: The Legacy of Jonathan Edwards*, ed. John Piper and Justin Taylor (Wheaton, IL: Crossway, 2004), 129–44.

formation, and sanctification. Rather than sulk in his humbler station, far below the influential position he once held, the older Edwards resolved to begin to prepare some of his greatest ideas for publication. Ironically, his firing provided him with more time for thoughtful writing and gave him a God-ordained opportunity re-preach some sermons, while teaching simpler, less demanding lessons to the Mahicans. Now he could write the books he had been thinking about for such a long time.

The glory of this affliction is in the fruit it bore. During this seven-year stage, Edwards wrote three of his most important books. *Freedom of the Will* engages the long-time debate about man's free will versus God's sovereignty.[10] Some say it has never been refuted. *The End for Which God Created the Word* is Edwards's biblical and theological explanation for why the universe exists in the first place, which I consider a masterpiece.[11] *The Nature of True Virtue* is his synopsis of ethics and morality from a purely philosophical perspective.[12] It is a first-rate work of philosophy. One wonders whether any of these books could have been written if Edwards had not been fired. Believers, whenever we suffer the trials of affliction, we should let this 67th Resolution come to mind, prompting ourselves to seek to discover what divine purpose God has for our good and for his glory.

❖ Confession and Renewal: Resolutions 8, 12, 29, 37, 47, 48, 49, 68

The word *confession* literally means to "declare together." It comes from two words *con* (meaning "with") and *fetari* (meaning "declare"). When we confess our sin, we join ourselves with all believers in aligning with what is right and true. We admit the truth about God and ourselves: that he alone is holy and that we are fallen creatures. In confessing this, we depose ourselves by the truth and openly renounce our former ways. We bring that which is true about ourselves verbally before the eyes and ears of God, and perhaps other mortal witnesses as well (James 5:16). Of course, most of our lives are spent trying to hide our real selves from the world. We often present ourselves in such a way to others that we minimize our foibles and show off our greatest strengths. This is why confession feels so good and relieving to troubled souls. Through confession, we give up on the preposterous idea that we can continue to project this false image of ourselves. It helps us sets aside our facades so we can say, "Here I am. I admit this is truly me. I am a sinner and I need to change."

---

10. *The Freedom of the Will* comprises WJEO 1.
11. *The End for Which God Created the World* can be found in WJEO 8:405–63.
12. *The Nature of True Virtue* can be found in WJEO 8:539–627.

When confession is combined with repentance, it becomes utterly trans-formative. We first admit that which is true about ourselves (we are fallen) and then repent (a word that means to change directions). We leave the false course and pursue righteousness. We ask God for help to live in a way that pleases him. The Greek word for repentance, *metanoia*, literally means to "change the mind." Of course, it is possible to confess (admit the truth) without repenting (changing our lives), but it is not possible to repent without first confessing. The one builds on the other.

Though there are many beautiful prayers of repentance in Scripture, probably none is more evocative than Psalm 51. In this text, David, con-fronted by the prophet Nathan, confesses his sin with Bathsheba and asks God to transform him by grace. Notice how David combines confession, "For I acknowledge my transgressions: and my sin is ever before me" (v. 3) with repentance, "Create in me a clean heart, O God; and renew a right spirit within me" (v. 10). The freedom of the forgiveness of sins that comes through repentance is dramatically pictured in the *Pilgrim's Progress* where Christian finally experiences the renewal of divine grace. As he approaches the cross, the heavy burden he had been carrying on his back snaps off, tumbles down Mount Calvary, and falls into the empty tomb where it is never seen again![13]

In this section, we will consider Jonathan Edwards's Resolutions on con-fession and renewal in grace, especially Resolutions numbered 8, 12, 29, 37, 47, 48, 49, and 68.

8. Resolved, to act, in all respects, both speaking and doing, as if nobody had been so vile as I, and as if I had committed the same sins, or had the same infirmities or failings as others; and that I will let the knowledge of their fail-ings promote nothing but shame in myself, and prove only an occasion of my confessing my own sins and misery to God. Vid. July 30, 1723.

It would be hard to argue that anyone was tougher on sin than the Pu-ritans, both in England and in Colonial America. And it would be hard to argue that anyone was tougher on himself for his own sin during this period than Jonathan Edwards. While preaching sin is a subject that has in many ways gone out of style in American pulpits today—as pastors prefer to focus more on positive subjects like love and grace—Edwards saw our ability to be honest about our own vile sinful nature as a Christian virtue. Let me explain.

As Edwards witnessed the revivals happening all around him (first lo-cally in Northampton in 1735 and then regionally between 1740 and 1741), one of the primary foci in his ministry became helping the citizens of the colonies to decipher which events were legitimate and which were extremes and ex-cesses. In other words, he took up the question of determining what would be

---

13. Bunyan, *Pilgrim's Progress*, 59–60.

the real distinguishing "marks" of true revival. Though he wrote several major treatises on this matter, especially his masterpiece the *Religious Affections*, we will for the moment consider a shorter work that preceded it. *The Distinguishing Marks of the Work of the Spirit of God (1741)* is by far the briefer of the two, and many scholars think the clearer of the pair.[14] In this sermon on 1 John 4, sketched out in long form for publication, Edwards provides readers with five "marks" that likely point to a true conversion experience. These marks are as follows: (1) The person loves God. God has become the all-satisfying hope and joy of their life. (2) The person loves Christ. It is not enough merely to be a theist; it is particularly the redemptive work of Jesus Christ in his cross and resurrection that matter. (3) The person loves the truth. This includes the truth about themselves. This love of truth includes a pursuit of historic Christian doctrine, especially in discerning between orthodoxy and error. (4) The person loves Scripture. Since the Scripture is the truth of God revealed to mankind in written form, a love and esteem for this message necessarily follows a change of heart. (5) Finally, in addition to the four "loves," there is one "hate": the hatred of sin; especially one's own sin.

If the person claims to have faith, but does not hate their own iniquities, then their professions of conversion are highly questionable. It is one thing to hate the sin of other people. Even unbelievers vex hot in displeasure when someone steals from them, maligns their character, or judges them with prejudice. But only a person under the conviction of the work of the Holy Spirit would hate their own sin most piercingly of all, especially as the four "marks" of love are growing in their life. As Edwards reasons through matters pertaining to revival, he supposes that if the revivals were manipulated and contrived, they would likely be the work of Satan, since this would involve such a widespread deception. But, he continues, it would be foolish of the devil to produce a movement that caused people to hate their own sin, since that would turn them to righteousness and to God! The devil would have to be a fool to bring about the kind of movement across the land that would cause people great discomfort with their own vices, lusts, and wickedness. Edwards writes,

> And therefore if we see persons made sensible of the dreadful nature of sin, and of the displeasure of God against it, and of their own miserable condition as they are in themselves, by reason of sin, and earnestly concerned for their eternal salvation, and sensible of their need of God's pity and help, and engaged to seek it in the use of the means that God has appointed, we may certainly conclude that it is from the Spirit of God, whatever effects this concern has on their bodies; though it causes them to cry out aloud, or to shriek, or to faint, or though it throws them into convulsions. (WJE 4:252–53)

---

14. *The Distinguishing Marks* can be found in WJE 4:226–88.

Though we don't have any record of Edwards himself fainting, shrieking, or convulsing, we do have plenty of evidence as early as the writing of the Resolutions to suggest that he was well aware of his own "vile" nature, reckoned openly with his "infirmities and failings," and sought to deeply repent of his shame, "sins and misery." The 8th Resolution and several others like it reveal the tender heart of a man who was realistic about his need for grace, forthright with his confession of trespasses, and therefore possessing the one negative "mark" of true conversion, a hatred of his own sin.

12. *Resolved, if I take delight in it as a gratification of pride, or vanity, or on any such account, immediately to throw it by.*

Pride and vanity are two repulsive attributes among the saints of God, and quite unbecoming in the otherwise pleasant and comely face of the bride of Christ. Christ's cherished one is to be beautiful in his eyes, purified, and made clean as she awaits his presence, "not having spot, or wrinkle, or any such thing; but that it should be holy and without blemish" (Eph. 5:26). When either pride or vanity are seen in the mirror of self-examination, they are like unseemly blemishes on an otherwise-beautiful face that can only be removed through washing in humility and repentance.

To change the metaphor to life-saving medicine, these self-aggrandizing sins must be surgically removed from the believer's heart through conscious confession the moment we realize they're present. As Edwards says, we ought to "throw it by" (the cause of pride), an expression I take to be synonymous with jettison, cast overboard, or toss in the garbage. The process of repenting of resident sins so as to remove them by the violence through heartfelt repentance was called "mortification" by the Puritans. In "Miscellany 635," Edwards describes this process:

> Bad wounds must be searched to the bottom; and oftentimes when they are very deep they must be lanced, and the core laid open, though it be very painful to endure, before they can have a good cure. The surgeon may skin them over, so that it may look like a cure without this, without much hurting the patient, but it will not do the patient much good. He does but deceive him for the present, but it will be no lasting benefit to him; the sore will break out again. This figures forth to us the case of our spiritual wound. The plague of our hearts, which is great and deep and must be searched, must be lanced by painful conviction. The core must be laid open. We must be made to see that fountain of sin and corruption there is, and what a dreadful state we are in by nature, in order to a thorough and saving cure [cf. Jer. 8:11]. (WJE 18:161)

What makes both pride and vanity such dangerous sins is that they constantly seek the central place of our lives: the honor and recognition that belongs exclusively to God. They have a gravity that pulls all attention and praise inward rather than yielding it outward to God, to Christ, or even to others who are more deserving. Pride tends to relish in our own accomplishments, achievements, and awards. Pride loves a plastic trophy and posts even the lamest paper "participation awards" on the refrigerator for the world to see. Vanity settles for even less, often savoring one's own image, swelling and engorging itself with little more than the superficiality of physical appearance. If pride is spurned in failing to gain the admiration of others, then vanity will console itself by prizing any glimmer of banality it can find in the mirror.

There are many other forms of pride, which Edwards acknowledges in his 1722/23 sermon "Poverty of Spirit."

> There are multitudes of such, as I believe everyone knows, so some are proud of their religion, others of their irreligion, and some are proud of humility. So pride will work one way or other in all natural men. (WJE 10:499)

True enough, there is a danger that even our meekness and lowliness can cause our hearts to swell with self-congratulations! Later in the same sermon, Edwards points out a cruel irony about these self-loving sins that's altogether too obvious: we hate pride in others but often cannot see it in ourselves.

> All men hate pride and covetousness in others and will praise the contrary values, however destitute they are of it; but how much more would they if they had their eyes opened and their blindness, that hinders them from beholding spiritual beauties? (WJE 10:505)

He is right. We can smell pride a mile away in someone else, but we are almost never aware of how reprehensible it makes us seem to those around us. The only possible solution—as the above citation from the closing paragraph of "Poverty of Spirit" suggests—is that we are captivated and overwhelmed by a beauty greater than ourselves. We must finally be overcome with the greater allure of what he calls true "spiritual beauties." These can be found only in Christ. When believers truly behold "the light of the knowledge of the glory of God in the face of Jesus Christ" (2 Cor. 4:6), placing themselves in proper context—only then will it be apparent where true beauty, glory, honor, and majesty reside. When Christ is seen for all of his greatness, pride melts to meekness and vanity wanes thin to shame, gladly yielding the position of honor to the bridegroom himself. In the light of his beauty, we must step back out of the spotlight, kneeling with poverty of spirit (Matt. 5:3) in the shadow of the Almighty.

29. Resolved, never to count that a prayer, nor to let that pass as a prayer, nor that as a petition of a prayer, which is so made, that I cannot hope that God will answer it; nor that as a confession, which I cannot hope God will accept.

We may find it somewhat shocking to notice that this is the only one of the Seventy Resolutions that mentions prayer. This comes as a surprise, given that the entire charter of the Resolutions is intended to govern Edwards's own spiritual life; and in the view of many of the Christian writers throughout the ages, a man's inner life very much consists in the vibrancy of his prayer. In my own view, the neglect of the topic of prayer in this document is largely accidental on Edwards's part and doesn't reflect any intentional or purposeful design to make little of this Christian duty and the delight of intercession.

The Diary receives far more treatment on prayer than the Resolutions, and the subject is one Edwards carefully monitored in his pursuit of holiness. For instance, on February 16, 1723, he warned himself by way of reminder not to neglect such a precious duty:

> At night. For the time past of my life, I have been negligent, in that I have not sufficiently kept up that part of divine worship, singing the praise of God in secret, and with company. I have been negligent for the month past in these three things; I have not been watchful enough over my appetite in eating and drinking; in rising too late a-mornings; and in not applying myself with application enough to the duty of secret prayer. (WJE 16:766)

On May 11, he similarly chided himself in a brief line for not staying mentally alert when praying in the gathered fellowship: "Have also been negligent about keeping my thoughts, when joining with others in prayer" (WJE 16:769). Toward the colder months of 1724, he wrote this short entry:

> Sabbath, Nov. 15. Determined, when I am indisposed to prayer, always to premeditate what to pray for; and that it is better, that the prayer should be of almost any shortness, than that my mind should be almost continually off from what I say. (WJE 16:787)

Most directly related to the present Resolution, he wrote in his journal,

> Saturday morning, June 29. It is best to be careful in prayer, not to put up those petitions, of which I do not feel a sincere desire: thereby, my prayer is rendered less sincere, less acceptable to God, and less useful to myself. (WJE 16:773)

In looking at these and other entries together, it seems Edwards's focus on the topic of prayer was largely concerned with the goal that his heart, mind, and lips be in true concert with one another. He should not allow mental wandering to ruin his times of prayer. He inferred (rightly, I think) in agreement with Matthew 6:5–7: that it is better to pray in short, sincere bursts, without any concern for the amount of time spent or the number of words babbled, lest we risk the "vain repetitions" of the pagans and hypocrites. Prayer should consist of true petitions, sincerely offered, with an entire trust and hope that God will answer. Any prayer of confession should be attended with the requisite lament of sin, empowered by a real desire to leave it and be lifted by God's grace to a higher obedience.

As Edwards grew in the faith and in maturity, his prayer life continued to build. Although he struggled in prayer like most believers, he sought to ensure that it was central both to his own life and to that of his growing family. George Marsden, in perhaps the best modern biography on Edwards, tells us that Edwards commonly rose early in the morning, held private prayer for some time, summoned his wife and children together to prayer by candlelight before the sun rose, and then held some devotion at every meal. Other than that, Edwards held to the secrecy principle of Matthew 6:6 and did not share with mortal ears what occurred between him and the Lord while he was in the study for those famous thirteen hours each day.[15]

Before closing this section, I want to speak kindly to you, the reader, for a moment. Often when we read of the lives of the great men and women of Christian history, we can find their stellar examples frustrating rather than encouraging. We tend to think of them as super Christians rather than ordinary people who sought Jesus in their time and era, with gifts as God was pleased to distribute them. But rather than exalting Edwards as some sort of a stained-glass saint, I find it more encouraging to know that he—like me— struggled with prayer. It was not easy, yet he persevered in this. Most of all, he reminded himself that if prayer would be fitting, it should be offered from a humble heart with no pretense. His 29th Resolution serves to encourage us to pray to the same God, with full expectation that our Father is ready and willing to hear our prayers, even if they are meager, short, and few.

37. Resolved, to inquire every night, as I am going to bed, wherein I have been negligent, what sin I have committed, and wherein I have denied myself: also at the end of every week, month and year. Dec. 22 and 26, 1722.

At some points in the Resolutions, Edwards seems obsessed with discovering the sin in his life. He desired to become a sin-sleuth and trail his errant footprints backward on his own path to their vile hideout. He would dust for guilty fingerprints on the window of his heart for transgressions. If he could, he would take a magnifying glass to his soul; he would track down the clues of iniquity wherever they went like a basset hound of holiness. He would watch and re-watch the security tapes of his actions in all their grainy detail. Despite this valiant effort to uncover all of his error, we know he was unsuccessful. There were gigantic "blind spots" of generational sin he could not see. Despite his resolution to search out any evil in his heart every night and to "inquire . . . wherein I have been negligent, what sin I have committed," Edwards still had faults he never recognized, notwithstanding his inten-

---

15. Marsden, *A Life*, 133.

tion to "trace it back to the original cause." One of those—one of the worst we know of—was his approval of slavery.

As much as it pains me to write this, Jonathan Edwards was a slave owner.[16] It wasn't just that he didn't speak out about slavery. It wasn't just that he was silent on the issue. It wasn't merely that Edwards never thought to speak against slavery as a moral application in one of his hundreds of sermons on sin, repentance, and holiness. (He never did preach against it, and the omission is glaring and alarming.) It's that he actually *owned* slaves himself. It seems unconscionable in our world today, as sensitive as we are to issues of race and injustice.

In those days, the evil of owning slaves was a vice few recognized, obvious as it is to us today. Generations of latent racism had led colonial Christians to fail to see what modern believers now know to be an obvious blind spot. In his financial account books, we have records of the Edwards family purchasing a female named Venus. So, too, we know he also had a young slave boy named Titus and another female named Leah. Leah was converted during the revival and actually joined the Northampton Church as a full member. Despite the Northampton Church having welcomed and received at least nine African slaves as members—which was fairly progressive for a church at that time—this still does not erase the stain from Edwards's legacy. Only the blood of Jesus can do that.

While there were some awakening to this radical social injustice, Edwards couldn't see it in his own heart. His position among the social elite led him to believe that clergy and landowners belonged to an exalted social class among civilization's hierarchical framework. Slavery, he thought, was simply part of that infrastructure. He was not alone in this. George Whitefield, the famed evangelical preacher of the Great Awakening, is also tainted by his connections with slavery. It's important to recall that Edwards lived before the Revolutionary War, much less the Civil War. In an era of kings and queens, most simply accepted the fact that people were born into ranks and classes as inherited from medieval feudalism.

Edwards accepted this layered hierarchy uncritically and was glad to be a member of the elite class of clergymen. In one of the rare times that he wrote on slavery, he defended the reputation of another minister whose integrity had been called into question on account of his slave ownership. Like a modern union representative, Edwards dutifully wrote to defend his pastoral colleague against charges of "manslaving," even though this particular pastor held some unsavory doctrinal positions and would otherwise have been Edwards's theological opponent. That he could not see this great hypocrisy in himself is tragic.

---

16. Much of what I will say here is a summary of Lowe, "Destruction and Benevolence," 87–110.

Thankfully, some of Edwards's own theological descendants did recognize this heinous sin and fought against it. Using some of Edwards's own ideas (his writings on the concept of benevolence), his son Jonathan Edwards Jr. and close disciple Samuel Hopkins carried the principles of Christian love farther than Edwards himself was willing to go and spoke out against slavery. While Edwards was a man of his time, this "New Divinity" movement was actually ahead of its time. In that sense, Edwards's own immediate disciples (his son and student) were on the leading edge of the abolitionist movement. Thankfully, these disciples of the famed Northampton pulpit were more consistently Edwardsean than Edwards himself.

Summing up this dark section, we might do well to remember that our own generation has moral blind spots we don't see. We may not yet be fully aware of what they are. Perhaps several generations from now, the church will shudder to think how we today may have been silent on important social issues on which few are willing to speak out.[17]

47. Resolved, to endeavor to my utmost to deny whatever is not most agreeable to a good, and universally sweet and benevolent, quiet, peaceable, contented, easy, compassionate, generous, humble, meek, modest, submissive, obliging, diligent and industrious, charitable, even, patient, moderate, forgiving, sincere temper; and to do at all times what such a temper would lead me to. Examine strictly every week, whether I have done so. Sabbath morning, May 5, 1723.

On a late spring morning as the weather began to warm, Edwards was up early before church, thinking about his personality and disposition. The 47th Resolution shares the distinction of being among the longest resolutions, topping the scales at seventy-one words. In length, it trails only the 1st Resolution (eighty words) and the 63rd Resolution (eighty-five words).

Here, Edwards piles up adjectives to describe the kind of man he hopes to be one day. This sentence would likely get red-penned heavily if it were submitted in many English writing courses, since Edwards awkwardly strings together some twenty successive adjectives, set like pearls on a necklace. Perhaps this resolution betrays the fact that he feared that few or many of these descriptors did not necessarily shine forth with any particular brilliance from his somewhat unsociable demeanor.

There may also be some personality projection here: *"Lord, let me be a more likeable person!"* We noted that Edwards wrote these lines on a particular Lord's Day morning, perhaps as he reminded himself to be as agreeable as

---

17. There is an excellent analysis of Edwards's problematic views of slavery by Sherard Burns titled "Trusting the Theology of a Slave Owner," in *A God Entranced Vision of All Things*, ed. John Piper and Justin Taylor (Wheaton, IL: Crossway, 2004), 145–71.

possible to the people who would soon be gathering in the Congregational church. For those of us who likewise struggle in the social graces, perhaps naturally predisposed to introversion, we need as much of the help of the Holy Spirit as possible—even when we're gathering with loved ones and fellow believers!

If the words in this Resolution didn't precisely describe its writer, they do at least adhere to our Savior! Every word Edwards chose here in this extended, run-on sentence is an exact match for the "sweet and benevolent" kindness of the Lord Jesus.[18] Look over them again if necessary. Think back to the ways Christ touched people's lives with his meek and gracious manner. Select a few choice scenes from the Gospels for consideration. Was he not beloved by both lepers and prostitutes, tax collectors and zealots? The crowds did not press in on Jesus, forcing him onto a boat just offshore, because he was rude or brutish. They loved him because of his obliging, charitable, and forgiving manner, even if they occasionally confused the gift with the Giver, as they did with the fish and loaves. People loved Jesus and were drawn to him because he possessed every attribute Edwards hoped to have.

In Edwards's 1740 "Personal Narrative," he thought back on the early years of his own Christian pilgrimage, often describing Christ in his writings as "sweet," the very attribute he prays for in this 47th Resolution.

> From about that time [the early 1720s], I began to have a new kind of apprehensions and ideas of Christ, and the work of redemption, and the glorious way of salvation by him. (WJE 16:793)

In an important passage, Edwards described having a nearly ecstatic experience of the glory of God in Christ. Look carefully at the adjectives he uses here:

> I walked abroad alone, in a solitary place in my father's pasture, for contemplation. And as I was walking there, and looked up on the sky and clouds; there came into my mind, a sweet sense of the glorious majesty and grace of God, that I know not how to express. I seemed to see them both in a sweet conjunction: majesty and meekness joined together: it was a sweet and gentle, and holy majesty; and also a majestic meekness; an awful sweetness; a high, and great, and holy gentleness. (WJE 16:793)

Edwards hoped to soak in these gracious attributes, basking in the glory of the Savior, and then to shine them forth more brilliantly in his own life thenceforth. For Edwards, this outdoor vision of God's graciousness was a turning point of sorts in his spiritual walk. He went on to note the momentous impact of this surprisingly ethereal visionary experience,

---

18. For a consideration of these attributes, see Edwards's marvelous sermon "The Excellency of Christ," in WJEO 19:560–94.

After this my sense of divine things gradually increased, and became more and more lively, and had more of that inward sweetness. The appearance of everything was altered: there seemed to be, as it were, a calm, sweet cast, or appearance of divine glory, in almost everything. (WJE 16:793)

Notice how he ascribes several of his pearly string of adjectives to God's own gracious nature, including "sweet," "meek," "and "gentle." Whatever Edwards saw of God's nature in his father's pasture that day, he craved to have more of it in his own life. In other words, Edwards was praying that the communicable attributes of God would blossom and manifest in a lively way in his own nature and character. This is the very essence of sanctification: that Christ would be formed in us (Gal. 4:19).

48. Resolved, constantly, with the utmost niceness and diligence, and the strictest scrutiny, to be looking into the state of my soul, that I may know whether I have truly an interest in Christ or no; that when I come to die, I may not have any negligence respecting this to repent of. May 26, 1723.

49. Resolved, that this never shall be, if I can help it.

Deep in the spring of 1723, Edwards was still questioning the state of his own soul—that is, whether or not he had truly been converted. In the 48th and 49th Resolutions, which we will deal with here together, Edwards once again provoked himself to continue to monitor the condition of his soul. In an abundance of caution, Edwards wanted to be as sure as possible that he had "an interest in Christ" (i.e., experienced conversion), even though he had articulated for some time that his own subjective experiences of the gospel were somewhat different from the standard Puritan model.

On just the previous day, Edwards had decided to look once again into some of the writings of the older theologians, hoping to find comfort or conviction that might help.

Saturday, May 25. In the morning. As I was this morning reading the 17th Resolution, it was suggested to me, that if I was now to die, I should wish that I had prayed more that God would make me know my state, whether it be good or bad; and that I had taken more pains to see and narrowly search into this matter. Wherefore, Memorandum, for the future, most nicely and diligently to look into our old divines' opinions concerning conversion. Made the 48th Resolution. (WJE 16:771)

Though most scholars consider Edwards's conversion to have taken place in 1721 (told by Edwards in his own words in the "Personal Narrative"; see especially WJE 16:792–793), the perplexing problem of certainty continued to eat away at him two years later. If Edwards were to go on toward a future in the ministry and not be truly saved himself, he would only be adding to his own guilt. After all, he knew full well what the apostle James wrote, "My brethren, be not many masters [ESV: teachers], knowing that we shall receive the greater condemnation" (3:1). So, on that Saturday morning, Edwards resolved to give the "old divines" another look, just to be sure. He dusted off a few volumes of reference works and sought to find some help for his tender conscience.

I can only hope that by delving again into the "old divines," Edwards was thinking of the Westminster Divines, for their section on assurance in chapter 18 is helpful indeed. I think it would have brought his soul some comfort, and perhaps may even be a salve to some of our own souls today as well. In the Westminster Confession, chapter 18, the Assembly of Divines addressed the topic of whether or not believers could be fully and finally assured of their salvation. That in itself is a good question and part of the dilemma: Was Edwards searching for something in the doctrine of assurance that was even possible to know? If that wasn't the case, then his self-examination in the 48th and 49th Resolutions was a fool's errand. Rather than linger in uncertainty, the Westminster Assembly came to the positive conclusion that yes, assurance of salvation is possible, even though many hypocrites might deceive themselves into thinking they had it (WCF 18.1). Given that possibility of self-deception, how could believers know that their salvation was a reality? The divines answered in three ways.

First, in the Westminster Confession, chapter 18, the divines counseled such men and women to look not into their own wavering experiences, but rather to the surer and more solid promises of God in the gospel (WCF 18.2). In this way, assurance is a matter of objective facts and promises, not conditioned upon our flimsier feelings. God gave his Son Jesus Christ in the gospel, and this is the greatest proof. His promises are backed up by his actions. This alone overrules our flighty emotions that scamper about like a paper in the wind. The question therefore is not "How do *I* feel?" but rather, "What has *God* promised? What has *God* done?"

Second, the Westminster Divines bid believers to look for evidence of faith and the fruit of obedience in their lives; that is, "the inward evidence of those graces unto which these promises are made." Do I believe these promises? Do I believe God gave his Son? Do I personally trust in his cross, and see the Holy Spirit giving me more "love, joy, peace, and patience" in my life (Gal. 5:22)? Can I observe his work blossoming on branches of my inward and outward life? These fruits are tangible and real, even if somewhat difficult to measure.

Third, the Westminster Confession encourages believers to listen for the voice of the Holy Spirit, "witnessing with our spirits that we are the children of God," since it is he who comes into our hearts and seals us for the day of redemption (Eph. 1:13–14). The Spirit whispers to us, calming our fears, and comforting us from terrors. His tender voice may be quiet and soft, gently assuring us, but it can be trusted—even when our ever-changing feelings cry out or the enemy screams in our face.

68. *Resolved, to confess frankly to myself all that which I find in myself, either infirmity or sin; and, if it be what concerns religion, also to confess the whole case to God, and implore needed help. July 23 and Aug. 10, 1723.*

This Resolution is simple in concept but exhaustive in scope. Edwards here promises and resolves to confess all of his sin openly, honestly, and with a posture of humility before Almighty God. To confess is to agree to what is truthful about ourselves, our proclivities; our tendencies and failures. When we confess, we vomit out the poison with the ipecac of honesty and purge the system of what is lethal. We cease to make excuses. We stop explaining away.

To confess is to admit "the whole case to God." Like an accused criminal before the bar, we start at the beginning and finally tell the whole truth to the judge, without obfuscating or sidestepping. To confess is to frankly declare before the courtroom of heaven the real condition of our soul without endeavoring to cover our tracks or obscure relevant facts. We let go of all fabricated alibis and acknowledge our secret motives.

To confess is soul-searching and difficult work that only the humblest and most daring among us can truly attempt. Notice that as Edwards confesses to God, he says he must also "confess frankly to *myself*" (italics mine), since part of remaining in sin is trying to fool ourselves into believing we're still okay. This annotated Diary entry from August 10, 1723, contains all of the 68th Resolution, but expands on it in three important ways:

> About sunset. As a help against that inward shameful hypocrisy, to confess frankly to myself all that which I find in myself, either infirmity or sin; also to confess to God, and open the whole case to him, when it is what concerns religion, and humbly and earnestly implore of him the help that is needed; not in the least to endeavor to smother over what is in my heart, but to bring it all out to God and my conscience. By this means, I may arrive at a greater knowledge of my own heart. (WJE 16:778)

Let's look at each of these expansions. In the first expansion, Edwards includes a reference to "inward shameful hypocrisy." This is interesting, because most hypocrisy is commonly thought of as those attempts to fool *others*. Hypocrisy is usually outward. The Greek word for "hypocrisy," we recall, literally means "one who wears a mask." Most of us aren't consciously aware of how much self-deception we commit on a regular basis. But with "inward hypocrisy," we are both the deceiver and the deceived, and the entertained member of the audience and the actor on the stage.

In the second expansion, Edwards admits the possibility that he might "smother over what is in his heart," which is another way of saying that we sometimes refuse to deal with the true problems as they exist. To return to a criminal analogy, we are merely bleaching the scene of the crime and wiping off the more obvious bloodstains. We attempt to cover up our most conspicuous boot prints. We do all this to prevent some curious detective from discovering the full truth about us. But we can never clean the surfaces thoroughly enough. The ultraviolet light of God's holiness sees all—even the smudged fingerprints we aren't even aware we've left behind. We put perfume on the corpse in the trunk, but the hounds are already on the scent.

For the sinner, there is no hope but to confess. True repentance rips off the mask and says, "It was me! Here is my real face! O God change my heart!" In the third Diary expansion of this resolution, Edwards says that the goal of such confession is that he would have a "greater knowledge of [his] own heart." This is true, isn't it? Part of confession is the self-discovery of what was never hidden from God, even for a moment. Edwards, then, is in concert with the writer of Psalm 19:

> Who can understand his errors? Cleanse thou me from secret faults. Keep back thy servant also from presumptuous sins; let them not have dominion over me: then shall I be upright, and I shall be innocent from the great transgression. (vv. 12–13)

Sometimes we confess what we know; other times we confess, that we might know more fully.

In an early sermon titled "True Repentance Required," which is contemporary to the writing of the above August 1723 Diary entry, Edwards speaks of the freeing effects of such heart-wrought repentance. The young minister admonished his congregation to do the very thing he sought to do in his own private life: experience the joy of true freedom by repenting *constantly*.

> Be persuaded to a constant repentance. None must think they have done with repentance when the first act of repentance is over. No, but we should frequently be reflecting on our old sins and lamenting of them before God. This frequent lamenting of sin will not decrease, but increase our comfort: for daily lamentation, contrition, and humiliation, we shall be largely repaid by the Holy Ghost, even [in] this world, by spiritual joys and delights. For by our thus frequently lamenting of our past sins, our hatred and aversion to sin increases and grows, and also our love to God, and consequently our joy and delight. (WJE 10:518)

We might tend to think of repentance as miserable agony, toilsome and loathsome, like a slug writhing in burning salt. But Edwards tells us that confession is far more like a release from prison: the key for release is inside the cell, and we are free to live a renewed and restored life, just as soon as we place the key in the lock of repentance and turn it.

❖ Heaven and Hell
Resolutions 9, 10, 18, 50, 51, 55

We end our survey of Jonathan Edwards's Seventy Resolutions, fittingly, where every one of us will end up one day: in either heaven or hell. If the Bible is correct, and I believe it is, then there are the only two destinations that await all of mankind in eternity. Both are worthy of our consideration. Both are shocking beyond imagination. Both should cause our hands to clap over our mouths in astonishment, but for different reasons. What makes heaven truly "heaven" is that God is there. He is present (Rev. 21:3). The reason we were made in the first place, as Edwards covered earlier in his Existential Resolutions, is that we would glorify the God who made us. We were made for him, and we will return to him, that we might praise him forever. Heaven will be shocking and startling to us in its joy, in its feasting, in its songs, and in its worship. At the very center of it all will be Christ, reigning and ruling among his redeemed people (Rev. 22:3).

According to Scripture, the other destination for human souls is hell. Hell is conceived of as a place of torment, regret, fear, darkness, worms, and fire. It used to be the case that Bible preachers could preach both heaven and hell with equal enthusiasm. Something has happened to our culture that makes most pastors leery of preaching on hell. Edwards, however, was not afraid to stare from a distance into the very mouth of hell, even if only to embolden himself to preach to others to avoid it!

Though we were made for heaven, Edwards would want us to be aware that hell awaits those who refuse to confess and repent, as we discussed in the last section. Therefore, let us be beckoned to the glories and joys of heaven, even as we are warned again (or perhaps for the first time) of the doom of hell. The young colonial preacher often used thoughts of both destinations to startle himself awake to live more consciously and fully for the glory of God.

9. Resolved, to think much on all occasions of my own dying, and of the common circumstances which attend death.

Many readers of the resolutions find the 9th Resolution dark, macabre, and possibly grotesque. Why—when many of these resolutions are so encouraging, uplifting, and inspiring—would Edwards throw in something so dismal and despairing? In our day and age, one of the most depressing things we can consider is death in general and our own demise in particular! But this isn't the only occasion when Edwards considered the concept of his death. The 7th and 17th Resolutions already dealt with this topic explicitly and others, such as the 6th Resolution, did so by implication. The simple answer to the "why" question is that Edwards chose not to think of death as something to dread, fear, or loathe. In fact, he could even view it as something of a relief. Consider this entry from his Diary: "Sabbath morning, Sept. 1. When I am violently beset with worldly thoughts, for a relief, to think of death, and the doleful circumstances of it" (WJE 16:780).

All of our worries and anxieties have a way of shrinking to a proper proportion when placed against the stark reality that this life will one day be over. Edwards is on good biblical grounds to think of death in such defanged and declawed ways, since a major part of the Christian gospel is the defeat of death's terrors through the resurrection of Jesus Christ. The apostle Paul wrote, "So when this corruptible shall have put on incorruption, and this mortal shall have put on immortality, then shall be brought to pass the saying that is written, Death is swallowed up in victory" (1 Cor. 15:54). The inevitable conclusion, then, is that through Christ's triumph over death at the tomb on Resurrection Morning, and in the light of his having given the promise of an incorruptible life to believers, death has lost its terrifying power over Christians. Paul concludes rhetorically, "O death, where is thy sting? O grave, where is thy victory?" (1 Cor. 15:55).

Edwards rejoiced in these truths, even if they prompted some concerted meditation on this topic that seems to fly in the face of our modern obsession with health, youth, and vitality. But this isn't always easy, is it? In fairness, contemplations of death did prompt even more soul-searching and self-examination from him as well, particularly when sleep eluded him. In another revealing entry, he wrote:

> Thursday morning, July 4. The last night, in bed, when thinking of death, I thought, if I was then to die, that, which would make me die, in the least degree fearfully, would be, the want of a trusting and relying on Jesus Christ, so distinctly and plainly, as has been described by divines; my not having experienced so particular a venturing, and entirely trusting my soul on Christ, after the fears of hell, and terrors of the Lord, encouraged by the mercy, faithfulness and promises, of God, and the gracious invitations of Christ. Then, I thought I could go out of the world, as much assured of my salvation, as I was of Christ's faithfulness, knowing that, if Christ did not fail me, he would save me, who had trusted in him, on his word. (WJE 10:773)

Although once again, Edwards seems to be questioning his spiritual condition based on the fact that his experience didn't exactly match that of some of the older Puritan writers, the last line in this entry is particularly clear and helpful and probably represents his stronger moments of confidence. Edwards consigns himself to trust fully that Christ won't fail to give believers what he promised in his word: complete victory over sin, guilt, fear, death, and the grave. Thus the "fears of hell" and the "terrors of the Lord" are deluged and overwhelmed by the gracious veracity and entire truthfulness of our covenant-making God, who does not lie and who promises to save those who trust in his Son.

Even if Edwards sometimes waffled in his confidence in his own faith in his private thoughts and personal musings, the same young man was fearless and confident when preaching on death from behind a pulpit. In a late 1722 or early 1723 sermon on the security of the believer in Christ, "Christian Safety," the twenty-year-old Edwards compared the cowardice of the atheist to the boldness of the believer when confronted with the surety of their mortality. We might even read into these words a bit of projected encouragement for himself to which he might cling in his weaker moments, even as he both preached the gospel and simultaneously clung to its promises:

> The most bold and daring of sinners are the worst cowards upon a deathbed. How do they fear and tremble; how do they shrink back; how do their proud hearts tremble at the sight of his frightful face: when those that they used to laugh at and ridicule as strict and precise, that dared not swear, or say anything, and dare not behave so courageously as they used to, yet can meet death as bold as lions, because they know they are safe, and nothing can hurt them because they trust in God, who, they know, is able to keep that which they have committed to him [2 Tim. 1:12]. (WJE 10:461)

Indeed, those who live now in the audacity of mockery and incredulity before Almighty God are commonly reduced to trembling wimps at their deathbed. Yet those who tremble before God and his holiness in this life—clinging desperately to Christ as they remind themselves of his promises—go through the corridor of death as "bold as a lion" (Prov. 28:1) when their time comes. Given Edwards's extraordinary regard for the holiness of God, no one could accuse him of being in the category of the former. Years later, at the actual moments of his death, he proved to be in the category of the latter.

10. Resolved, when I feel pain, to think of the pains of martyrdom, and of hell.

Every papercut we receive, every hangnail we carefully pull loose, is an invitation to consider the seriousness of the human condition, the lostness of mankind apart from the gospel, and the everlasting nature of the eternity waiting on the other side of death. Pain is a natural reflex given to both man and animal alike as an evidence of God's common grace. Its purpose is to deter us from actions that can result in even greater harm. The reason that a boiling jug is hot to the touch, causing us to instinctively jerk our hand away from it, is to warn us of the greater danger of the fire below it on the stove. The reason why jagged rocks hurt our bare feet when we walk on them is so that we may be sufficiently warned to traverse more carefully in the future. Indeed, pain involuntarily alerts the mind to those things that may increase our future misery. And there is no *worse* future misery than to be damned.

Edwards therefore resolved to allow even the smallest injuries to the body to be an alert mechanism to his soul to consider those spiritual realities that we would rather forget or suppress.

He mentions two such spiritual realities in particular here: martyrdom and hell. Suppose Edwards was working outside in the bare sun in the heat of July. He begins to feel the searing heat of the sun on the back of his neck. That pain, dull at first, but growing sharper as the evening dawns, is a reminder that cannot be ignored: another day like this could result in serious injury. But there is more: that sunburn might also raise his sensory awareness to the contemplation of something more serious yet, perhaps the flames of the fires of martyrdom.

Surely many had literally died on such burning stakes, including thousands in the days of ancient Rome's cruelest emperors. So, too, did the Protestant martyrs more recently suffer under the pope's devices in the Counter-Reformation.[19] Some were burned, others beheaded for professing Christ. Edwards would not coddle his mind by protecting it from thinking about such dreadful facts. He would invite these thoughts. Muse upon them. Even draw strength from them.

I have read that leprosy in the days of the New Testament caused one's nerve endings to grow numb to the dangers of the physical world all around, allowing these poor souls to further maim themselves by accident and by ignorance. How much worse, though, when a person's spirit grows dull to Scripture's warnings of the dangers of hell! Edwards would not allow his spirit to grow insensitive to the vast suffering of those martyrs who endured for Christ's sake, nor would he allow himself to grow comfortable with the fact that multitudes would die without Christ and suffer forever in hell. He wouldn't walk around like a spiritual leper, unable to feel pity or remorse, unwilling to entertain difficult questions about his own ability to endure torture for Christ. He would actively prepare his mind for such eventualities; for if he whimpered *now*, what would save him from crying out for mercy *then*?

In Edwards's last Diary entry, penned in the summer of 1735, he was still both permitting and encouraging himself to think such dark and foreboding thoughts:

> June 11. To set apart days of meditation on particular subjects; as sometimes, to set apart a day for the consideration of the greatness of my sins; at another, to consider the dreadfulness and certainty, of the future misery of ungodly men; at another, the truth and certainty of religion; and so, of the great future things promised and threatened in the Scriptures. (WJE 16:789)

19. The reader would do well to consider the history of William Tyndale, for instance, or Calvin's letter to the Five Martyrs of Lyons, France.

No, Edwards would not allow himself to rationalize away the doctrine of hell, under hypothetical or theoretical notions that accord with our own sensibilities rather than the revealed will of God in Scripture. Perhaps this partially explains why many churches today have lost their zeal for evangelism; they have already "explained away" the church's historic doctrine of hell, preferring more sentimental versions of the afterlife. Edwards would have disdained that doctrinal fuzziness as heresy. Part of the reason why he was such a successful evangelist during the revivals is that he preached as though there was a real, terrible pit of fire that must be avoided through the cross. In "Miscellany 280," written in 1727 while an associate pastor under Solomon Stoddard, Edwards spelled out his belief that the torments in hell are literal and incomprehensibly grave:

> I am convinced that the torments of hell are literally as great as they are represented by fire and brimstone, a lake of fire, and the like—and that without any hyperbole—by the greatness of the agonies of Christ in the garden. I am ready [to] think that such agonies of mind as are sufficient to put nature into such a violent commotion and ferment, so as to cause the blood to strain through the pores of the skin, are as great affliction as one would endure, if they were all over in a fiery furnace. I think the souls of the wicked must endure greater agonies than Christ in the garden, because they have despair and many other dreadful sensations of mind, that it's impossible an innocent person should have. (WJE 13:379)

Few write like this today. Fewer speak like this aloud. We may think that these and other of Edwards's descriptions of eternal suffering are base and distasteful, but that's exactly why he preached them. If we soften our doctrine of hell, then we have already compromised the necessity of the cross to the same degree. Further, if we soften our doctrine of the cross, then we will ultimately compromise our view of God's holiness and glory too. This, the Puritan preacher believed, must never be done.

18. Resolved, to live so at all times, as I think is best in my devout frames, and when I have clearest notions of things of the gospel, and another world.

We don't always see as clearly as we should. This is why we sometimes rub our eyes, wash our glasses, or visit the ophthalmologist. The fact that we see the leaves on the trees as smudged green globs doesn't mean they're that way in reality. My eyes sometimes deceive me. With a better prescription, however, the world comes into sharp relief again. The world has not changed, but my view of it has become more accurate. Likewise, we suffer from spiritual myopia as well. In the 18th Resolution, Edwards admits he doesn't always see the spiritual world as he ought, and yet he should live as though his vision of the world is as sharp and crisp as revealed in Scripture.

There are certainly times when we perceive the Lord to be close, and other times when we can't perceive him at all. There are some moments when we feel the very presence of God in gathered worship, as though he were near and tangible, and other times when worship feels cold and remote. There are days when our sin feels particularly burdensome to the conscience, like a searing, hot brand; and other days when the conscience fails to set off its warning alarms to awaken us to our own depravity. There are some moments when prayer feels powerful, emitted from our lips as both intrepid and sincere. And there are other moments when we are barely going through the motions, mechanical and stale. Our open Bibles seem to us as so many blank pages.

Here in the 18th Resolution, Edwards resolves to live "at all times" as if he were always under the "clearest notions of things of the gospel, and another world." Even if he cannot quite see it that way all the time. Suppose we are walking on a wooded trail at midnight. The fact that we can't see our way clearly doesn't mean there isn't a sure path home. We ought to walk as though the path were straight and safe, even when the shadows have grown dark. Edwards is right, of course. We think back all too fondly on the great spiritual writers, preachers, saints, and martyrs of church history as if they were *always* acutely aware of the imminence of eternity, the presence of the angels, the holiness of God, and the quickening power of the word. But in reality, even the greatest of Christian saints experienced what is called the "dark night of the soul."[20]

Edwards, like all of the notable ones before him, recognized that there are seasons of life when spiritual matters appear blurry, like a microscope or telescope poorly adjusted. And yet, just as suddenly, perhaps even unexpectedly, all comes into view again. The precious gift of spiritual sight is unexpectedly restored. In these moments of clarity, we can perceive that our souls are immortal, that our God walks in our midst, and that we are not alone in the dark of the universe. It is then, in these rare, precious instances of utmost clarity, that we must capitalize on our renewed perspective and refocus the whole of our Christian walk and life.

Notice in this late Diary entry how he longs to seize such moments to recapture the focus and aim of his whole life:

> Apr. 4, 1735. When at any time, I have a sense of any divine thing, then to turn it in my thoughts, to a practical improvement. As for instance, when I am in my mind, on some argument for the truth of religion, the reality of a future state, and the like, then to think with myself, how safely I may venture to sell all, for a future good. So when, at any time, I have a more than ordinary sense of the glory

---

20. This phrase is often associated with the writing of St. John of the Cross. See *John of the Cross: Selected Writings* (New York: Paulist Press, 1987), 155–210.

of the saints, in another world; to think how well it is worth my while, to deny
myself, and to sell all that I have for this glory, etc. (WJE 16:789)

If we too could see spiritual realities all the clearer, would we be so much
more willing "to "deny ourselves, and to see all that we have for this glory"?
And what exactly would we see more clearly? The 18th Resolution mentions
two items: "the things of the gospel" and the things "of another world." We
would wipe the fog from our glasses and see ourselves as sinners, depraved
and hopeless, when relying on our own strength, but greatly beloved of God
and redeemed through his blood. We wouldn't waste time wallowing in self-
pity, but we would view ourselves more sharply and accurately as men and
women filled by the Spirit and commissioned for great acts of witness and
compassion in the world. We would see Christ as glorious and strong, a Redeemer standing well above our troubled world. We would long for heaven
and the joy of God's saints, desiring to sing the songs of glory. We wouldn't
allow the rain, snow, and mud of the world's troubles to smudge or obscure
the windshield of our worldview. If we could see more clearly, we would
throw off the hindrances of temptation and courageously plod forward as if
heaven were glorious and hell were terrible. For indeed they are.
    Lord, grant us eyes to see what is real.

*50. Resolved, I will act so as I think I shall judge would have been best, and most
prudent, when I come into the future world. July 5, 1723.*

When a hiker is lost, one of the best things he can do is to climb a tree or
trek to a higher position to see the landscape below. Height grants perspective. On Friday morning of July 5, 1723, Edwards was thinking about death
again when he wrote,

Last night, when thinking what I should wish I had done, that I had not done,
if I was then to die; I thought I should wish, that I had been more importunate
with God, to fit me for death, and lead me into all truth, and that I might not be
deceived, about the state of my soul. In the forenoon, made the 50th Resolution.
(WJE 16:774)

Here, Edwards picks up on the concept of accurate spiritual perception,
which he began back in the 18th Resolution. He admits that we will have the
fullest, best, and most accurate perception of reality when we finally have
the comprehensive knowledge of the eternal life that has been waiting for us.
    But we ought not wait until then to act rightly. What if we could some-
how capture that perspective early? In the 50th Resolution, Edwards states
that he should resolve to act *now*, as he will see as "most prudent" *then*. He
hopes to be able to place himself in the frame of mind he will one day have
in eternity, seeking to live his finite life nobly now in the same way he knows

he will in the future. The future, of course, has a way of making the past seem obvious and predictable. As they say, "Hindsight is always 20/20." I'm sure we'll all regret wasted time and missed opportunities. We will be embarrassed then of the ways we think, act, behave, and feel now. Although what Edwards resolves to do in the 50th Resolution is unfortunately impossible for anyone, there are some things we can do to bring about greater clarity. The last paragraph of the Westminster Confession of Faith helps us climb to the higher ground by thinking forward to the judgment to come.

> As Christ would have us to be certainly persuaded that there shall be a day of judgment, both to deter all men from sin, and for the greater consolation of the godly in their adversity: so will he have that day unknown to men, that they may shake off all carnal security, and be always watchful, because they know not at what hour the Lord will come; and may be ever prepared to say, Come, Lord Jesus, come quickly. Amen. (WCF 33.3)

Let's consider three details from this paragraph. First, eternity will expose the insanity of sin. Sin is ultimately insane because it attempts to manipulate us into thinking that there is something more precious than our eternal reward—or worse—than Christ! But when we finally stand before his glory, it will be obvious we have chased mirages and mined for fools' gold.

Second, the confession emphasizes the ways that eternity will make clear the purposes behind our sufferings. These current agonies are finite because they will end, and they are purposeful because through them we may glorify Christ. We often struggle to see the purposes in many of our afflictions as we walk through them in "real time," but looking back on them will make manifest the ways we glorified Christ by endurance. Third, the confession reminds us that we will have to endure an intense scrutiny of judgment—even though ultimately delivered by grace—and this reality beckons us to "shake off all carnal securities" all the sooner.

Edwards, more than any other writer, has helped me to live in view of eternity, and for that I am grateful. His sermons on heaven, his miscellanies about eternity, and even his personal writings that we have been studying in these chapters, have continually helped me place my own struggles and trials next to the greater context of heaven's joys. On May 1, 1723, just after Edwards suffered the loss of his most intimate friendships in New York, he wrote these thoughts down in his Diary:

> Lord, grant that from hence I may learn to withdraw my thoughts, affections, desires and expectations, entirely from the world, and may fix them upon the heavenly state; where there is fullness of joy; where reigns heavenly, sweet, calm and delightful love without alloy; where there are continually the dearest expressions of their love: where there is the enjoyment of the persons loved, without ever parting: where those persons, who appear so lovely in this world, will really

be inexpressibly more lovely, and full of love to us. How sweetly will the mutual lovers join together to sing the praises of God and the Lamb! How full will it fill us with joy to think, this enjoyment, these sweet exercises, will never cease or come to an end, but will last to all eternity. (WJE 16:768)

Although I am not sure we can ever "learn to withdraw our thoughts, affections, desires, and expectations *entirely* from the world," I absolutely concur with Edwards that we should fix our minds on the heavenly state as often and as deeply as possible (cf. Eph. 4:23; Phil. 4:7; Col. 3:2). The mere promise of heaven's eternal joys has a way of overwhelming and overcoming our temporary agonies here in this life.

> Beloved, now are we the sons of God, and it doth not yet appear what we shall be: but we know that, when he shall appear, we shall be like him; for we shall see him as he is. (1 John 3:2)

One day, we will think clearly at last when we come into the glorious future world. We will know ourselves more honestly than ever before. All of our worldly struggles will be recontextualized in the light of eternity. We will see clearly *then*, because we will see Christ *as he is*.

51. *Resolved, that I will act so, in every respect, as I think I shall wish I had done, if I should at last be damned. July 8, 1723.*

This is a terrible thought and one that many Christians will have difficulty to countenance. What if I am lost at the end? What if I should have severe regrets in the last moments of my life? What if I die and go to hell? Edwards considers—even if merely theoretically—the possibility that he might be damned after all. Personally, I believe that Edwards was gaining an increasingly greater understanding of his own assurance, and that the seminal thought contained in this resolution speaks more toward Christian ethics than salvation. The thrust of this resolution is that he should continue to live in such a way that would be commendable, even if all should turn out to be a lost cause at the end.

This is a noble idea.

Soldiers ought to fight in battle in such a manner that, even if they are captured or killed, they have done their nation proud. Husbands should care for their wives in such a manner that even if they lose them at the end, they will have done what is right the whole time. Christian parents should raise their children in such a way that even if their children walk away from the faith when they become adults, they will have no shame in their decisions and actions. I often tell my son before he steps on the wrestling mat that he should fight as hard as he can, so that even if he loses or gets pinned, he can be proud of his effort. In one place in his writings, the apostle Paul briefly considers the idea that he would even be willing to be condemned *himself* if it would result in the salvation of his Jewish brethren:

> I say the truth in Christ, I lie not, my conscience also bearing me witness in the Holy Ghost, that I have great heaviness and continual sorrow in my heart. For I could wish that myself were accursed from Christ for my brethren, my kinsmen according to the flesh. (Rom. 9:1-3)

I have to admit that I too have had similar thoughts to those articulated in the 51st Resolution. Suppose on one hand that I'm wrong and there is no God. Perhaps Christianity was all a lie, and when we die, we cease to exist after the mortal body gives way. Suppose there is no consciousness after death. No reward or punishment. Or suppose on the other hand that God is real, but I'm among those who have deceived themselves into thinking that I believed when I really didn't know him. After all, Matthew 7:21-23 suggests that there will be many—multitudes perhaps—that are self-deceived in such ways. If either of those contingencies were to prove to be the case, Edwards suggests that he should still desire to live in such a way that he truly loved people as sincerely as possible, that he acted honorably toward his family and neighbors, that he spoke the truth at all times, and that he endeavored to live as conscientiously as possible for the good of mankind in general.[21] These sorts of behaviors suggest themselves as intrinsically commendable. In other words, he hopes he would have lived like a Christian, even if it turned out that he wasn't one.

Of course, if one were to actually be damned, there would be no amount of pride of accomplishment one could hold up before the righteous face of God. There would be no "nice try" efforts or "moral victories" that can avail before the judgment seat of God. If God were to damn any of us, he would be just and right to do so, and no amount of protestation would vindicate us before his righteous gaze. Edwards warned his congregation in his spring 1723 sermon, "The Way of Holiness," that there would be many such persons deceived about the condition of their souls until the last possible moment:

> What a pitiable, miserable condition are they in: to step out of this world into an uncertain eternity, with an expectation of finding themselves exceeding happy and blessed in the highest heaven, and all at once find themselves deceived, and are undeceived, finding themselves sinking in the bottomless pit! (WJE 10:477)

Though Edwards makes a strong, and even compelling point about Christian ethics in this resolution, we should be mindful of the fact that no

---

21. Here, we might think of Edwards's thesis in his 1755 work *The Nature of True Virtue*, that man's primary ethical duty is to live in such a way that he displays "benevolence to being in general," which, for Edwards, meant living in love toward God and all the creatures he has made. See WJE 10:539-627.

one can stand on moral high ground before a righteous God aside from grace. This is all the more reason to continue to hope and trust in the life, death, and resurrection of Jesus Christ. These truths—these unconditional bedrock presuppositions of the Christian gospel—are so necessary and transformative, Paul describes the Christian life as vain, futile, and pitiable if they were not so (1 Cor. 15:12–19).

55. Resolved, to endeavor to my utmost to act as I can think I should do, if I had already seen the happiness of heaven, and hell torments. July 8, 1723.

Without any doubt, the most famous sermon in American Colonial history is also the most infamous piece of Jonathan Edwards's corpus of writings, the 1741 sermon "Sinners in the Hands of An Angry God." In the academy, this sermon is often reprinted in American literature anthologies as an example of typical Puritan dour. Among believers, this sermon is equally well known for the effect it produced on its audience, advancing the fervor of the First Great Awakening. It is also known for its vivid, terrifying imagery that produced shrieking, howling, and even fainting fits in the gallery. God, Edwards suggested, is so angry with rebellious sinners that he holds them like a spider on a web over a fire. There is nothing keeping God Almighty from letting us fall into the fire at any moment. Our foot may at any instant slip into an eternal abyss. God aims his bow at our faces with the arrow pulled back. He may let fly his righteous justice at any time.[22]

The very title of the sermon is objectionable to many Christians today. *How can God be "angry"?* a modern interlocutor might strenuously object. *Isn't he the God of love?* Edwards would reply that if love is the only attribute of our thrice-holy God that our preaching is capable of conveying, then we fall well short of the fully orbed and richly textured portrait of God that the Scriptures give us. It is true, after all, that the Bible *does* portray God as angry (Exod. 32:11; Ezra 5:12; Jer. 10:10; John 3:36; Rom. 1:18), and that he *has* determined a time to pour out his judgment on the world (Ps. 9:8; 96:13; Acts 17:31). Moreover, it was Christ himself who warned of the fires of hell more often than any other biblical preacher, be it an Old Testament prophet or a New Testament apostle (in Matthew's Gospel alone, Jesus mentions hell eight times in the KJV, with each occasion attended by the utmost seriousness).

But if we still think it is cruel for preachers to inflict this kind of hellish imagery on their church congregation through such fiery preaching, we should keep several things in mind. First, Edwards believed that a true preacher would rightly announce to his people both the good (the gospel) as well as the bad (the judgment), because preaching the full truth of God demands that pastors preach the entire panoply of divine revelation. Since judg-

22. See WJEO 22:404–18.

ments and warnings are a ubiquitous part of Scripture, preachers would be a failure at best and a rebel at worst to refuse to relay these sterner messages. Actually, Edwards preached "Sinners" twice. The first time was to his home congregation in Northampton. Nothing much happened, perhaps because they had heard it all before from Edwards. Ironically, it was the *second time* he preached this sermon to another congregation in Enfield, Connecticut, as a visiting pastor that it hit the mark. This perhaps goes to show how often our hearts can grow calloused to familiar themes from familiar voices.

Second, we can say with some confidence that Edwards subjected himself to the same warnings as often as he subjected his people to it. Notice here in the 55th Resolution that he wants to live as though he had personally seen the very fires of hell with his own eyes and escaped to talk about it! His preaching of the "Sinners" sermon in 1741, eighteen years after his original writing of this resolution, seems to validate the notion that he kept his promise. From where else could these vivid images have come but his own sanctified imagination, ruminating on these powerful Scripture texts and themes? Edwards often imagined the pains and tortures of hell so he could preach effectively to his people. This frequent meditation on hell likely also kept him on the faithful path of obedience as a Christian man, as well as keeping him stocked with images with which to sharpen his judgment sermons.

Third, we should keep in mind that by preaching hellfire and brimstone, unleashing terrible images of snakes and spiders and open fiery pits on his people's imaginations, Edwards believed he was doing something gracious and merciful: he was showing his people *the way out* of such judgment. For Edwards, as well as the other Puritans and the Reformers before them, preaching hell and judgment regularly was a gracious way to show God's people his redeeming love. He has, after all, provided us a way out of this judgment: salvation by grace through faith in Christ.

All told, my only quibble with reprints of the infamous "Sinners" sermon is how infrequently it is paired with another sermon that should be complementary required reading. "Heaven Is a World of Love" is a tremendous sermon, filled richly with images of heaven's joy, happiness, and glory (WJEO 8:366–97). Would that these two sermons—one on heaven the other on hell—be read together side by side more often. That way, modern thinkers would have a fuller picture of Jonathan Edwards, as well as Edwards's tremendous and awesome God.

Conclusion: Why Jonathan Edwards Stopped Using the Resolutions

In late 1722, Jonathan Edwards began writing his Seventy Resolutions and continued adding to them until August 17, 1723, at which point he abruptly stopped. Most of them he wrote between December and January that winter, while serving in a temporary New York City pastorate. When he finished, he had written exactly Seventy Resolutions, though he sometimes referred to "resolving" more generally in his writings.[1] The Diary also began abruptly at virtually the same time as the Resolutions (December 18, 1722), and although this notebook carried on for several more years, Edwards ceased writing there eventually as well. Through 1724, he steadily continued to add entries to his Diary, but he began to slow down notably as he began serving as a full-time tutor at Yale (May 1724–September 1726). The entries trickled to a halt, as one might slowly close off a spigot, with seven entries in 1725 and then one each in 1726, 1728, and 1734, finally grinding to a complete stop with three entries in 1735.

The two questions we will consider in this closing section of our study are: why did Edwards stop writing his Resolutions, and why did he apparently cease examining himself so excruciatingly in his Diary by those Resolutions he had already written?

Several obvious answers present themselves to the first question. It is entirely possible that Edwards viewed the "canon" of his resolutions as complete with the 70th Resolution, which he composed in the heat of August 1723. There were already seventy in total, which is a nice, round, and biblically appropriate number.[2] Not only that, but the more he wrote, the harder it would be to assess his conduct with his Resolutions. Therefore, a finite number of Resolutions to work through seemed appropriate. The simplest solution to the first question is that Edwards viewed the collection of Resolutions as

---

1. See WJE 16:787 for a couple of examples of such resolutions.
2. E.g., Exod. 24:1; Num. 11:16; Deut. 10:22; Ps. 90:10; Dan. 9:2, 24; Zech. 7:5.

complete. By August 1723, he had already written what he thought to be most helpful to his own soul and considered the project a done deal.

The second question, why Edwards appears to have stopped examining himself in his Diary using these Resolutions, is a bit harder to answer. One suggestion is that his life gained complexity and purpose as his ministerial duties increased. He simply had less time to work on these primarily inward issues. The more his outward duties in the pastorate and his family life increased, the less time he had for such exhausting introspection. Moreover, much of his intellectual rigor transferred from self-examination to outward theological production. For instance, by the end of 1725, he had written almost two hundred miscellanies, and he was obviously preoccupied with this new outlet for creative expression and theological expansion. By 1727, his production of sermonic material would necessarily increase exponentially, and from that point forward, preaching and writing theological treatises would become his all-consuming passion.[3]

This suggestion certainly comports with the data, and it is notable that Edwards was called to the Northampton Church to serve under his grandfather, Solomon Stoddard, in the fall of 1726, the year in which the Diary entries drop off most precipitously. On July 28, 1727, Edwards married Sarah Pierpont, and his new role and calling as a husband explains why there are no Diary entries recorded that entire year. Marriage has a way of changing a man, redirecting his affections, and turning him outward to the direct care and tender love of another human soul besides himself. In August 1728, he became a father as Sarah gave birth to the first of their eleven children! Needless to say, life would never be the same again as it had been for the intensely introspective, soul-searching bachelor. Duties both domestic and pastoral would command his attention as he grew as a Christian and as a man. His meager attempts to revive the Diary project as a more mature minister in 1734 and 1735 seem half-hearted and disconnected (WJE 16:789), and his interest in further self-analysis appears to have dried up entirely. That is, until December 1740, at which point Edwards again took up his pen to muse about the inner workings of his own soul as he wrote his beautiful and winsome "Personal Narrative," in direct response to the request of Rev. Aaron Burr.[4]

Yet even within the Diary itself, Edwards appears to have changed directions early on, using it for reasons other than to review his Seventy Resolutions. This seems apparent by the time he went to Yale College to serve as a tutor in June 1724. Although after this date, he would still occasionally refer to "resolving" to do this or that in his Diary,[5] he no longer used the formal

---

3. See the dated sermons in the appendix of WJEO 14:543–50.
4. For the "Personal Narrative," see WJE 16:790–804. For more information on Rev. Aaron Burr, see JEE 77–8.
5. See the entries of November 22, 1724, and May 21, 1725.

list of the Seventy Resolutions to check his spiritual progress or monitor his failures. His last direct reference in the Diary to his Resolutions is in February 1724 (WJE 16:785). This means that Edwards only actively used the Resolutions—as brilliant and as inspiring as they are—for a brief period of just over a year (December 1722–February 1724). Before Edwards began his tutorship, there are eighty-eight references to the Resolutions, or "resolving," and only two afterwards. Ironically, easing his regular use of the Resolutions was in itself a breach of the preamble and the 3rd Resolution, in which he vowed to use them perpetually.

Deeper Reasons

This leaves some Edwards scholars to consider the possibility that there were deeper reasons for leaving off of his self-examination project centered on his Resolutions. Early on in the Diary, Edwards began to sense that this process may be more discouraging than he had initially hoped. Barely two weeks into the project, he wrote:

> Wednesday, Jan. 2, 1722–23. Dull. I find by experience, that let me make resolutions, and do what I will, with never so many inventions, it is all nothing, and to no purpose at all, without the motions of the Spirit of God: for if the Spirit of God should be as much withdrawn from me always, as for the week past, notwithstanding all I do, I should not grow; but should languish, and miserably fade away. I perceive, if God should withdraw his Spirit a little more, I should not hesitate to break my resolutions, and should soon arrive at my old state. There is no dependence upon myself. Our resolutions may be at the highest one day, and yet, the next day, we may be in a miserable dead condition, not at all like the same person who resolved. It is to no purpose to resolve, except we depend on the grace of God; for if it were not for his mere grace, one might be a very good man one day, and a very wicked one the next. I find also by experience, that there is no guessing out the ends of providence, in particular dispensations towards me—any otherwise than as afflictions come as corrections for sin, and God intends when we meet with them, to desire us to look back on our ways, and see wherein we have done amiss, and lament that particular sin, and all our sins, before him–knowing this, also, that all things shall work together for our good; not knowing in what way, indeed, but trusting in God. (WJE 16:760)

Two weeks later, he added a similar disparaging sentiment to his Diary:

> Jan. 15, Tuesday, about two or three of clock. I have been all this day decaying. It seemed yesterday, the day before and Saturday, that I should always retain the same resolution to the same height. But alas! how soon do I decay. O how weak, how infirm, how unable to do anything of myself. What a poor, inconsistent being! What a miserable wretch, without the assistance of God's Spirit. (WJE 16:765)

This is an important realization that came rather early in the project: if he thought he was going to be able to improve himself by willpower alone, then he would fail miserably. He could do nothing without the Holy Spirit of God working within him. Resolutions alone would not be able to sustain him during dull and dry times when his sanctification seemed to wane rather than wax, and the fresh power of a new obedience seemed impossible. By January 20, he had written dozens of Resolutions and the project had just gotten started. But less than a month in, he was already feeling overwhelmed. He seems to have been walking heavily in this entry, as though uphill like John Bunyan's character Christian when he still carried that great burden on his back. Edwards felt low. Discouraged. Negligent. Dreadful. Could he let this project continue to weigh him down? Just five days after his "decaying" comment, he wrote:

> Jan. 20, sabbath day. At night. The last week I was sunk so low, that I fear it will be a long time, 'ere I shall be recovered. I fell exceedingly low in the weekly account. I find my heart so deceitful, that I am almost discouraged from making any more resolutions. Wherein have I been negligent in the week past; and how could I have done better, to help the dreadful, low estate in which I am sunk? (WJE 16:765)

Throughout the years 1723 and 1724, when Edwards was most committed to his Resolutions/Diary projects, we read several such concerns. On Saturday night, April 7, 1723, as he prepared for the following Lord's Day worship services, he wrote in his Diary:

> This week I found myself so far gone, that it seemed to me, that I should never recover more. Let God of his mercy return unto me, and no more leave me thus to sink and decay! I know, O Lord, that without thy help, I shall fall innumerable times, notwithstanding all my resolutions, how often so ever repeated. (WJE 16:768)

The spiritual weight these self-imposed vows seemed to place on him only grew. On June 22, he wrote, "I take notice, that most of these determinations, when I first resolve them, seem as if they would be much more beneficial, than I find them" (WJE 16:772). But lest we think that Edwards was ready to give up the fight and abandon the entire project too early, he had an idea that just may have helped. What if he were to put the Resolutions into some form of acrostic that could be easily memorized and summoned when he was under temptation or given to spiritual despair? In a Diary entry of July 25, 1723, he notes this idea as a possibility: "Memorandum. At a convenient time, to make an alphabet of these resolutions and remarks, that I may be able to educe [evoke] them, on proper occasions, suitable to the condition I am in, and the duty I am engaged in" (WJE 16:776). Whether or not he followed through on this idea, we don't know. But this example, among others, demonstrates his willingness to creatively seek solutions on how he could apply the Resolutions to his daily life.

On December 27, the second-to-last entry of 1723, Edwards again fortified his determination to press on in the self-examination project, this time adding scriptural cement to the dam of Resolutions to hold the flood of the sinful nature back: "At the end of every month, to examine my behavior, strictly, by some chapter in the New Testament, more especially made up of rules of life." Since he was now facing the turn of the calendar year, he added, "At the end of the year, to examine my behavior by the rules of the New Testament in general, reading many chapters. It would also be convenient, sometime at the end of the year, to read, for this purpose, in the book of Proverbs" (WJE 16:783). It appears then that Edwards was making a turn toward using more of the Bible to analyze his life and less of the resolutions. In the end, we can conclude that Edwards had been placing more spiritual pressure on himself than any nineteen-year-old could realistically tolerate. As Jesus said, "The spirit indeed is willing, but the flesh is weak" (Matt. 26:41).

Stained-Glass Saints

Our stained-glass saints are just that: they are stained, and they are glass. They are stained because their records of righteousness are markedly imperfect, tainted through and through by their own sinful nature. Temptations, failures, and character defects are present even in the great ones. They are also glass because their image is fragile, and just a bit of exploration reveals them to be far less resilient and strong than we like to think. Should anyone come to the looking glass of history to find "the real" Jonathan Edwards, they will find him—like Luther, Calvin, Spurgeon, Wesley, and others—to be all too human. Weak, breakable, and prone to failure.

Edwards's experience with his Resolutions project should remind us of how even our heroes from Christian history can ultimately disappoint us. We can be thankful, though, that his experience with the frailty of his own human flesh and the victory given to him by the Holy Spirit are chronicled for us in these scant personal writings. Together, the resolutions and the Diary give us helpful insight into the love of holiness at once possessed by this man, as well as the impossibility of attaining it on his own. As George Marsden wrote, "Despite his massive intellect and heroic disciplines, he was, like everyone else, a person with frailties and contradictions."[6] Douglas Sweeney agrees:

> Edwards would later come to believe that in this period of his life he grew too cocky spiritually, "which afterwards," he wrote (quoting the "Personal Narrative"), "proved a great damage to me." He came to regret that his "experiences had not then taught me, as it has done since, my extreme feebleness and impotence."[7]

Perhaps Edwards needed the extreme rigor of the Resolutions project to expose for himself the need of increased humility to temper his spiritual

6. Marsden, *A Life*, 45.
7. Sweeney, *Ministry of the Word*, 44–45.

ambitions. As we see in a March 2, 1723, Diary entry, this message of spiritual humility and Spirit-dependence does seem to get through to him:

> O how much more base and vile am I, when I feel pride working in me, than when I am in a more humble disposition of mind! How much, how exceedingly much, more lovely is an humble, than a proud, disposition! I now plainly perceive it, and am really sensible of it. How immensely more pleasant is an humble delight, than a high thought of myself! How much better do I feel, when I am truly humbling myself, than when I am pleasing myself with my own perfections. O, how much pleasanter is humility than pride! O, that God would fill me with exceeding great humility, and that he would evermore keep me from all pride! The pleasures of humility are really the most refined, inward and exquisite delights in the world. How hateful is a proud man! How hateful is a worm that lifts up itself with pride! What a foolish, silly, miserable, blind, deceived, poor worm am I, when pride works! (WJE 16:767)

In my own view, Edwards needed the Resolutions project to expose how much he actually needed the Holy Spirit in his life. It was not wasted effort as it showed him just how desperately he needed the Lord to persevere in the faith and pursue holiness. Though it does perhaps reveal the spiritual ambition of an enthusiastic young man, all too prone to personal optimism given his gifted intellect and exceptional upbringing, the failures he learned through trial and error in this formative year taught him valuable lessons about the indispensability of the Holy Spirit's work in the hearts and lives of his people.

Between Antinomianism and Legalism

I have no doubt that Edwards understood that justification is by faith alone through grace alone. In fact, he wrote an orthodox master's thesis on that very topic.[8] He didn't need to learn head knowledge. He needed to experience what Paul was talking about when he exhorted the Philippians to "work out your own salvation with fear and trembling. For it is God which worketh in you both to will and to do of his good pleasure" (2:12–13). This is a tightwire balancing act.

There is a memorable scene in *Pilgrim's Progress* when Christian sees two lions on the road in front of him.[9] He is terrified, of course, and believes that either of them can eat him alive. He's right. As Christian approaches these two lions, he realizes that the only way to avoid these fearsome beasts is to go directly between them. Only as Christian gets closer, however, does he realize that both lions are chained and can't attack him if he stays exactly in

8. See Edwards's *Quaestio* in WJEO 14:47–66.
9. Bunyan, *Pilgrim's Progress*, 69–71.

the center. Throughout the book, staying directly on the straight and narrow way is a theme Bunyan develops in ever more creative ways.

There is something profound in the idea that we must stay safely between the two extremes, where the ground is straight and narrow. The dual errors of antinomianism and legalism stand ready to maul unsuspecting Christians if they don't cling to the *via media*—the way of life. Legalism, or any form of strict and personal rigorism, has caused too many Christians to be flayed to shreds by the sharp claws of self-righteous pride. Antinomianism (Greek: lawlessness), on the other hand, has likewise torn apart many believers as they grew all too lax in their walk of faith, refusing discipline and growing careless. Only the center path—properly balancing grace and obedience—is the sure way.

There are many instances in the Diary where we see Edwards so proud and arrogant that he believes he is overcoming his spiritual foes, perhaps even on his own strength. In this January 14, 1723, Diary entry, he boasts to himself of his recent victories over the flesh. This is the young Edwards at his most confident:

> At night. Great instances of mortification are deep wounds given to the body of sin, hard blows that make him stagger and reel: we thereby get great ground and footing against him, and he is the weaker ever after. And we have easier work with him the next time. He grows cowardly; and we can easily cause him to give way, until at length, we find it easy work with him, and can kill him at pleasure. While we live without great instances of mortification and self-denial, the old man keeps whereabouts he was; for he is sturdy and obstinate, and will not stir for small blows. And this, without doubt, is one great reason why many Christians do not sensibly increase in grace. After the greatest mortifications, I always find the greatest comfort. . . . Such little things as Christians commonly do, will not show increase of grace much. We must do great things for God. It will be best, when I find I have lost any former, ancient, good motions or actions, to take notice of it, if I can remember them. Supposing there was never but one complete Christian, in all respects of a right stamp, having Christianity shining in its true luster, at a time in the world; resolved to act just as I would do, if I strove with all my might to be that one, that should be in my time. (WJE 16:764)

Here, he seems valiant. Victorious. He has met the "old man" (Rom. 6:6) on his own terms and clubbed him down in brutal hand-to-hand combat. He is ready to offer advice to "common" Christians, who are not yet as advanced as he is. He even considers the possibility that he might be that *one* true Christian in his time! Sweeney comments that these kinds of statements "tend to weary middle-aged and older Christians, but they thrill the young at heart, the most extreme disciples of Christ."[10] The very next day, however, the young man has lost his swagger and laments:

---

10. Sweeney, *Ministry of the Word*, 45.

What a miserable wretch, without the assistance of God's Spirit. While I stand, I am ready to think I stand by my own strength, and upon my own legs; and I am ready to triumph over my (spiritual) enemies, as if it were I myself that caused them to flee. When alas, I am but a poor infant, upheld by Jesus Christ; who holds me up, and gives me liberty to smile to see my enemies flee, when he drives them before me; and so I laugh, as if I myself did it, when it is only Jesus Christ leads me along, and fights himself against my enemies. And now, the Lord has a little left me; how weak do I find myself. O let it teach me to depend less on myself, to be more humble, and to give more of the praise of my ability to Jesus Christ. (WJE 16:765)

Here, we see Edwards wobble between sweet victory and utter despair. One day, he could write, "O how weak, how infirm, how unable to do anything of myself. What a poor, inconsistent being! What a miserable wretch, without the assistance of God's Spirit" (WJE 16:764–65). Then a few entries later, he would wax eloquent: "Near sunset. Felt the doctrines of election, free grace, and of our not being able to do anything without the grace of God; and that holiness is entirely, throughout, the work of God's Spirit, with more pleasure than before" (WJE 16:767). William S. Morris states the matter with precision when he writes,

> The search for personal holiness through self-discipline must not be allowed to blind one to the truth that only God's sovereign grace acting in and on the soul to strengthen and nourish it could enable the soul to possess that creature holiness for which it so much yearned.[11]

Reflections of a More Mature Saint: The "Personal Narrative"

When Edwards began his 1740 "Personal Narrative" to describe his spiritual growth over the years, he hoped to write a new introspective document that could encourage younger ministers like the Rev. Aaron Burr. Perhaps a revised spiritual account, now from the perspective of a far more mature Christian, could help other men more successfully stride between the two lions of legalism and antinomianism. And so, Edwards wrote a winsome and honest account of his spiritual life and allowed others to read it. This document is helpful to scholars, because though it is a stylized account (though not nearly so raw as the Diary), it has the advantage of mature reflection. Edwards looked back on the 1722/23 with both fondness and candor. He describes this time in his life as some sort of high point, a pinnacle of spiritual thrills that gave him sustained energy. His spiritual experiences were *real*. Time had shown that now.

---

11. Lawson, *Unwavering Resolve*, 53.

I had an eager thirsting after progress in these things. My longings after it, put me upon pursuing and pressing after them. It was my continual strife day and night, and constant inquiry, how I should be more holy, and live more holily, and more becoming a child of God, and disciple of Christ. I sought an increase of grace and holiness, and that I might live an holy life, with vastly more earnestness, than ever I sought grace, before I had it. I used to be continually examining myself, and studying and contriving for likely ways and means, how I should live holily, with far greater diligence and earnestness, than ever I pursued anything in my life: but with too great a dependence on my own strength; which afterwards proved a great damage to me. (WJE 16:795)

Note that last line: "but with too great a dependence on my own strength; which afterwards proved a great damage to me." In my view, this refers to his Resolutions project and the regrets attached to it. In his youth, Edwards truly believed he could make vows, drawing up personal rules and guidelines that would keep him on the faithful path. But these attempts showed more of his human failures than accomplishments and his weaknesses rather than his strengths. Thankfully, he learned the lesson from this and was able to move on with his pursuit of sanctification. He continues:

I have vastly a greater sense, of my universal, exceeding dependence on God's grace and strength, and mere good pleasure, of late, than I used formerly to have; and have experienced more of an abhorrence of my own righteousness. The thought of any comfort or joy, arising in me, on any consideration, or reflection on my own amiableness, or any of my performances or experiences, or any goodness of heart or life, is nauseous and detestable to me. And yet I am greatly afflicted with a proud and self-righteous spirit; much more sensibly, than I used to be formerly. I see that serpent rising and putting forth its head, continually, everywhere, all around me. (WJE 16:803)

Now a pastor for some thirteen years, in the very throes of the Great Awakening, Edwards has seen the work of God in his ministry in dynamic ways. But he does not lament that he attempted these extreme measures. It is too late to change the past, and he is thankful for what the Lord has shown him. Besides, his intense spiritual longings were legitimate despite his failures. In some ways, the vigor and enthusiasm of youth is still to be admired and fondly recalled. He even allows himself to admit that he might have even been at his peak of divine zeal and spiritual fervor then:

Though it seems to me, that in some respects I was a far better Christian, for two or three years after my first conversion, than I am now; and lived in a more constant delight and pleasure: yet of late years, I have had a more full and constant sense of the absolute sovereignty of God, and a delight in that sovereignty; and have had more of a sense of the glory of Christ, as a mediator, as revealed in the gospel. On one Saturday night in particular, had a particular discovery of the excellency of the gospel of Christ, above all other doctrines; so that I could not but say to myself; "This is my chosen light, my chosen doctrine": and of Christ,

"This is my chosen prophet." It appeared to me to be sweet beyond all expression, to follow Christ, and to be taught and enlightened and instructed by him; to learn of him, and live to him. (WJE 16:803)

Let's not miss the crucial point here: Though the joys of newfound conversion are indeed beyond compare, so too are the constant graces of steady Christian maturity. "Yet of late years, I have had a more full and constant sense of the absolute sovereignty of God." Each season of life comes with its own blessings. Many readers will doubtlessly sense that this parallels their own faith journey. I know I do. When I was first saved, my longing for the presence of God and my passion for the evangelization of the world—and even my willingness to suffer for him—were at an all-time high. But now, as an older minister myself, my emotions have tempered to a more constant, balanced, assured confidence in the goodness of the Lord as I have seen him work in my life through the decades.

Edwards's Resolutions and a Gospel of Grace

We will close our adventure with Jonathan Edwards and his Seventy Resolutions here. Some may see the project as an example of self-righteous willpower gone wrong. Others see this early document from the pen of one of history's great ministers as a true inspiration, a model to be emulated. Perhaps there is room here for both sentiments. Don Whitney writes:

Does the relentless self-examination border on the obsessive? Was Edwards too self-critical in his concern for the mortification of sin? Were he confronted with such a charge, likely his defense would have been that no earnestness is too great in the pursuit of God and that no zeal is too stringent for those who believe that a day of judgment is coming when every word, deed, thought, and motive in a person's life will be examined. In any case, the fact remains that the variety and amount of Edwards's journal-type writings provide a broad, clear window into the interior of his spiritual life.[12]

Personally, I am convinced that the Resolutions are both a warning of the excesses of self-confidence in one's own willpower, as well as an inspiration to pursue the holy life in the brief time we live here on planet Earth before eternity dawns. Having read and studied this unique document from one of my own personal heroes now for several years, I am all the more willing to join Jonathan Edwards in declaring: *Resolved: to live with all my might while I do live!*

---

12. Don Whitney, *Finding God in Solitude*, 94.

APPENDIX

The Older Puritan Model: A Morphology of Salvation

Several times in this book, we have referred to the common morphology (or "shape") of the conversion experience as articulated by the older Puritans. Readers more familiar with Reformed theology might assume we are talking about the "golden chain of salvation" as articulated by the Paul in Romans 8:28–30 (predestination, calling, justification, and glorification), as well as in the Westminster Confession of Faith, chapters 10–17. But the older Puritans had something else in mind here. For them, the very experience of conversion itself didn't usually happen in one moment, contrary to the expectations of most American evangelicals in our settings.

Today, we often tie salvation to a dramatic moment in time, a life-changing decision, such as walking forward at a crusade, trusting Christ at a summer camp, or signing a pledge card in the front of a Gideon Bible. But for the Puritans, coming under the conviction of the work of the Holy Spirit, ultimately resulting in being born again, was considered an arduous process. This transformation might take weeks, months, or years. Sometimes this is referred to as "the steps."[1] As refined theologians and extraordinarily precise thinkers, many of the Puritans attempted to break this process down into something that could be described in detail. Their concern, of course, was to identify the anatomy (so to speak) of a real conversion versus one that was likely to result in a false or temporary profession of faith. The result of this thinking was a defined series of expected steps or stages one would most likely go through in the very throes of the conversion experience itself.

---

1. For a more complete evaluation of the Puritan concept of morphology or preparationism, see the chapter titled "Puritan Preparatory Grace," in Joel R. Beeke and Mark Jones, *A Puritan Theology* (Grand Rapids: Reformation Heritage, 2012), 443–62. See also "Preparationism" in JEE 461–63.

It seems obvious that Timothy Edwards, Jonathan's father, held to a standard form of this view, as did Solomon Stoddard, Edwards's esteemed grandfather. Both of these men were highly revered both as pastors and as defenders of traditional and conservative Puritanism. In fact, both were considered experts in their own time on this matter, which is the root cause of much of young Jonathan's spiritual angst since his own experience evidently didn't accord with the expected series of spiritual agonies.

Timothy Edwards had a somewhat flexible understanding of the conversion morphology, and his view included three (or four) primary steps, depending on how one grouped them.[2] Kenneth Minkema, one of the most respected Edwards scholars today, has analyzed dozens of verbal testimonies given in Timothy Edwards's early eighteenth-century congregation. He summarizes the expected morphology as containing four basic steps: (1) Conviction/Awakening, (2) Legal Terror, (3) Humiliation, and (4) Light/ New Spirit. Minkema arrived at this conclusion by having reviewed dozens of remaining verbal testimonies, which were given to the congregation orally and in public by the inquirer and then reduced to written form by Rev. Timothy Edwards himself as he listened. Since many of these testimonies were the only public speech many common farmers and laborers would be expected to give in their whole lives, much attention was given to saying everything "just right" in front of the gathered congregation. Minkema copiously poured through these extant testimonies looking for the shared patterns in each. Common to all or most of the approved public professions of faith were an awareness of "one's present sad estate in sin," a realization of God's anger against sin, a recognition that God has every right to condemn sinners to hell, and finally repentance.[3]

George Marsden combines Kenneth Minkema's series of four steps into three for the sake of clarity: (1) Conviction/Awakening, (2) Humiliation, and (3) Light/New Spirit. Perhaps Marsden is attempting to make Minkema's summary of Timothy Edwards's congregational material harmonize with another Puritan, Thomas Shepherd, who had identified three distinct steps in the process—namely, conviction, compunction, and humiliation (WJEO 2:57). Indeed, even among the Puritans themselves, there was no clear agreement as to exactly how many steps there were (three, four, even seven!), or what their titles should be, but there was a general consensus of the direction and trajectory of the spiritual crisis and turmoil that the soul had to go through in order to truly see the light. Sticking with Minkema's

2. See Marsden, *A Life*, 26–29, 57–58.

3. Kenneth P. Minkema, "The East Windsor Conversion Relations," *The Connecticut Historical Society Bulletin* 51.1 (Winter 1986).

summary of Timothy Edwards's congregation, let's describe the process in more detail.

Conviction

The first step was called conviction. Conviction was usually impressed on the hearer by the outward ministry of the preached word. Churchgoers would fall under the power of the sermon and begin to sense a new awareness of their fallen spiritual condition. Sometimes this was called "awakening." We note here that this term is appropriate since the revivals themselves were often called "awakenings"; that is, large-scale groupings of men and women under conviction. At this point, new believers don't yet embrace the gospel savingly, but they begin to recognize that they are mortal. They realize they are going to die. This may also be caused by some sort of personal tragedy or community event, such as an outward misfortune, accident, death, or security threat. Perhaps they lost a loved one and realize that life is short and eternity is long! At this point, they begin to be more aware of good and evil, life and death, heaven and hell. But these realizations are themselves no guarantees of salvation. They might easily slip back into their old way of life again here. They must proceed to the next step.

Legal Terror

This is an important step in our study of Jonathan Edwards, because from the best we can tell, this is the step Edwards skipped and the gap in his testimony that made his own father suspicious of his conversion story. Without this step, Timothy Edwards would have been reticent to accept his own son into visible church membership, even though young Jonathan was already on the way to vocational pastoral ministry! But Jonathan was too honest to describe what he did not personally feel. He wasn't going to fake it, for the sake of the old Puritan schema. Legal terror included a knowledge of the law of God and the absolute dread that one could not uphold the moral demands of the Scriptures, especially the Old Testament. The reading of the law, particularly the Sinai covenant, was supposed to terrify the individual. They were supposed to feel what the Israelites themselves felt when the law was revealed in Exodus 19, as the mountain trembled, lightning rippled, and men and women fell into dreadful fear. Here, one realizes one cannot keep God's law, no matter how hard they try. Once again, John Bunyan's *Pilgrim's Progress* can be invoked by way of illustration. Christian dreads that Sinai itself would fall upon him.[4] Many readers find it strange that Moses comes along and beats Faithful down with blows of violence.[5] Why would Moses do that? Because without the terror of the law, the gospel will not be viewed as a relief.

Humiliation

The third step is humiliation. This step can be switched in order with the previous or perhaps combined with it. Here, the would-be converts come into a greater awareness of their own peculiar and proper sins. They see that they are sinners not only theoretically but in specific and particular ways. It becomes obvious that "getting religion" is not enough. They truly become desperate for a Savior. If they had any initial enthusiasm during their awakening process earlier, it may even give way to backsliding as they realize that they are completely incapable of reforming their behavior on their own. Therefore, the legal terrors of the previous step are often exacerbated, and they slide downward into further despondency. They are humbled greatly. Though they repent of sin, it is more often the occasion that they fear temporal chastisements and worldly punishments. They may be tempted to believe that the gospel is for others, but not for them. They think themselves too far gone to save. They realize they have no possible way to save themselves through any devotion, church attendance, or reformative behavioral patterns. Finally, at their lowest moment, they sink down to the realization that God would be just and righteous to cast them into hell. They have realized their total unworthiness before the great and Living God. They have no hope in the world to be saved at all, until the final step.

Light

Suddenly, perhaps triumphantly, even unexpectedly, the new converts realize that the gospel is a message of hope and light for sinners such as themselves. This is truly a dawning realization that only the Holy Spirit can bring about.[6] They see themselves as unworthy sinners, but it suddenly strikes upon them in pure grace that Christ came to save such unworthy wretches (1 Tim. 1:15). A new principle is instilled from above and their nature is transformed by grace. The Spirit of God does a tremendous work in the heart. The new

---

4. Bunyan, *Pilgrim's Progress*, 34–35.
5. Bunyan, *Pilgrim's Progress*, 106.
6. For an excellent treatment of this power of regeneration, see Jonathan Edwards's sermon "A Divine and Supernatural Light" in WJEO 17:405–26.

converts fully and finally repent for sin because they have grieved the heart of a holy God; not merely because they fear the consequences of sin in this life. They now embrace the gospel, their eyes having been enlightened, and they hope and trust in Christ alone for salvation. Obedience from this point on will be an attempt to show proper gratitude as an act of worship, and not an attempt to earn or deserve such saving favor in the first place. Doubts may still come and go at this point, but the newly saved believers move closer and closer to a position of full assurance as they mature. Once being saved, they never fall from grace, though they may err and stray occasionally. They show true growth in the faith, and they manifest more and more of the fruit of the Spirit in their lives.

About the Author

Rev. Dr. Matthew serves as the senior pastor of Gospel Fellowship PCA in Ascension Presbytery, Pennsylvania. He is also a regular writer for *Modern Reformation* (web-exclusive articles). Matthew is a graduate of Reformed Theological Seminary (Orlando, Florida), Ashland Theological Seminary (Ashland, Ohio), and Malone University (Canton, Ohio). At Malone, he majored in Bible and theology, at ATS he concentrated in the field of spiritual formation, and at RTS Orlando, he did a directed study on Jonathan Edwards and wrote his doctoral dissertation on Edwards's theology of joy, supervised by Dr. Michael Allen. His dissertation was later published as *A Theology of Joy: Jonathan Edwards and Eternal Happiness in the Holy Trinity* (Fort Worth, TX: JESociety Press, 2018). Matthew is also a contributing editor for *A Collection of Essays on Jonathan Edwards* (JESociety Press, 2016), and a contributor of four entries (Joy; Hell; Original Sin; Predestination) in the comprehensive *Jonathan Edwards Encyclopedia*, published by Eerdmans in cooperation with the Jonathan Edwards Center at Yale University.

Native Ohioans, he and his wife Kelly have three children: Soriah (an aspiring neonatal nurse and artist), Elijah (an aspiring physical therapist and Olympic wrestler), and Simone (likely an aspiring lawyer, since she talks so much!). Deeply committed to world missions, Matthew has served in Equatorial Guinea (Central West Africa), El Salvador, Mexico. Ukraine, the Bahamas, Scotland, Thailand, and the Cayman Islands.